Ecology, Ethics, and Interdependence

Ecology, Ethics, and Interdependence

The Dalai Lama in Conversation with
Leading Thinkers on Climate Change

JOHN DUNNE *and* DANIEL GOLEMAN, *Editors*

Wisdom Publications
199 Elm Street
Somerville, MA 02144 USA
wisdompubs.org

Library of Congress Cataloging-in-Publication Data
Names: Bstan-'dzin-rgya-mtsho, Dalai Lama XIV, 1935– | Dunne, John Anthony, 1986–
    editor. | Goleman, Daniel, editor.
Title: Ecology, ethics, and interdependence : the Dalai Lama in conversation with leading
    thinkers on climate change / John Dunne and Daniel Goleman, editors.
Description: Somerville, MA, USA : Wisdom Publications, [2018] | Includes bibliographical
    references. |
Identifiers: LCCN 2017059972 (print) | LCCN 2018029169 (ebook) | ISBN 9781614295143
    (e-book) | ISBN 9781614294948 (pbk.: alk. paper) | ISBN 9781614295143 (ebook)
Subjects: LCSH: Environmental ethics. | Climatic changes—Moral and ethical aspects. |
    Environmentalism—Religious aspects—Buddhism.
Classification: LCC GE42 (ebook) | LCC GE42 .B84 2018 (print) | DDC 179/.1—dc23
LC record available at https://lccn.loc.gov/2017059972

ISBN 978–1–61429–494–8   ebook ISBN 978–1–61429–514–3

22 21 20 19 18   5 4 3 2 1

Cover photo by Olivier Adam. Cover design by Jim Zaccaria. Interior set in Chaparral Pro 10.5/15.

Wisdom Publications' books are printed on acid-free paper and meet the guidelines for permanence and durability of the Production Guidelines for Book Longevity of the Council on Library Resources.

✪ This book was produced with environmental mindfulness. For more information, please visit wisdompubs.org/wisdom-environment.

Printed in the United States of America.

MIX
Paper from
responsible sources
FSC
www.fsc.org FSC® C013483

Please visit fscus.org.

Publisher's Acknowledgment

The publisher gratefully acknowledges the generous contribution of the Hershey Family Foundation toward the publication of this book.

Table of Contents

Introduction

John Dunne, *University of Wisconsin*

When the present Dalai Lama was young, Tibet teemed with wildlife. He has written fondly of seeing wild yaks and herds of rugged *kiang* (a wild donkey) roaming the vast plains of his homeland, and even in the capital of Lhasa he had many opportunities to enjoy wildlife, including the striking sight of wild cranes nesting behind his summer palace, the Norbulingka. Other travelers in Tibet from the early twentieth century have likewise recalled this natural abundance, and some even report catching glimpses of rare species, such as the unique snow leopard, that lived in the hills and higher altitudes of the Tibetan Plateau. But by the late twentieth century, all this had changed. The great Tibetan plains no longer hosted large herds of kiang or wild yak, and the snow leopard itself had become severely endangered. Along with these and many other abrupt changes, the ecosystem of Tibet, as with the rest of our planet, was already showing the jarring impact of a new era in natural history: the "Anthropocene age," or the "Human age," so called because human activity plays such a central role in the ecological changes we are witnessing.

Now, in the early twenty-first century, the effects of the Anthropocene age have become even more obvious throughout the globe. Average global temperatures are on the rise, with the top ten hottest years in history all occurring since 1998, and the trend seems likely to continue. Warmer temperatures mean that ice is melting at both poles, and the seas are rising, already threatening some island nations and low-lying coastlines. The increased atmospheric energy from higher average temperatures is

1

shifting weather patterns and producing more intense storms, longer droughts, and other effects such as the spread of tropical diseases. And climate change from global warming is only one of the many impacts of the Anthropocene age. Pollutants in the air pose a significant risk to health, and in some cities the air quality reaches the point that schools must be closed to protect children from the ill effects of the dense urban smog. Our water and soil are likewise laced with pollutants, with consequent disruptions to the food chain and to human health. Deforestation has led to huge habitat losses and a high rate of extinction, involving the loss of hundreds of species in recent years. We face, in short, an ecological crisis of such profound proportions that it is easy to feel overwhelmed.

Despite our dire ecological circumstances, however, there is still some good news: just as human activity has played a significant role in producing this crisis, so too can we humans work actively to lessen or even reverse the effects of what we are witnessing. With that hopeful view in mind, His Holiness the Dalai Lama requested that Mind and Life Institute (MLI) organize a weeklong dialogue with top-level scientists and scholars so as to inquire into our ecological situation and clarify ways that we can move forward constructively. In conversation with experts in various disciplines, we at MLI soon saw that this historic meeting must approach the problem from multiple perspectives. A key theme emerged: interdependence.

The very notion of an ecosystem presupposes a deep level of interconnection. Through complex interactions, the living beings and elements that constitute an ecosystem are tightly linked—relatively small changes in one part of the system can have profound implications for all else in the system. When those changes come about through conscious, deliberate actions, an additional implication emerges: in ecological terms, our actions involve a clear ethical responsibility. When we make choices about how we live our lives, we are having an impact far beyond our own immediate circumstances. Those impacts can extend not only to the rest of the planet but also to future generations. As we uncovered these and other ethical implications of ecological interconnectivity, we realized that our dialogue would require a deep inquiry into ethics from both philosophical and spiritual perspectives.

Finally, our dialogue needed more than an understanding of our ecological crisis in both scientific and ethical terms; we also needed to explore the question of concrete action. Many of us understand a great deal about the ecological dangers that we face, and we can also appreciate the ethical responsibility that we bear toward the rest of the world and toward future generations. Yet concrete action may still be hard to come by. Why so? When we asked various experts this question, we learned that there are well-known psychological barriers to action when faced with the peculiar, long-term dangers that arise from the ecological crisis. To learn how to overcome those barriers, our meeting needed to include expertise in the psychology of danger assessment and decision making. The context of action, however, does not just end with the commitment to act. It also requires sound strategies and techniques that can succeed in our complex, globalized communities. To that end, we also needed participants with firsthand experience about what works—and what doesn't work—to bring about beneficial and lasting change in relation to our environment.

With all these considerations in place, the contours of our meeting became clear. For the best possible dialogue, we needed to find and invite participants with the highest level of expertise in three overall areas: environmental science, ethics, and action. Fortunately, our invitations were readily accepted because our invitees—all renowned in their respective fields—saw great potential benefit in a weeklong discussion of these issues with the Dalai Lama at his home in Dharamsala, India, where he resides in exile, in 2011. This book is a record of those remarkable conversations.

The conversations were divided into three parts, and so are the chapters in this book. The first chapters focus on presenting scientific evidence related to the impact humankind is having on the planet Earth and the effects of changing environmental conditions on both human beings and the natural world. The next chapters turn to ethical considerations related to environmental issues. And the final chapters discuss how we can enable effective action to address these crucial matters.

In the first chapter from a presenter, environmental scientist Diana Liverman presents data on the impact of human beings on Earth, particularly in the last seventy years, focusing on a matrix of interrelated factors such as climate change, pollution, and loss of biodiversity. She reveals the great acceleration of changes that have occurred in that period, which signal the shift to the new, Anthropocene era in planetary history.

In chapter 3, Dr. Jonathan Patz speaks of his work in measuring the impact of climate change on public health in ways that point to the importance of understanding the complex interdependence of ecosystems. Without such an understanding, even well-intentioned attempts to regulate an ecosystem can have unforeseen consequence. On that basis, Dr. Patz then surveys the kinds of actions that can be taken to reduce negative impact, and how such actions often have concomitant benefits.

Chapter 4 is presented by industrial ecologist Gregory Norris, who introduces the developing "science and art" of calculating the environmental "footprint" of human products and activities—as well as the potential "handprints" of creative actions to offset such footprints. As it turns out, wise choices in the marketplace are not necessarily the most obvious choices. But with access to the right kinds of analyses, both businesses and individuals obtain clear guidance and incentive for choices that can serve to ameliorate ecological degradation and benefit the environment.

The section of the book focused on ethical considerations begins in chapter 5 by introducing the developing field of environmental ethics. Professor Clare Palmer explores both human-centered and nonhuman-centered approaches in this new area of philosophy, presenting three key issues for discussion: whether we should act now to benefit those who do not yet exist ("future people"), how we should place value on individual species versus ecosystems, and what kind of intention we should hold for the global environment into the future.

Matthieu Ricard's presentation in chapter 6 lays out the compelling evidence that humanity's ever-increasing consumption of animals as food—

enabled through industrial farming techniques—has become a major factor in environmental deterioration, as well as a significant generator of suffering altogether. Venerable Ricard's background brings together the perspectives of Western science and Buddhist practice to highlight the deep impact that the simple choice to eat a vegetarian diet—or even to reduce one's consumption of meat—can have in the world.

Christian theologian Sallie McFague gives the final presentation on ethics in chapter 7, addressing particularly the rampant consumerism that fuels the global ecological crisis. She proposes that religions can make a special contribution in this area by calling upon their basic insights of restraint and compassion as a means to enable "abundant life" in an interconnected world by curbing the "heresy" of unchecked consumption. For individuals who practice conscious restraint, or "self-emptying," she argues, a new way of thinking and being in the world can take hold.

Chapter 8 begins the transition from the discussion of ethics to the discussion of action with an address by His Holiness the Dalai Lama on the Buddhist perspective on the environmental crisis faced by all beings on the planet. His Holiness especially points out the role that unbiased compassion can play in our efforts to live in a way that is not only more sustainable, but ultimately more fulfilling.

Professor Elke Weber brings, in chapter 9, deeper understanding of the psychology behind behavior change and motivation for taking action—or more specifically the failure to take action—as these relate to addressing ecological issues. She examines various obstacles to taking action, many of which emerge from fundamental aspects of human psychology and the way in which our decision-making capacities have evolved. She then proposes some specific strategies, including the need for positive attitudes about the possibilities for the future, that can enable us to be more effective in making and implementing long-term decisions about the environment.

In chapter 10, Thupten Jinpa, who otherwise served as translator to His Holiness the Dalai Lama during the meeting, offers a counterpart to Professor Weber's presentation, addressing the psychology of change and decision making from a Buddhist perspective. Discussion in this chapter focuses on what Buddhism can offer to the process of addressing the global environmental crisis, especially in terms of contemplative approaches that enhance and harness our fundamental motivation for flourishing.

His Holiness the Karmapa has instituted several initiatives within Buddhist monastic communities to make environmental protection central to their life and practice. In chapter 11 he describes these in brief and also speaks to how various Buddhist teachings support a deeper understanding of interdependence that can be supportive of environmental conservation.

Chapter 12 is a presentation by environmental activist Dekila Chungyalpa, focused on how to engage activism as "skillful means" to address problems caused by climate change and other environmental issues. As an example, she specifically details the work the World Wildlife Fund (WWF) has engaged in to protect the ecosystem of the Mekong River and guide development in an environmentally sustainable manner. Among the important lessons that emerge from Dekila Chungyalpa's work are the importance of understanding local contexts and the need to involve all stakeholders in environmental initiatives.

Documenting a final conversation among the participants, the concluding chapter offers concrete suggestions for addressing our ecological crisis. Here, much of the emphasis is not on the dangers, but rather on what we can do in a positive and forward-looking way to live together on our planet sustainably. In this same spirit, the afterword catches up with each of the principal participants and looks at how his or her work was affected by the meeting and has developed in the years since.

As we turn now to the opening chapter of this powerful meeting, it is helpful to recall the mission of the Mind and Life Institute: "to alleviate suffering and promote flourishing by integrating science with contemplative practice and wisdom traditions." This inspiring mission can be realized in many ways, but of all the many dialogues that the Institute has organized, perhaps this conversation around ecology, ethics, and interdependence has the greatest potential for the widest-ranging impact. There is no question that we face a global ecological crisis, and it is equally clear that we are struggling to engage effectively with this challenge. In the chapters that follow, the enormity of this challenge becomes apparent, but through this dialogue we will also be inspired by the tremendous capacities and hope for the future that emerge when we bring together all of our various perspectives and commit ourselves to collective, long-term well-being.

1 Ecology, Ethics, and Interdependence

Daniel Goleman

HIS HOLINESS THE DALAI LAMA: In order to explore ethics, we must first depend on research for facts about reality. We can rely on scientific methods to uncover reality with no concept of right or wrong, no positive or negative. Then, after finding the unbiased facts, the next questions we can ask are "What are the implications?" and "What is the value?" So I think we must first approach these issues with research, simply trying to find out reality. Even phenomena such as anger, fear, suspicion, and distrust should be investigated without bias. We should investigate without considering anger as bad or compassion as good, but simply with the aim of discovering reality and its causes and effects. Then we can consider the ethical implications for our well-being.

When considering ecology, I think that—in combination with science, interdependence, and philosophical view—ecology offers a way to explain reality. Things exist due to many factors. That's the basic concept of interdependence. As with research, with interdependence there are no notions of good or bad, just reality.

So for the next few days our discussion will be serious, and eventually we can share our ideas with others who have similar interests in this field. It is our responsibility to create more interest and awareness in other people's minds.

So let's talk about ethics. Everybody agrees that there are a lot of problems on the planet. Every morning when I listen to BBC, I hear about some problem, some killing here or there. Recently I heard about unrest in England and I was really shocked. I was shocked and surprised, you see, because I had the impression that the British had become very mature. On several occasions when I visited England, I hardly saw any police. I had the impression that English people were generally self-disciplined. So when I heard about this unrest in England, I was very surprised.

And just this morning I heard on a BBC broadcast about flood victims in Pakistan and the fact that the aid workers trying to help these people are about to run out of funds to continue their help. Very sad, isn't it?

If we investigate why such things happen, of course there are natural disasters beyond our control. But we could also prepare better, care for people better, and create an overall higher standard of living. And this, I think, can help reduce suffering.

Another point is that corruption contributes to these problems and makes them worse than they already are. Corruption is creating serious consequences in Africa and in many areas. In a way, corruption is like a disease, like a cancer for the whole planet, for humanity.

What is wrong? This corruption is not due to the lack of a judicial system, or the lack of police forces, or the lack of government organizations; ultimately, it is due to a lack of ethics. It is due to a lack of self-discipline, for self-discipline is entirely based on ethics. We have the responsibility to bring awareness to the fact that the many problems we are facing ultimately result from the lack of inner discipline, of moral ethics.

And while the primary way to promote moral ethics is through religion, many religions, including Buddhism, have had opportunities over the last thousand years or so to promote ethics—and have often failed. So now we must find new ways and means to create conviction in others that behaving ethically is in our own best interest and for our own well-being. That's the main goal.

We have moral responsibility to create this awareness in more people, and in this way, I really appreciate the efforts of all the participants, particularly the scientists.

I think Richard Davidson, for example, has made such a great contribution with such motivation that I feel that I want to not only acknowledge you, Richie, but also repay your kindness. And you remain humble. That's very good. That I like. If a good scientist becomes too proud, he may lose respect. The same is true with religious leaders.

DANIEL GOLEMAN: This is a quite an unusual forum. Here we have an integrative, collaborative dialogue between science, spiritual traditions, and the humanities. We are going to use these multiple perspectives to address the current environmental crisis. This is a very unusual topic for Mind and Life.

Out of twenty-three meetings, I think this is only the second to address the "life" side of Mind and Life. As you will hear from the scientists, there is sad and bad news, and also some very hopeful news. But at the beginning we are going to make the scientific case that, as a species, we are engaged in what amounts to a slow-motion suicide if we continue the way we are now. It's because of this urgency, and the moral importance of the situation, that we felt this was a compelling topic for a Mind and Life meeting.

Your Holiness, in your talks, you often cite the love of a mother for her child as a basis for compassion. Today, we're facing a real paradox: even though we love our children as much as anyone in human history has, every day, each of us unwittingly acts in ways that create a future for this planet and for our own children, and their children, that will be much worse. The problem is rooted in a very important term that we are going to hear this morning: the Anthropocene age. So what does *Anthropocene* mean?

Diana Liverman will go into that in more detail later, but for a basic understanding, consider that geological history extends over millions of years, and that in the last few hundred years we've entered into a unique time in history. This is the first time the actions of one species are altering the planetary systems that support life in a negative way. That's the slow-motion suicide. And we are confronted with the dilemma that we have an urgent, compelling need to save ourselves from our worst enemy: ourselves.

The problem from an evolutionary psychology point of view is this: Our brains were formed over several hundred thousand years, and the alarm system in the brain, the system that recognizes threat and danger, was designed for detecting snarling tigers, not for detecting the very subtle causes of this planetary degradation. Our sensory system does not actually register the danger. It's too big, or it's too small, and therefore it's invisible to us. Our amygdala and its brain circuitry—the alarm system of the brain—doesn't realize there's a danger and doesn't activate.

This makes it very hard to motivate people to do anything about what is perhaps the worst crisis in human history. Rather, many people go through their daily lives as though nothing were happening. We're all in a kind of trance. Because of this design flaw in the brain, there's no sense of immediate threat.

In exploring this, I feel that Buddhism and Christian theology, as well as philosophy and psychology, have very important perspectives to offer science. Science documents what's happening, but it doesn't necessarily have within it the mechanisms to mobilize people to act in a skillful way. And that's the particular aspect of reality, or truth, we're seeking to explore over the course of the week.

2 The Science of Climate Change

PRESENTER: Diana Liverman, *University of Arizona*

DANIEL GOLEMAN: Diana Liverman is an environmental scientist, formerly at the University of Oxford and now at the University of Arizona, where she directs the Institute of the Environment and is a professor of geography and development. She looks at how environmental changes are affecting the developing world, and she has written many books and scholarly articles on the subject. She's a coauthor of the article "A Safe Operating Space for Humanity" (*Nature*, 2009), a paper that details how human activity is driving the degradation of the handful of planetary systems that support life. While we often hear about and talk about global warming, it is actually only one dimension of eight or nine world systems that support life.

DIANA LIVERMAN: Humans are changing the global environment and transforming the planet in many ways that affect the potential for our survival and the survival of other species. I represent an international group of scientists who are working very hard to try to understand what's happening to the earth, to the earth's systems, and how humans are changing these systems for better or for worse.

I want to set the scene for the conversations this week by showing how the rate of human impact on the planet has been accelerating over the last sixty years in a new era that we are calling the Anthropocene age. I'm going to make the case that these changes are not just affecting climate but also creating multiple risks to life: threats to water supplies and to ecosystems, increased pollution, and overuse of resources.

I will then discuss "planetary boundaries," which is the idea of setting limits that could guide the way we use the planet. In this context, I will discuss a set of environmental thresholds that we want to avoid.

I'll end with an update on the latest findings about climate change, and particularly some results about the Himalayan region. In the past five years, since the last big study on climate change was done by the Intergovernmental Panel on Climate Change (IPCC), we have new scientific results that give us even greater concern.

A Look at Human History

DIANA LIVERMAN: Figure 1 is based on chemical data from ice cores that show how the earth's average temperature has changed over the last 100,000 years. What you can see here is that 100,000 years ago, the earth was much cooler than it is today. The average temperature of the earth, from a few thousand years ago to as recently as 1950, was about 13.5 degrees Celsius.

HIS HOLINESS THE DALAI LAMA: As I understand it, some parts of the world today, such as Siberia, are very cold, but there are indications, based on archaeological findings, that at one time it was a very hot plateau. Similarly, was not India once under the sea? Are these changes within the time frame you are showing us?

DIANA LIVERMAN: Not really. The changes you are talking about took place over millions of years. What we are talking about includes two relatively recent geologic periods within the past 100,000 years: the ice ages and our current climate and weather patterns.

If we look at the graph (figure 1), at the left is the oldest period, starting a period of 90,000 years when it was quite cold. This was the period of the last ice age, the Wisconsin glaciation that ended around 12,000 years ago. There were very few humans during this period, and they migrated

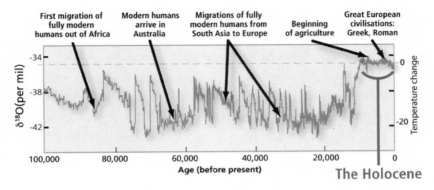

Figure 1. 100,000 years of human history

around the earth in small groups. They were living from hunting, gathering plants, and fishing.

The next point I want to show is on the right-hand side of the graph. There's a 10,000-year period where it warmed up to a much more comfortable temperature of just less than 15 degrees Celsius. What's interesting is that this is the period when agriculture developed. It's when the great civilizations developed, and many people think of this as an ideal period for human development and for many other species. This period was very good for humanity. It's the period when our populations grew, when we were able to grow food. This good period is what we call the Holocene.

The reason I wanted to show you this is because this Holocene period was a period of balance for humans and the planet. It was a period when we lived in relative harmony. I'm showing you this to set the stage for what we are doing now, which is taking ourselves out of the Holocene and into a period that could be much more challenging for the planet; for humans and for plants and animals.

So for the last 10,000 years the earth's systems have been in balance; human activities were moderate, and they did not have global impacts on the planet. Then, about 250 years ago, things changed, particularly with the Industrial Revolution and with advances in medicine that allowed populations to grow.

The Great Acceleration

DIANA LIVERMAN: What I'll do now is talk about the last 250 years. I want to show you a series of graphs that chart human activities and how they've grown over this period. Each graph shows growing human activity on the planet. On each of these graphs I've put a dotted line at 1950. On almost every graph you can see significant acceleration in growth at about 1950. This is the work of my friend Will Steffen, executive director of the Australian National University Climate Change Institute. He put together a series of graphs, and when we sat down and looked at them, we suddenly realized that there was a real change in the rate of growth at around 1950. We've had a "Great Acceleration" in our human impact on the planet.

This Great Acceleration is due to the growth in human population and consequently to the growth in resource use, particularly in the industrialized world. The impact is not only based on the number of people on the planet but more precisely on how much each person consumes, which varies from country to country. We'll look more closely at this later.

The first graph in figure 2 shows the world population. You can see the rapid growth. But this is actually one graph where we do have some good news. We know now that the population is likely to level off sometime around 2050 at about 9 billion people. It's one of the few activities where we see, perhaps, some good news.

HIS HOLINESS THE DALAI LAMA: Is it the result of family planning, or is it simply naturally occurring?

DIANA LIVERMAN: It's the result of millions of women around the world choosing to have fewer children.

HIS HOLINESS THE DALAI LAMA: Yes, through awareness, through education.

DIANA LIVERMAN: Yes, and it's often because women have more opportunities. There's more health care for them and they have been educated.

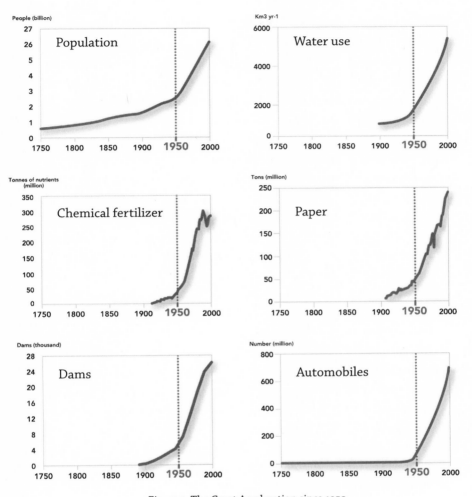

Figure 2. The Great Acceleration since 1950

When this happens they can make the choice if they would like to have fewer children.

This next graph shows the increase in water use. The left-hand side of the graph is blank because we didn't have any good data on water use until around 1900, but you can see the rapid increase since 1950.

The next graph is the use of chemical fertilizers, not traditional fertilizers. And here again you can see great growth. The change in 1950 is associated with the green revolution, which was the large increase in agricultural production, particularly in places like India. This increase in food production, while fewer people were hungry, also meant the use of a lot more agricultural chemicals. We can see this change begin around 1950. There is an interesting decline later, which has to do with economic problems in the developing world and the fact that many people can't afford fertilizers now.

The following graph is another indicator of human activity. This is the consumption of paper, which is of course linked to the destruction of the world's forests. Here again you can see a rapid increase. Perhaps that will decline a little bit with the use of computers, if they lead us to print less.

The next graph depicts the damming of the world's rivers. Again, you can see a rapid increase since 1900, and particularly since 1950, where we've made this decision, for better or worse, to control the rivers of the planet.

The final graph is very dramatic; it's the growth in the use of the motor vehicle. Of course, motor vehicles produce all sorts of pollution, both in the cities, such as Delhi, and in the atmosphere, because the fuel they burn produces greenhouse gases that are warming the planet. We have had a very dramatic increase in the use of motor vehicles.

So to sum this up, the point I want to make here is that human activities have been growing and growing in magnitude and size, particularly since 1950. We have coined the term "the Great Acceleration" to describe this trend. The Great Acceleration is not only a period of acceleration in human activity but also a period of acceleration in environmental consequences on the earth's system.

The Earth's System

DIANA LIVERMAN: The earth's system really relates to interconnection, one of the themes this week. It's the earth's interacting physical, chemical, and biological processes. The earth's system consists of the land, oceans, atmosphere, and living things, all of which are interconnected. It also includes the planet's natural cycles. Naturally occurring compounds and chemicals cycle through the earth; through rocks, through life, through the atmosphere. The most important of these are the carbon cycle, the water cycle, the nitrogen cycle (which occurs naturally and in fertilizers), and other cycles that I won't mention here, such as the cycles of phosphorus, sulfur, and others.

The way we live is an integral part of every one of these chemical cycles. We affect the carbon cycle because we exhale carbon dioxide and we grow crops that take up carbon dioxide. We affect nitrogen in the way we practice agriculture. We affect the water cycle in many ways, through consuming water and through building dams that change the flow of water. It's very important to remember that the earth's system is not separate from us, but rather that we are part of it. The earth's system includes human society, but our impacts are such that we are disturbing the balance of these natural cycles. And for scientists, while the complexity of all these cycles is beautiful, that complexity also makes it very difficult for us to understand exactly what's happening throughout the interconnected system.

Impacts from the Great Acceleration

DIANA LIVERMAN: Let's take a look now at what the great acceleration in human activity has done to the environment and to the planet. The first graph in figure 3 is one with which you may be familiar. It represents the concentration of carbon dioxide in the atmosphere. This is one of the greenhouse gases that are warming the planet, in the same way a greenhouse can warm the plants growing in it or a blanket can warm a person in bed. What we see here is that the use of fossil fuels, including the driving of vehicles, and the cutting of forests has led to this rapid increase in carbon dioxide. Again, you can see the Great Acceleration after 1950.

Figure 4 shows a graph of a second greenhouse gas, methane. It's not only carbon dioxide that is warming the planet; there are other gases.

The increase in methane is particularly associated with an increase in the world's livestock numbers; for example, cows and sheep. There has been a great growth in the population of animals, particularly because of people eating meat.

HIS HOLINESS THE DALAI LAMA: And chicken?

DIANA LIVERMAN: Yes, but chickens produce much less methane. Different animals emit different amounts of methane. Chickens are only responsible for the methane produced from their manure, but cattle are probably the most serious in terms of the amount of methane because of their emissions. In some parts of the world, cattle are kept in one large building, and the methane is captured and used to heat the building or the farmhouse. It can be recycled in this way.

The other sources of methane are waste dumps and landfills. As rubbish decomposes, it releases methane gas. There are many human factors that are causing a rise in the methane concentration, including our choice to raise livestock and eat meat, as well as the fact that we throw so many things away. This increase in methane, in addition to carbon dioxide, is warming the planet.

HIS HOLINESS THE DALAI LAMA: We know that a percentage of global warming is a natural cycle of the whole system that happens over millions of years, and this cycle is gradually and always changing. So is one factor in global warming this cycle? Can scientists calculate the percentage or the rate at which global warming is taking place that is actually the result of human impact versus the natural cycle the earth's climate goes through?

DIANA LIVERMAN: Yes, we can. One of the most important things to consider is that we're changing the greenhouse gas composition of the atmosphere much faster than the natural cycles. The natural cycles change the atmosphere over many thousands of years, yet we've changed it in a period

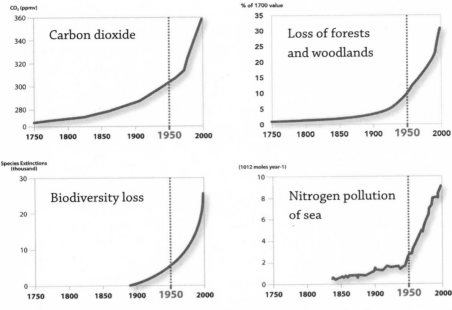

Figure 3. Environmental impacts from the Great Acceleration

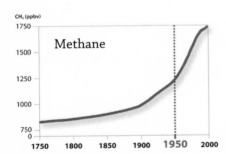

Figure 4. Atmospheric methane (CH_4) concentration

of just one hundred years. Also, the concentration of carbon dioxide in the atmosphere is now the highest it has been in 650,000 years as a result of human activity. And by looking at the chemistry of the atmosphere, we know that our greenhouse gases have created this level of carbon dioxide.

The Warming World

DIANA LIVERMAN: The impact of all of these gases can be seen on this graph, the observed warming of the planet (figure 5). This is the average temperature of the planet since 1880 in degrees Celsius. The graph is show-ing the variation around the average. The trend to notice is the growth in the temperature, particularly in the last ten or so years. Since 2000, we've had eleven of the warmest years on record. The year 2010 tied with 2005 as the hottest on record since record keeping began. And as we will hear this week, global warming has tremendous impacts on the world's system: on our glaciers, water, health, and lives.

There are other cycles that also affect global temperature. For example, when there's a volcanic eruption, it often gets a little cooler. And when we have changes in ocean currents that happen naturally, we can have a cooler year as well. Right now we have surface temperatures in parts of the Pacific Ocean that are cooling some areas of the planet. This is called

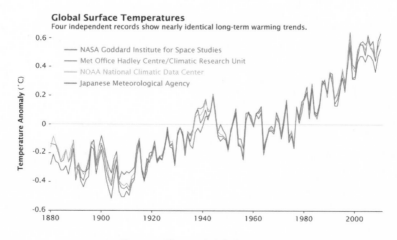

Figure 5. Observed global warming

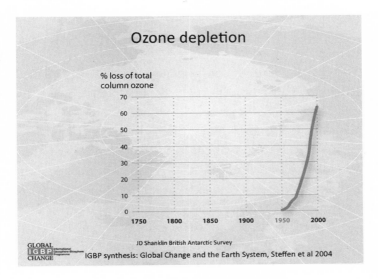

Figure 6. Depletion of the ozone layer

La Niña. There are variations from year to year, but the long-term trend, and what we should focus on, is that it's getting much warmer.

I also want to show you a few more impacts that are not related to climate change. Figure 6 shows an impact associated with our use of chemicals for refrigeration and air conditioning: the depletion of the protective ozone layer, which is what protects us from skin cancer. Since 1950 there has been a loss of the ozone layer, and this has increased the risks of cancer.

If we refer back to figure 3, we see another very dramatic impact of human activity: the loss of tropical rainforests around the world. Here, again, you can see the Great Acceleration—human activity creating a great acceleration in the impact on the planet.

Another cause of impact is the exploitation of fisheries (see figure 7). We are taking more and more fish, not just for ourselves, but we also feed great amounts of fish to our pets.

Figure 3 also shows the pollution of our coastal waters due to our use of nitrogen-based fertilizers. When these waters get polluted by fertilizers, some organisms take up all the oxygen and dead zones are created for other species.

Figure 3 has one more: the loss of biodiversity, which means the loss of species through extinction, including plants and animals, insects, fish—all of the fellow species on the planet.

To sum up, we've shifted from the Holocene period to a new geologic epoch, which Nobel Prize–winner Paul Crutzen called the Anthropocene, where human activity shapes the planet more than any other factor. The term *Anthropocene* comes from *anthro*, which means "human," and *cene*, which means "new." So it's the new human epoch we believe we have entered, which is defined by a planet completely shaped by humans.

Figure 8 is a very powerful photo that was created from satellite images. It shows the human impact on the planet through our use of energy for

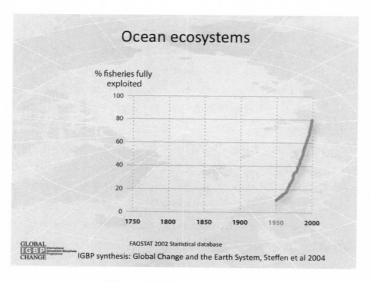

Figure 7. Exploitation of fisheries

Figure 8. Satellite image of the Anthropocene world

light. It's actually a photograph of the Anthropocene, if you like. You can see how the industrial world is brighter. And because most of the electricity that powers these lights is produced from coal, oil, and gas, these lights also represent greenhouse gas emissions and air pollution. The photo shows that some regions are much more responsible than others for energy use and related pollution. One of the interesting things you can see is that much of Africa, Latin America, and the Tibetan Plateau is dark. These are areas that are not contributing to greenhouse gases and to air pollution. It's because either people are not there or people are poor or people are living in harmony with the planet.

HIS HOLINESS THE DALAI LAMA: This is more due to the fact that they do not have the resources and ability to use as much energy, not so much out of awareness or self-discipline.

DIANA LIVERMAN: I think the planet is grateful, whatever the reason. You can also see that North America, Europe, India, Japan, and the coast of China are much brighter. Clearly, some people and regions are placing a much greater burden on the planet than others, but overall this photograph is a good example of what we mean by the human-dominated planet of the Anthropocene. And the fact that we now dominate the planet brings great responsibility.

Planetary Boundaries

DIANA LIVERMAN: There's a further reason for concern. We think that the growing impact of human activity on life-supporting systems may take us to dangerous thresholds. Figure 9 is a photo of a child looking over a waterfall, which symbolizes what we're worried about: by warming the planet, by destroying species and earth systems, we may actually take ourselves to thresholds where change will be very sudden and rapid, and even irreversible.

Examples of the abrupt and rapid changes that we're worried about include the possibility that global warming may trigger the breakup of the great ice sheets in Antarctica and the large-scale release of greenhouse gases from frozen ground where they've been trapped. As the ground warms and melts, these could be released, and that would add to the warming of the planet. We're also concerned that some of the world's great forests, which currently absorb carbon dioxide, may become drier and may not be able to play their role in the carbon dioxide cycles. Some of these changes could be very difficult to reverse. We want to avoid getting near those thresholds.

Another example would be the ocean threshold, where we have combined effects on the world's oceans. Carbon dioxide is making the oceans more acidic, and that's affecting species in the oceans, particularly in and around coral reefs. We're also overfishing the oceans and putting fertilizer into the oceans. Fertilizers get into the oceans through the great rivers of the world. For example, the Mississippi River in the United States carries all of the agricultural pollution from the Midwest into the Gulf of Mexico and poisons life in that aquatic region. All of these actions can combine to destroy parts of the oceans.

So these sudden, rapid, and possibly irreversible thresholds need to be understood, monitored, and avoided. Sometimes we call them "tipping points," as if I leaned forward on the chair and then fell off. We're very worried about these tipping points. A group of us came together to try to set some guidelines for avoiding falling over these thresholds. We created what we call a set of "planetary boundaries" to guide the management of the planet.

Of course, you don't want to set the threshold right at the edge of the cliff. You want time to change, time to put on the brakes. You want to take account of the fact that we may not be exactly sure where the boundary is. So we've set the thresholds at a safe distance from where we think the actual boundaries of collapse may be.

Figure 9 is a diagram of the planetary boundaries that we have established. We identified this set of boundaries to create a safe operating space for the planet. This project was led by my friend Johan Rockstrom,

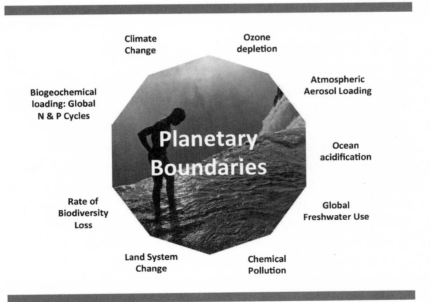

Figure 9. Planetary boundaries

executive director of the Stockholm Resilience Centre and professor at the University of Stockholm. The idea is to set limits that will keep us away from the danger zones. We've identified a set of thresholds that define a safe space for humanity, and I'll tell you briefly what each of them are. I won't go into scientific details; the general idea is that we have a set of boundaries.

- The first boundary is to avoid the risks of dangerous climate change. We've set that at a technical limit of **350 parts per million of carbon dioxide** in the atmosphere.
- The second boundary is to prevent the depletion of the ozone layer to avoid the risk of cancer, and we've set the boundary at **276 Dobson Units**.
- The third boundary is one that we haven't been able to define yet, but it has to do with aerosols, dust and soot, in the atmosphere. These can be dangerous to human health and to the environment.
- The fourth boundary is designed to save the oceans from becoming acidic: **2.75 aragonite saturation**.
- The fifth boundary is to prevent us from using too much water. It sets a limit on what the planet, as a whole, can take in terms of human water use: **4,000 cubic kilometers per year**.
- The sixth boundary is difficult to define (in figure 9, it's referred to as "chemical pollution" and in figure 10 as "novel entities"), but it has to do with all the toxic chemicals that we're putting into the environment, including plastics and poisonous heavy metals such as lead. We need to limit these, but we haven't been able to calculate the exact boundary yet.
- The seventh boundary has to do with the conversion of lands for agricultural use—constraining the conversion of forests and other wild lands to agriculture at no more than **15 percent of total land**.
- The eighth boundary—defined as the loss of no more than **ten species each month per year**—is to limit the loss of biodiversity, to try to prevent species from going extinct.

· And the final boundaries limit pollution from nitrogen (no more than **35 metric tons per year**) and phosphorus (no more than **11 metric tons per year**), which occur as pollutants from various sources such as chemical fertilizers.

The diagram in figure 10 is a little complicated, but what I want to show you is the history of our march toward these thresholds and danger zones. Each of these lines is the walk toward the cliff, so to speak. The inner thick line is the safe boundary. The collapse would be somewhere out beyond the safe zone.

What we can see here is that in the 1950s we were already marching the planet toward the danger zone with the conversion of forests to agricultural land use. We were starting to put greenhouse gases into the atmosphere and approaching that boundary, and our use of nitrogen fertilizer was taking us toward its boundary. Some of the variables, such as phosphorus flow, ozone depletion, aerosol load, ocean acidity, and chemical pollution were not being measured yet in 1950. We've estimated undocumented levels for the 1970s and 1990s where possible. And as we look at the present day, it is very dramatic. In fifty years we have gone out of the safe zone on three variables: biodiversity loss, nitrogen flow, and climate change.

Though this looks terrible, there is some good news. There are some boundaries where we are still well within the safe zone. For example, in terms of our freshwater consumption, we still have some capacity as a whole planet. The complication is that there are some areas where we have gone over the boundary of water use already, and others where we haven't.

There's another piece of good news here, which has to do with ozone depletion. In 1990 we were closer to the danger zone than we are now, and that's because the world got together and agreed to control the chemicals that were damaging the ozone layer. Today, the ozone layer is beginning to heal. This shows that we can, in fact, not only stay away from the danger zones but also bring ourselves back away from the boundaries.

But it's very important that we move back from these boundaries before we hit the thresholds, because once we go over a threshold, it could be very difficult to reverse the course and impacts.

Himalayan Glaciers and Carbon Emissions

DIANA LIVERMAN: We're now going to the final part of my presentation, which brings us back to the Himalayas. I want to end with a brief update on some of the latest research results on climate change. I know you are already very aware and concerned about global warming and its impact on the landscapes and lives of the people in this region. We are working very hard to monitor and explain what's happening, and what may happen in the future, to the climate in different areas of this region.

The first thing I wanted to mention is that, despite the fact that the countries of the world have met regularly to try to control greenhouse gas emissions, and some efforts have been made to control emissions, the gas levels are continuing to rise. The concentration of carbon dioxide in the atmosphere is now almost 40 percent above where it was before the Industrial Revolution. As I mentioned earlier, it's the highest it's been in 650,000 years. China has just become the largest emitter of greenhouse gases at 2 billion gigatons, followed by the United States, and then India. If Europe were treated as one country it would be higher than India, but being English, I treat Europe as separate countries. However, European nations combined would still be lower than China or the United States. And Japan has actually reduced its emissions slightly. It has a very efficient economy that is helping with that output.

It's very interesting to note that the per capita emissions vary greatly in different regions. In the United States, we produce 5 tons of carbon per year, per capita. In China it's 0.6 tons per capita, per year, and in India 0.2 tons. Therefore, each person in India is less responsible than each person in the United States for carbon emissions.

There's another interesting result I wanted to share with you about China's emissions. We estimate that one-third of China's emissions are

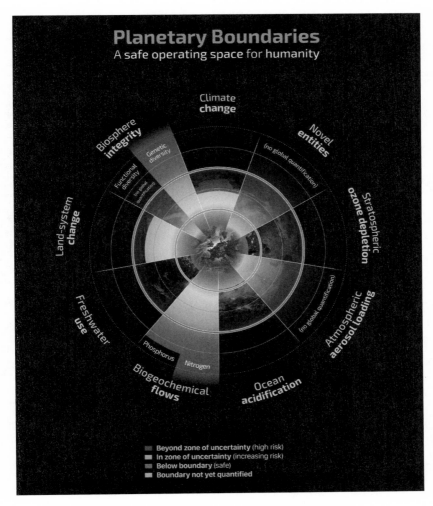

Figure 10. Human activity and planetary boundary limits

stimulated by the United States through demand for manufactured goods exported from China to the United States. So, in a sense, American consumers are responsible for one-third of China's emissions as well.

If these trends continue, in terms of overall increase in greenhouse gases, the latest computer models suggest that the world could warm by

5 degrees Celsius, that is 9 degrees Fahrenheit, by the end of this century. Also, we could have a world that could be warmer by at least 4 degrees Celsius within fifty or sixty years. This is a significant change over previous estimates, such as those in the IPCC report from 2007. The latest results are pushing up the temperature estimates because of both the increase in emissions and better scientific methods and models for measuring and estimating. Unfortunately, better models seem to give us more troubling results in terms of what we think may happen to the climate.

We're worried that it will be warmer than we even thought it would be.

One example in a recent paper suggests that the temperatures during heat waves that we get today, such as those in Delhi when it can reach 45 degrees Celsius, will become the average in the future, and that the extremes could be 50 degrees Celsius. In other words, the future summer average would be what the most extreme conditions are today. This is of great concern, because heat waves especially affect the poor.

In terms of the glaciers in the Himalayas, I wanted to confirm the scientific results that suggest that many of the glaciers are losing their volume, especially those that are at lower altitudes. This is linked to global warming. The Tibetan Plateau, for example, has warmed more than anywhere else on Earth, 1.8 degrees Celsius in recent years.

But there's a new factor that's contributing to the melting of the glaciers: deposits from air pollution, such as dust and soot, on the glaciers, which makes them melt more rapidly because darker surfaces warm more quickly. So it's not just global warming, it's also air pollution that is contributing to the loss of the glaciers.

However, I did want to tell you that some of the popular myths that all of the ice will disappear are unlikely to come true. Many of the glaciers are so high in the Himalayas that even warming will not cause them to fully melt. We do think, however, that we could lose 40 percent of the volume of the glaciers, perhaps as soon as the middle of this century. This could create problems with lakes filling up and spilling over and increase the risk of flooding in places like Bhutan. It's also eventually going to cause problems with the flow of rivers.

Even so, we don't need to worry about all of the rivers in the same way, because many of the rivers in Asia get most of their water from the monsoon rains, not from the glaciers. The two rivers connected to glaciers that we're most concerned about are the Brahmaputra and the Indus.

The final thing I wanted to share with you is that although many people in this region of Asia are worried about melting glaciers, we need to be much more worried about what climate change would do to the monsoon. This is where I feel a little unable as a scientist to tell you what's going to happen. There are some very contradictory results recently about what will happen to the monsoon.

What we think is that climate change will mean that wetter areas will get more rain and drier areas will get less. The monsoon might become more intense. This is a new scientific frontier, and it's one of the areas where we're doing a lot of research because we now understand how important the future of the monsoon will be to this part of the world.

With that I will finish, and I hope this provides a good context for our discussion. I look forward to any questions you might have, and thank you very much for the opportunity.

Leaders Need to Know the Facts

HIS HOLINESS THE DALAI LAMA: As I mentioned, leaders should know more about these serious matters. Sometimes the problem with the environmental movement is that it can become a kind of political fad. When we look at the data, it's a very serious matter. Global leaders should be exposed to this kind of data so that people who are responsible for countries will become fully convinced of the seriousness of the situation. More awareness needs to be created, particularly awareness in free countries where leaders are chosen through election. Also, the United Nations, a world body, should have a much clearer awareness of these issues. Then they can take these issues more seriously and perhaps act upon them effectively.

DIANA LIVERMAN: As you are aware, Your Holiness, the next big UN meeting on the environment is in Rio in June. Scientists are doing what they can to provide scientific input on these issues to the meeting, but I have noticed that there seems to be less attention to this meeting than to previous meetings. It almost seems as though the world's attention has turned away from the environment for the moment. It's a little frustrating because it seems as though people aren't as prepared to listen.

DANIEL GOLEMAN: Well there's another dimension, too, and that is that many of these reports are commissioned by governments, or by the UN, for leaders, but leaders exist in a political atmosphere where there are also pressures from vested economic interest—oil companies, gas companies—and so the findings have become politicized.

Diana, I think you have some experience with questions being raised about the credibility of the climate science, and people, for political reasons, trying to create doubt in other's minds about this data. So what's happening now in terms of climate? I know that was a very big issue, in fact the data about Tibet was particularly called into question.

The Credibility of Climate Science

DIANA LIVERMAN: Yes, about three years ago there was an orchestrated attack on climate science, which tried to undermine the credibility of much of the science that I've presented to you. It's been very difficult for climate science over the last three years because the media overplayed some of the criticisms. While there were some errors—perhaps a few errors in three thousand pages of documents—more recently, there have been reports to respond to the criticism showing that the science was correct.

We have been trying very hard to reestablish the credibility of climate science over the last few years. It's particularly difficult in the United States, where there is a very strong criticism of climate change and an unwillingness to accept that global warming is happening. Also, it's part of the political debate; the issue has become very politicized. Scientists are having a hard time figuring out how to respond. How do we regain the trust of politicians and of the public?

Perhaps it's because the science is telling people things they don't want to hear; telling them that they need to change. I'm not sure what the origins of this attack on the science were, but I would say that we're more and more confident about what we know, not less confident. We're confident that Earth is warming. We know that the ice is disappearing. We know that it's a result of human activity. So scientists are just as confident as we always were, but it seems as though some leaders have lost confidence in what we're saying.

DANIEL GOLEMAN: Also, there's the assumption that awareness alone will be enough to cause leaders to act, or cause anybody to act. But, as we're going to hear in more detail over the course of the week, there's good evidence (including the fact that the acceleration is continuing) that this may not be the case for most people. I wonder if any of our panelists might speak to the gap between awareness and action. Elke?

Awareness versus Action

ELKE WEBER: Good morning, Your Holiness. I just want to reiterate what Diana said, that it's true that climate change, or other environmental disaster messages, are very uncomfortable for many of us. We don't want to hear about them because the implications are so severe. We all have to change our way of life, and we don't like change. I'm going to say much more about that in my upcoming presentation.

HIS HOLINESS THE DALAI LAMA: But I think for most people, if their physician said, "Based on your physical condition, you should not smoke," they would listen. I think once awareness and conviction develop, people will change. It is in their best interest, in humanity's best interest. I think we still need to make greater efforts to create awareness, including working with the media.

ELKE WEBER: Unfortunately, people are not so easily convinced by this environmental data. They're convinced by the physician when they're hurting. When you're hurting, you realize you're sick and you need to do something. But when we say there's climate change and you look out of the window and it's snowing, it's easy for people in Washington, DC, to say there's no climate change.

HIS HOLINESS THE DALAI LAMA: They can see the weather changing and the extreme melting of glaciers. These are visible facts.

ELKE WEBER: Think about tobacco and smoking. It took us fifty years to realize that we should ban tobacco, even though the scientific data existed long before. Statistics are not very convincing. People like to believe their own senses, and with climate change, by the time our senses tell us that there's a problem, it's going to be too late. And that's a real problem.

HIS HOLINESS THE DALAI LAMA: In any case, we must make extra effort to find a way to get through to those who are not listening. We have no other alternatives. We must make them listen and convince them of the issues. In these modern times, the scientist can sometimes be considered a guru, a person of authority on these issues. The gurus need to come out and speak.

DIANA LIVERMAN: I think that at the moment, we scientists who work on climate change are doing a lot of evaluation of ourselves. In particular, we know that we need to reach out more to ordinary people, to speak in schools and community centers. But also we need to listen. It's important to understand what's confusing people. And we've learned that we make big mistakes. For example, many scientists talk in degrees Celsius because that's the scientific term, but in the United States, everybody thinks in Fahrenheit. So when I say it's going to warm up 4 degrees Celsius, they think that's very little, because they're thinking Fahrenheit. It's actually about 7 degrees Fahrenheit. We have to change our language in order to communicate better.

MATTHIEU RICARD: Considering a combination of the evolutionary and Buddhist perspectives, we often speak of reacting both from the cognitive aspect and the emotional aspect. As Dan said at the beginning, emotionally we fear things that are immediate. If an elephant is running through the room, we are afraid and react. If someone says an elephant will be here in ten years, nobody moves. And that's why we need the cognitive as well as the emotional. Change in the cognitive comes with deep investigation, and that's more challenging. And that's the dilemma. The future doesn't hurt, not yet. It is somehow too far away for us to be moved emotionally; we need more of the cognitive aspect to consider the future consequences.

THUPTEN JINPA: It's true that the environmental evidence and the science of environmental degradation are not that visible, but, on the other hand, it is also true that a lot of people do experience effects right now. For example, with health conditions, people may have difficulty breathing or experience some other kind of environment-related disease.

DIANA LIVERMAN: I think that climate change will be experienced very much through extremes. When people begin to experience natural disasters such as floods and droughts, then they will start to believe that the climate is changing. Also, people who live closest to the environment are often already convinced, because they can see what is happening to them. People who live further away from nature may be less aware. One of the studies Elke may be familiar with found that the people who are most aware that the climate is changing are those who have gardens. They see the change in their gardens. Perhaps if more people were gardeners, more would be aware of the changing climate.

JONATHAN PATZ: Your Holiness, you made the analogy of when your doctor tells you you're sick, you change your behavior. This was followed by some comments from Elke and Matthieu about the difficulty in perceiving the problem. I was actually a physician before I trained as an environmental scientist, and I have an analogy from a physician's point of view. When patients come to you and they're bleeding, and you can see the problem, you can sew them up and treat them immediately; that's very obvious. Or if they are having a heart attack and short of breath, it's obvious.

But I see the problem of global environmental change and degradation, its direct and indirect effects on human health and well-being, as very insidious and, as Matthieu said, nearly invisible in many cases. I think the analogy is more akin to high blood pressure: when you have high blood pressure, you feel fine, but inside it's killing you. It's harming every system in your body over a long period of time. It's called an "insidious killer."

And so in some regards this problem of global ecological climate change will be more difficult to deal with than the ozone layer. Diana mentioned how we've solved that problem, or nearly solved that problem. Well, you could see the hole in the ozone by satellite, and it had a very direct impact. The environmental destruction of the ozone layer caused skin cancer and eye cataracts. We could see it, so it was simpler.

Climate change affects a broad range of things, and except for possibly heat waves, we'll have many more indirect, invisible, and insidious problems. I think that's why this is so challenging, and why it will be more difficult to reverse.

Our Minds Can Help Us Plan and Change

HIS HOLINESS THE DALAI LAMA: Actually, consider that this specialized human brain is able to think in terms of long-term interests. We can't expect animals to have the same forethought. They have little or no conceptual long-term intelligence; they live day by day. But we have this marvelous brain. So we must think about what will happen in ten years, in a hundred years, perhaps even a thousand years—or maybe that is too long. Eventually the sun will change in a serious way too; then we can give up hope. And then it will be better to just meditate on impermanence. There will be no need for worry then! But for now the obvious, serious changes in the climate, such as wet areas getting wetter, floods, and some dry areas getting drier, need to be addressed. How can you make the connection between those changes and global warming, and tie that connection to human actions? What is the causal link and why would global warming produce those kinds of weather extremes?

DIANA LIVERMAN: There are several quite complex reasons. One is that warmer air holds more moisture. Another is that when some parts of the world warm more than others, stronger winds are created, which build storms, which in turn release more moisture from the warmer air.

Also, the great cycles of the atmosphere, such as air rising at the equator and sinking over the subtropics, are accelerated. Where it rises, you get rain and a wetter climate. The sinking air will be stronger, drying things out.

But it's extremely complicated, because we also have phenomena like the monsoon, which depends on the difference between the temperatures of the ocean and the temperatures of the Tibetan Plateau. We're still trying to understand how those dynamics will change.

There are certain parts of the world that we know will get warmer and drier. We're thinking of those as the hot spots of the planet. These include places like southern Africa, the Mediterranean, and the part of the United States where I live, Arizona. In India, it looks as if some areas will get wetter because of an increase in moisture that will be in the atmosphere.

It's as if the cycles get more intense because there's more energy from the warming. Another example would be the formation of hurricanes and typhoons. As the oceans warm, heat feeds the energy of the storms. We think that hurricanes and typhoons will become fiercer and more intense. Not that we will necessarily have more of them, but they will be stronger.

We Are Not Our Own Enemy

SALLIE MCFAGUE: Your Holiness, I am wondering whether it helps to think a bit about another great crisis that human beings faced, which was World War II. You and I were both children during then. It was a terrible time, but people thought, "Well, we're going to get together, and we're going to fight this enemy." The problem now is that the enemy is us, and it's so much more difficult to fight our own tendencies and our denial, our desire to have the comfortable lives that we have, than it is to fight something that's outside of ourselves. What do you think?

HIS HOLINESS THE DALAI LAMA: We should not consider ourselves our own enemy, no. Within our emotions and ideas some parts can be our enemy, such as ignorance. But as human beings, as sentient beings, I think we are primarily positive, that we want to survive. That is why we are discussing these issues. If we really are our own enemies, then it is better to finish this off and not bother seriously discussing these issues. For human beings to survive, I believe you have to see things positively.

SALLIE MCFAGUE: Well, doesn't one have to free that good part of us? I mean, there's one part of us that doesn't want to face difficult things, and says, "It's too hard for us to do all these things," and the other part says, "No," as you're saying, "we've got to do it together." But it's difficult in this case, because we don't see it as clearly as we did with a war, or if the enemy were outside.

HIS HOLINESS THE DALAI LAMA: Oh yes, that's right. But to a large degree, it's really a question of understanding and awareness. The more we understand, the more we become aware. As human beings, we have the ability to develop long-term visions and think of the future. That's our sort of special "gift from God." So we must utilize it.

We have such wonderful capacities for memory and language. We record outcomes using scientific methods. We now know about the previous hundred thousand years, about what happened. Only human beings have this ability and knowledge. Maybe angels know these things, but that is at a mysterious level. We have the ability to look back several centuries and similarly to consider several centuries into the future. With that sort of knowledge, with that ability, then we must make proper plans.

SALLIE MCFAGUE: I couldn't agree with you more. The question is how to get people willing to make those proper plans, because we're not doing it right now. Why aren't we doing it?

HIS HOLINESS THE DALAI LAMA: I think it requires constant, tireless effort. If, each year, we increase the number of people who are clearly aware of these things, their awareness and enthusiasm will lead them to do something. If each year we reach a hundred thousand people, then in ten years we can reach a million. Eventually this will have an effect. It's like education. When education was first deemed important, very few people were in fact educated. Now education is universal.

Similarly, with ecology, very few people showed concern during the last century. But gradually, as scientists share the seriousness of our current state, awareness will grow.

To use myself as an example, when I came from Tibet in 1959, I had no concept of problems with the environment. I would freely drink any surface water in Tibet—it was very clean and pure. When we would travel, whenever we came across a river or stream, we would drink and enjoy it.

It was only after I left Tibet and came to India that I first heard, "You cannot drink this water." I was surprised that it was polluted. I had never experienced that in Tibet. And through awareness, I now feel a deep concern about the environment, as it has become a question of our survival. Not just for me, not just for a few hundred, but for the survival of nearly 7 billion human beings. So it is quite serious.

I learned about this through awareness—not through meditation, but through awareness with help from scientists. That is why I call scientists "gurus."

Another good thing about scientists is that they tend to have an open mind; they're not as fixed about ideas as some of us. Sometimes we religious people are a little bit fixed, but scientists try to be unbiased. That is very good. So when they find facts, they accept them.

How Do We Create Awareness?

DIANA LIVERMAN: I teach very large classes of students and one source of optimism I've found is the level of interest and concern the students have for these issues. When I give this talk to a group of undergraduates, they immediately ask, "What can we do? What can we do?"

This is really meaningful, and in light of what you just said I feel I should be teaching even more classes. I also wanted to make a couple more comments. One is that scientists sometimes wish that carbon dioxide were a colored gas, so that people could see it. Unfortunately, it's a clear gas.

HIS HOLINESS THE DALAI LAMA: Yes, that is unfortunate. If people could somehow see or be exposed to the levels of carbon dioxide in the atmosphere, perhaps they would be more motivated to take the issue seriously.

DIANA LIVERMAN: Interestingly, even overexposure to carbon dioxide may not have the intended effect. Near where I live in Arizona, we have a facility called Biosphere 2, where we tried to simulate a miniature planet. When people went into Biosphere 2 with no exchange from the outside, the carbon dioxide levels did go up. But one thing that happens with increased carbon dioxide levels is you start laughing; carbon dioxide makes you silly before it kills you.

CLARE PALMER: This goes back to Sallie's comments. I'm thinking about these environmental problems being caused by the "bad" side of us. But one of the problems with carbon dioxide emissions is that we don't intend to produce them, and we would behave in the same ways even if we weren't producing the carbon dioxide emissions. We don't drive our cars in order to emit; it's a side effect of what we do. So it's a more complicated problem about being aware of things that we don't intend to happen, as well as things that we actually intend.

DANIEL GOLEMAN: So we don't intend them, we don't see them, and we don't perceive them. That makes it very difficult to raise awareness.

People Are Concerned But Need Direction

DIANA LIVERMAN: We're acting as if nobody is concerned, but Elke and I have a friend, Tony Leiserowitz, who does surveys all over the world. His surveys show that the majority of people are concerned about climate change; they are aware. (*Climate Change in the American Mind*) It's not everybody, but even in the United States with all of the politics, the majority of people think the world is warming and would like something to be done. It's perhaps the citizens who understand it and somehow the leaders are not quite responding to that understanding.

ELKE WEBER: Can I add something to this? When Al Gore released his movie *An Inconvenient Truth*, there were many people who were very concerned about the problem. They came out of the movie theaters and wanted to act. So I think one other important thing we have to talk about is not just getting people's attention, but once we have it, we have to tell them what to do. And the solutions are not simple.

One of the reasons the ozone problem was solved, and we now actually have a reduction of the ozone hole in the atmosphere, is because there were simple solutions. There were two or three simple things that industry could do, such as substitutes for the ozone-depleting gases. When we can do something about a problem, we will. When we have no simple solutions, we try to deny that it's a problem, because we feel powerless.

More Than Climate Change

DIANA LIVERMAN: Though we're talking a lot about climate change, one of the intentions of my talk was to show that even if we solved climate change, there are many other problems, and we have to learn how to manage them all together. For many scientists, there are other risks such as biodiversity loss and the extinction of species.

We've almost become so focused on climate change that we've forgotten about these other thresholds. Part of the point of the planetary boundaries was to remind us that we need to be focused on all of these very, very serious problems. The problems of water use, of species extinction, of pollution: we have to manage all of those together. I think they all have similar roots in human consumption of resources. And from a scientific point of view, it's the multiple stresses that we're concerned about. What happens when climate interacts with deforestation, which interacts with water scarcity? How do we give guidance on all of those stresses together?

One affects the other. Biodiversity loss and forest loss is affecting climate, and vice versa. We need to have international action on all of those. You've mentioned the United Nations, Your Holiness. The UN has conventions on climate and on oceans, but in many of these other areas we still haven't even been able to get the United States to take a position.

JOHN DUNNE: If I may ask a question? We heard the notion that perhaps it is very important to have something to do, so to speak. The science tells us a lot about the dangers. We have a case of a successful intervention in the context of ozone. So what's the next thing that might be like ozone? What's the most promising area in which advancement could be made quickly? Because, of course, the more successful cases we can demonstrate, the more good news we have, probably the more people will be willing to really accept and look more carefully and gain the knowledge necessary to reverse some of this environmental degradation. So is there an area that's the most promising? Or is it all hopeless?

DIANA LIVERMAN: It's not all hopeless. I was trying to think of which one of those boundaries it could be. I think it could be the loss of forests that we are really starting to tackle, in part through increasing the amount of protected areas. Matthieu was talking about Bhutan, and many countries, such as Brazil, for example, are making very serious efforts to protect their forests. Even Indonesia, which had very bad loss of forests, is now taking that issue seriously. I think there's a combination of a commitment to protect forests with investment in allowing more food to be produced on the same land. That doesn't necessarily mean plant breeding. It can just mean reducing losses and pests, or helping farmers get a little more yield. So perhaps the forest boundary might be the one that would be relatively easy to solve, and it's something that a lot of individuals are already taking action on. Perhaps others might have a boundary that they're more optimistic about, but that's my choice.

How Do We Make Sustainability a Norm?

DEKILA CHUNGYALPA: Your Holiness, I'm thinking about what Diana was talking about earlier, the fact that there are individuals who are very concerned about climate change. There is a program called Earth Hour, in which one-fifth of the world is actually participating. They switch the lights off for one hour each a year to demonstrate their concern about climate change. Some of our monasteries participate in it. At the individual level, the concern is there. The challenge is at the institutional level, because there are so many reasons at an institutional level why nobody wants to change. If you look at the oil, mining, and gas industries, you see a pattern of development that persists. In many ways, it seems as though we are only being given one blueprint for economic growth.

So the challenge really is, how do we make sustainability a social norm? The individuals are already there; how do we engage the institutions? My own hope is that religion will play a very big role.

I think, especially where I live in the United States, most people really want to live the good life. That means you want more and more things for yourself. How do we bring sustainability into this way of thinking? It seems to me that the only area where we naturally embrace sacrifice is religion. You fast because you want to evolve spiritually, or you take on robes and vows because you want to enlighten other living beings. If religions can come together and institutionally start transforming other institutional minds, maybe there is great hope there.

HIS HOLINESS THE DALAI LAMA: There are people who are serious about their religious faith, and these people are acting in accordance with what they believe, but that is a limited number of people. For example, here in India, there seems to be a significant portion of religious-minded people, but equally there are a lot of corrupt people. Even supposedly religious people often do not hesitate to get involved with corruption. That's a clear sign that they are not serious about their religious faith.

When you believe in God, Buddha, Vishnu, or other faiths, you must act honestly. The common messages or practices in all religions are justice, honesty, and truthfulness. But these common themes don't always manifest in the behavior of individuals. Therefore, I think religion could present difficulties. My greater hope is education.

In Bhutan, and some other smaller countries, such as some of the Baltic states, there seems to be the development of a different lifestyle. Recently I was in Estonia. As usual, I woke up early in the morning and was out at around four or five in the morning. There were no cars on the street, just a few people walking and riding bicycles.

I thought, the lifestyle here appears to be very good, it should be preserved. In New York, Los Angeles, or San Francisco, you see cars almost twenty-four hours a day. That lifestyle is actually unrealistic.

Meanwhile, on a global level, there are a lot of poor people in areas such as India and China. That is immoral. We must improve their standard of living. But at the same time, if these poorer people—I think they number more than 2 billion human beings now, between China and India probably close to 3 billion—want cars and other First World material possessions, that's impossible. We can't handle 3 billion more cars. And yet we cannot say, "Oh, we're rich people. We have a special right to have these things. You should remain poor." We must reduce this gap between rich and poor. But the reality is that the Western, American lifestyle is impossible to copy in the rest of the world.

So some of these smaller nations could be a good example of how to create sustainable lifestyles and economies where people are more equal and happy, and live in a just society. Then, gradually, other nations might follow that example. What do you think, Matthieu?

MATTHIEU RICARD: Recently Jonathan Patz, Richie Davidson, Susan Davidson, and I went to Bhutan and met the environment minister. He said that more than half of the country is now national parks and 80 percent is natural land. This has been increasing over the past twenty years. In five years they are going to completely phase out pesticides and fertilizers and farming will be 100 percent organic. In ten years, they will have zero carbon emissions. So that's an example of a more sustainable country.

There are also cities that are good examples. I just read something about Portland, Oregon. There are 20 percent fewer cars, they grow organic gardens in parts of the city, and all this has the support of the citizens. So these efforts can also come at the community level. Perhaps other cities can learn from that.

And just to add to what Your Holiness was saying about greed and corruption, the problem is that greed and corruption needs immediate satisfaction. You're not greedy for something in a hundred years. So in the United States, most of those who finance campaigns to make people believe that there's no climate change are those involved in reaping immediate benefits from oil and similar industries. To protect those benefits, they give millions and millions to these campaigns. So that's one of the problems.

But we also have to consider the holistic view. There is a social psychologist named Tim Kasser, professor at Knox College, who studied how strongly people are inclined to consumption and consumerism. He studied tens of thousands of people over a period of twenty years. What he found is that people who have more also have a greater desire to consume more. They place more value in possessions, in identity and reputation, and having nice cars and so forth. They are much less concerned about holistic values. They don't care much about the environment. They are only looking for immediate pleasures.

And somehow they also often have fewer friends and frequently worse health. So, in fact, they seek too much value and hope outside of themselves, and they don't have enough of a sense of intrinsic value. That's an interesting study, because it's not about ethics, but if you want to be happy, to have many friends, to be in good health, and to be concerned about the big picture, just live a little bit more from a place of voluntary simplicity.

DIANA LIVERMAN: Considering the question of India and China, and people's aspirations for a motor vehicle or for other consumer items, I feel as though there's another question to consider here: suppose we have a car that was all electric and used solar energy, would we then find that acceptable? Is it okay for people to consume more if it doesn't damage the environment?

That's the contradiction, and as Gregory will discuss, there are ways to calculate the impact of different consumer goods. If a consumer good has low impact, does that make it acceptable? That's one of the questions I have. I know from my work in Latin America that for some people a car means a better life. They can get to the hospital faster; they can take their children to school.

I think that there are some very interesting questions here. You've also given me an idea with your report on Bhutan. We should do a paper on how Bhutan is staying within the planetary boundaries as an example of how to achieve that goal.

JONATHAN PATZ: Just to follow up, Your Holiness, about the change in cities, and specifically about the automobile, which I'll be speaking to a little bit in my presentation: Sometimes it's not so good to have an automobile, especially in a big traffic jam. The city of Bogota, in Columbia, a developing country, came to a point maybe ten years ago where there was so much traffic that they didn't have enough capacity for all the cars. It was awful. Mayor Penalosa of Bogota was faced with a decision to either build more roads and highways or to take a cheaper route and develop a bus-train, and to take one lane away from the highway for this. He opted for the bus-train. It's called TransMilenio, and it includes a full system of mass transportation, as well as bicycle paths.

This is a case study in a developing country where they actually made a decision to get away from the automobile, and there are now follow-up studies to see if the population is happier and healthier. We don't know the answer yet, but there are, as Matthieu said, some great positive developments.

Chicago is one city that's very green; for example, building green roofs and living roofs, where, with vegetation on top of the building, you have less heat intensity and you also control the rain better. You don't have flooding and contamination from runoff. You've got multiple benefits from some of these interventions. So at the local level, there are some positive developments around the world.

HIS HOLINESS THE DALAI LAMA: As I mentioned earlier, in Estonia, in the early morning I noticed city buses but no private cars. During the day, the number of cars increased a little, but still, I was very impressed with the limited traffic. Of course, this is a smaller country with a smaller population, which is more manageable. But as you mention, these things really are happening. This is encouraging.

One of the big problems is that people often take things for granted. They take whatever the current situation is, the status quo, for granted without knowing there may be an alternative.

When they see more luxury cars and luxury houses, this looks very pleasant and attractive. But once they understand the long-term consequences of 100 thousand cars, or 100 million cars, then perhaps they will start to question the value and implications of these things. Once you start thinking along those lines, then there will be questions in your mind.

JONATHAN PATZ: Just to follow up that very nice comment, and getting back to what Elke said, it's a matter of changing the norms. The norm right now is this: when you get richer, you get a car and the status that comes with it. But the new norm could be that as you get wealthier and advance, you live closer to a train or are able to bicycle to work. So we have to change the mental norm.

THUPTEN JINPA: Often only physical, material measurements are used to create a standard for quality of life. We do not bring into the equation one's own internal sense of well-being, of mental well-being.

HIS HOLINESS THE DALAI LAMA: Quite often among very rich people, when I talk to them, at first they are very nice and pleasant. But as we get to know each other, there are frequently many complaints. It's not uncommon that a very wealthy person, even a billionaire, can be very unhappy.

And then there are people who are not so affluent, but they have a very happy family, full of trust and friendship. This is wonderful. More money and power can lead to more suspicion, more distrust, and more jealousy.

DIANA LIVERMAN: People sometimes ask me how I can keep doing this science, because it seems to have such depressing outcomes. Actually, being a scientist makes me happy, because it's so fascinating. Even though these things we're studying are very worrying, they're so interesting and intriguing that it's a very happy life to be a scientist, I think.

DANIEL GOLEMAN: We've hit many of the themes that will continue through the week. We've had some bad news, some good news, and some very good news. We've talked about the ethical dimension and the dilemma about what leads to action. Is awareness enough? We will continue with these issues and explore them more deeply as the week continues.

3 The Ethical Burden of Climate Change

PRESENTER: Jonathan Patz, *University of Michigan*

DANIEL GOLEMAN: Now we're going to look at a different aspect of environmental science: the health consequences of some of the changes Diana talked about. His Holiness made the point that if a doctor said a change was necessary for better health, more people listen. Dr. Jonathan Patz has the scientific findings that make this case at the global level. Jonathan is a professor and the director of the Global Health Institute at the University of Wisconsin–Madison. His specialty is ecology and health. He is cochair of the group that wrote the health report of the US National Climate Assessment. He was one of the lead authors on the United Nations' Intergovernmental Panel on Climate Change (IPCC) that won the Nobel Peace Prize with Al Gore for their efforts to share knowledge about climate change. He is also founding director of the International Association for Ecology and Health, a global group of scientists who are studying climate change. And he's written many scholarly books and papers on this subject.

JONATHAN PATZ: Your Holiness, I'd like to pick up on a question that you asked in your introductory remarks: Given the science, what are the implications?

My role here is to take the environmental science presented by Professor Diana Liverman and ask the question, what does that mean for human health and well-being? I'm going to try to answer your question

51

about the implications, and look at the risks and ethical aspects. We'll see that certain people and populations will be disproportionately affected. And in the end, we'll look at the interdependence of environment and health: the interdependent risks, as well as the interdependent opportunities.

First, we'll look at the health impacts of climate change, a key topic explored by Professor Liverman. I use climate change as a case study of the ethical dimension of environment and health. Second, I'll talk about the interdependence of environment and global health, giving some examples of how complex these relationships really are. And third, we'll look at possible benefits found in interdependencies. Since everything is interrelated, if we can solve one problem, maybe we can solve two or three at the same time. So let's begin with the case study of the health effects of climate change, and why this is a huge ethical consideration.

Climate, Health, and Consequence: An Ethical Dilemma

JONATHAN PATZ: The World Health Organization (WHO) did an analysis that looked at global warming from 1960 to 1990, a thirty-year period of greenhouse gas emissions and warming. They asked the question, what would that small amount of warming mean for these climate-sensitive diseases: malaria, malnutrition, and diarrheal diseases?

For example, malnutrition can be caused by crop shortages, which can be a result of climate change and droughts. And something like malaria is very sensitive to external environmental conditions. With a mosquito-borne disease such as malaria, much of the life cycle of that biological system, including the parasite and the insect, is responsive to the temperature outside. As I will show in a minute, the local air temperature can affect the parasite in the mosquito.

Indirectly transmitted diseases, insect-borne or water-borne diseases, are more environmentally sensitive than directly transmitted diseases, and that's why the WHO picked those diseases.

The question the WHO asked is, based on what we know about malaria and changes in temperature, where have we seen the biggest increase?

In Africa, India, and the Middle East. These are the areas where the WHO believes climate change over the last thirty years, from greenhouse gas warming, will have an impact going forward.

Who's Responsible and Who's Affected

JONATHAN PATZ: The next question is, who is causing that climate change? What they learned is that even though Africa will be disproportionately affected by climate change, they're not really producing greenhouse gases, not burning a lot of fossil fuels, as Diana mentioned. But the United States—and this is where I'm embarrassed to be from the United States—has been the number-one contributor to greenhouse gas emissions over the last fifty years, from 1950 to 2000. So you could say that we, in the United States, are the most responsible for causing climate change, and for causing ill health in other parts of the world. China is number two. India, the former Soviet Union, and Canada are also up there. But this is where you see that the countries that will suffer the most are not responsible for the original problem.

Now let's take a look at this same data in a different format. What you're seeing here is a data-driven map (figure 11). We call this a cartogram because the size of each country is determined by a number. On the bottom are mortality numbers in malaria, diarrheal disease, and malnutrition. And the bigger the country is shown in the figure, the bigger the increase in those diseases from warmer climates.

HIS HOLINESS THE DALAI LAMA: Could hygiene also be a factor in some of these countries?

JONATHAN PATZ: Well, that's true, and in fact the poorer you are, the more directly affected you are by changing environments. In a heat wave, if you're wealthy, you can have air conditioning; if you're poor, you're exposed. If you have an increased risk of malaria and mosquito-borne diseases, and if you have no shelter, no windows, no screens, you're at higher risk. Poverty definitely plays a role in your exposure and your risk for exposure.

What we see is a lot of suffering. Look at all the suffering in Africa and India. But now look at the greenhouse gas emissions in the cartogram at the top of figure 11. Africa and the developing world are not really responsible for causing global climate change, and yet they're the ones most vulnerable initially. I'm not an ethicist, but after traveling with Matthieu and others, I'm becoming more ethical. To me, this difference between those most vulnerable being the least responsible for the problem is the largest ethical challenge that I can imagine. And when I look at this map and I learn more about Buddhism, I'd say this is where there's a huge role for compassion across nations.

When we began the Industrial Revolution 170 years ago and we built the steam engine, burned coal and oil, and developed the automobile, we didn't know it was a problem. We didn't know that burning would pollute the air; we didn't know it was harmful. But now we know. And with the knowledge that what we do in one place affects an innocent person

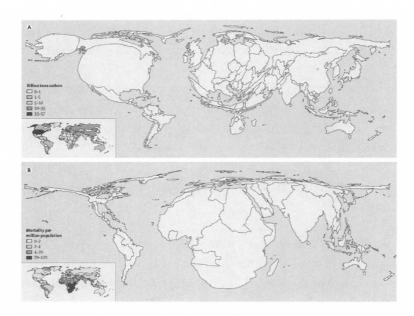

Figure 11. Cartogram of CO_2 emissions versus disease impact

somewhere else, we need compassion at the United Nations and all over the world to look at this suffering and balance it.

HIS HOLINESS THE DALAI LAMA: This clearly shows the relationship between an ethical responsibility and knowledge. If you were ignorant in the past, then of course there's less moral responsibility, but once you have the knowledge, then the ethical responsibility becomes even more important.

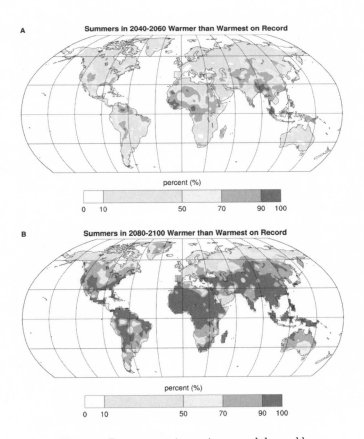

Figure 12. Temperatures increasing around the world

The Trend Is Heating Up

JONATHAN PATZ: Let's look at some examples of the health effects of climate change. We know that people die in heat waves. In 2010, India had a record temperature, 50 degrees Celsius (122 degrees Fahrenheit). Hundreds of people died. We know that there are some significant health effects from extreme weather. Where else in the world are we having record-breaking summer temperatures?

Figure 12 is a map that shows the areas in the world in the future—in the next few decades and during this century—where we may experience the hottest summers ever recorded in history. In the top part, the darkest areas have more than a 70 percent probability of experiencing the hottest summer ever recorded by the middle of this century, within only thirty to fifty years from today. In the bottom half, the dark areas indicate places with a greater than 90 percent probability of being hotter than ever recorded in history by the end of the century.

What we're concerned about, from the public health point of view, is that already today 800 million people are at risk from hunger, and these types of extreme temperatures in the summer would be devastating for crops. According to scientists published in the very prestigious journal *Science*, one of the top two science journals in the world, the risk of hunger could double by the middle of this century.

Another example of public health effects related to climate change is the risk of malaria. We talked about malaria and why malaria is so sensitive. Figure 13 is a graph that shows the relationship between temperature and the parasite as it develops inside the mosquito. What you see is that as temperature increases, the number of days that it takes for the parasite to develop inside the mosquito decreases. So as temperature rises, mosquitoes become infectious quicker. Therefore, warmer temperatures can lead to malaria epidemics. However, while the right temperature is needed to have the development of malaria, temperature is not the only cause. Other issues also contribute to epidemics, including population migration, bed-net therapies, drug resistance, and many other factors.

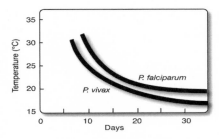

Figure 13. Temperature increase versus malaria parasite gestation period

Even so, malaria requires the right temperature, and malaria kills between 1.5 and 2 million people every year, most of whom are children. From this perspective, climate change and its impact on temperature-sensitive disease like malaria become an ethical consideration and an intergenerational problem.

According to the WHO, nearly 90 percent of climate change health risks would affect children. Diarrheal disease, malaria, malnutrition—these are all diseases that especially affect children.

Warming Oceans Will Have an Impact

JONATHAN PATZ: There's another element to the ethical aspect, including different types of risk to different populations and regions.

Figure 14 is a map of Bangladesh. Bangladesh is a very low-lying country in a river delta. What this map shows is that all the dark areas would be underwater with a 1.5-meter rise in sea level. Rise in sea level is another issue related to climate change in addition to the issues Dr. Liverman mentioned, extremes in temperature and extremes in water cycles such as floods and droughts.

Temperature increases would lead to a warming of the ocean. Warming salt water creates thermal expansion, and the estimates right now show that even without glaciers falling into the ocean, thermal expansion would lead to a rise in sea level of a meter or more. If land-based glaciers, like those on Greenland, slip into the ocean, we may have 5 to 10 meters of rise in sea level. But even only considering thermal expansion and the warming oceans rising a meter, 17 million Bangladeshis would be displaced. In addition to displacement, there are health issues related to moving populations; environmental refugees face tremendous health burdens.

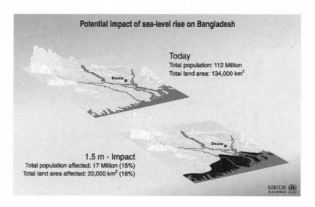

Figure 14. Potential impact of sea-level rise on Bangladesh

Health and Environment: An Interdependent Relationship

JONATHAN PATZ: Now that I've raised some ethical questions on climate change, I want to talk about some other environmental health issues and show the interdependence between the environment and our health. First, here is an example of what happens when you try to solve a health problem without understanding the interdependencies. In this example, the WHO initiated a malaria-control program in Borneo in the 1950s. They sprayed a pesticide called dieldrin to kill mosquitoes. It seemed like a good idea. They sprayed the pesticide and malaria declined. Not only did the mosquitoes die and malaria drop, but the flies and the cockroaches disappeared as well. Everyone was happy.

But soon after, the straw-thatched roofs in the village collapsed. And not only did the roofs cave in, there was a typhus epidemic. The question was, why did this happen?

The answer is based on the interconnectedness of life. When they sprayed the pesticide, dieldrin, it killed the mosquitoes, and it killed all sorts of other insects including cockroaches, but also ants and wasps.

As the pesticide killed those insects, the poison went up the food chain. Animals that ate the contaminated insects got sick and the pesticide got concentrated. Cats that ate contaminated lizards and geckos died. And when the cats died, the mice and rat population exploded. With rats come fleas, which carry the organism that causes the deadly disease typhus.

Now, what about the straw-thatched roofs? Well, remember the wasps that also died from the pesticide? This particular wasp normally lays her eggs in caterpillars that live in the thatched roofs. When the eggs are laid in the caterpillar, the caterpillar dies. But when the wasps died, and they weren't laying eggs in the caterpillars, the caterpillar population took off, and they devoured the straw roofs. That's why the roofs caved in.

So if you go in and try to solve a problem without understanding the interdependencies and interlinkages, you can cause more harm than good. This is why we need to solve each problem with a very interconnected, interdependent approach and with many perspectives at one table.

HIS HOLINESS THE DALAI LAMA: Is there a middle way in this situation? Can we control malaria without these side effects?

JONATHAN PATZ: You are asking a very important question. There are usually tradeoffs and we need to optimize, to find the way that has the fewest unintended consequences. There's rarely a perfect solution.

There are many scientists who are looking at these interlinkages, and hopefully, as we learn and understand more about the complexity of how everything is linked, we will find solutions with fewer negative outcomes. Because everything is interconnected, we need to have knowledge of the interrelationships to find a middle road.

Ecosystem Services from Nature

JONATHAN PATZ: There is some good news, however. There is a group, similar to the IPCC, of more than a thousand scientists from ninety-five different countries who conducted something called the Millennium Eco-system Assessment. They asked the question, how do intact, functioning ecosystems provide services for human health and human well-being? This led to a report, "Ecosystems and Human Well-Being," which is where we've developed some terminology such as "ecosystem services," how function-ing ecosystems provide services directly to human society, and "natural capital," the financial value of intact nature. These are free services from nature, so to speak. For example, an intact ecosystem will purify water, will regulate climate, will provide food, and more.

While there are global climate issues, to understand regulating cli-mate, consider a local example. Here in Dharamsala, if you cut all the trees, your local climate would change. You'd have less moisture; it could be hotter. If you have a steep hillside leading to a river, the plants and trees hold the water back, so that when it rains the hillside doesn't slide into the river. Flood protection from an intact hillside with plants is an example of an ecosystem service. There are other ecosystem services, such as having a spiritual and beautiful natural environment to walk in, and to recreate and exercise in. The effort is to try to understand these free services, which are extremely valuable but up to now have not really been evaluated.

Some of the work I do is researching how intact ecosystems protect us from diseases. Many people are beginning to look at these linkages. Here is one. In the work that we've done in the Amazon we asked the question, is there a link between the rise in malaria and the destruction of rainforest? What we found is that a dangerous species of mosquito, *Anopheles darlingi*, which carries malaria, is more present in deforested areas.

We controlled for the number of people. So we know that it's not more people in these locations driving the increase in mosquitoes; it's actually the change in the landscape. Not only did we find more mosquitoes in locations with deforestation, we also found more mosquito larvae in the water in deforested areas. Based on this research, we think there's a link between cutting the rainforest and an increase in malaria in this region.

Interdependent Benefits

JONATHAN PATZ: As the last part of this talk, I'd like to look at interdependence and consider that if everything is interdependent, then perhaps we could solve multiple problems or create co-benefits with appropriate solutions.

Professor Liverman talked about fossil fuels causing global climate change and greenhouse gases, but she also said that burning oil and coal causes air pollution. From this example, we see that if we work to reduce greenhouse gases by burning less fossil fuel, we will also have a co-benefit of cleaner air. According to the WHO, we know that today millions of people die prematurely every year from air pollution around the world.

Further, many cities are now designed for the automobile. And because we drive a car so often, many of us are not walking or bicycling enough, and that's a health concern. The WHO estimates that almost 3 million deaths occur prematurely from lack of physical activity each year. Another way to look at it is 30 million years of healthy life are lost due to lack of physical activity.

So if we were to progress on mitigating or reducing greenhouse gases in an effort to solve the global warming problem, we could also have some immediate, major health benefits. We've already seen this happen in areas.

In 1996, the Olympics were held in Atlanta, a city that had bad air pollution. Because of the Olympics, traffic controls were put in place that resulted in a 23 percent reduction in traffic. This, interdependently, produced a 28 percent drop in air pollution and a 42 percent decrease in emergency room and hospital visits for asthma, including lower incidence of childhood asthma. These were wonderful co-benefits of traffic controls.

HIS HOLINESS THE DALAI LAMA: By reducing the traffic by that percent, what was the impact on the economy? Has that been measured? For example, we hear and read about calculations of a negative impact on the economy when people go on strike, and so on. Are there ways of measuring the economic impact of changing transportation behavior, for example?

JONATHAN PATZ: I don't know the answer to that. I don't know the economic impact, but I will tell you that traffic-related air pollution is well recognized as a big problem. So based on these findings, I think more laws can help. I've been to Delhi twice. The first time was nine years ago for an air pollution meeting. At that time, the air pollution in Delhi was very bad. But in Delhi they've made major beneficial changes by requiring natural-gas vehicles and eliminating two-stroke engines. The air quality is getting better due to these interventions.

HIS HOLINESS THE DALAI LAMA: I'm wondering if there is a difference in the air pollution from airplanes because of the length of their flights and the fuel they use.

JONATHAN PATZ: Yes, the emissions from airplanes are affecting the climate. Airplanes are bad for two reasons: one, they affect the climate, but also on the ground they contribute to ground-level air pollution.

HIS HOLINESS THE DALAI LAMA: So in terms of the impact on the ozone layer, are airplane ground emissions and emissions at high altitude equally impactful?

JONATHAN PATZ: I'm a public health scientist, so I will defer that question to Diana. But I do know that the chlorofluorocarbons, the chlorine that goes into the upper stratosphere, affects the ozone layer, and that is different from the ground-level ozone, smog, pollution, and so forth.

One other quick example is the Olympics in Beijing. We don't have health numbers yet, but after the government of China spent 17 billion dollars to clean up the air quality to have a greener Olympics, pollution fell substantially. Nitrogen dioxide fell by 38 percent and particulate matter fell by 20 percent.

Particulate matter is the black smoke coming out of a diesel truck or from burning wood. You can see the black smoke; it's very dangerous. The smoke contains especially small particles that have been shown to be very harmful when breathed in. Nitrogen dioxide, and other gases such as sulfur dioxide, come from burning fossil fuels and are found in factory smoke. Those gases can form aerosols that are also harmful to breathe.

In addition to these examples from Atlanta and Beijing, my research team has also looked at air pollution where Richie and I live: Madison, Wisconsin, not far from Chicago.

We asked the question, if Atlanta had that amazing health benefit of less asthma by reducing traffic 23 percent, what would the outcome be if we could reduce car trips in our region by 20 percent? These would be short car trips of less than 8 kilometers round trip in city areas. How would that change the air quality? And further, how would the change in air quality affect the population's health?

We found that if we could eliminate these short car trips, we would save five hundred lives every year in the region. We would also avoid hundreds of thousands of illnesses such as respiratory illness and heart disease just by eliminating the short car trips.

HIS HOLINESS THE DALAI LAMA: If you biked instead, how long would it take to do that 4-kilometer trip each way? Some people will argue that driving saves them time.

JOHN DUNNE: Your Holiness, I cycle to campus from about 3 miles away, or about 5 kilometers, so that's actually the distance we're talking about. If I drive, because of the traffic in the morning and the afternoon, it takes me at least twenty-five minutes to get to my office door. On the bike it takes me twenty minutes. It's actually faster on the bicycle.

JONATHAN PATZ: Because this is a flat area, it's faster by bike. You avoid traffic and you don't worry about parking. One problem is in the wintertime, when you have ice and snow. So we narrowed our question to ask,

What if half of these short car trips were made by bicycle in the best four months of the year; what would be the added benefit? We found that if half of those short trips were made by bicycle, in addition to the air quality improvement from not taking the car, the benefit from physical fitness would still save 1,100 lives every year.

This is a great example of interconnectedness. If we think about mitigating climate change by burning less fossil fuel and by reducing greenhouse gases, we also can enhance personal fitness and reduce air pollution. And this is why I think that this interdependence of solutions could be one of the greatest public health opportunities we've had in a century.

I want to offer a vision of change here. We need to begin to think about how to make our cities not just for automobiles, but also for people. This is where I look to your wisdom and some of your writing, Your Holiness. As you often say, everything starts with the individual. I like Gandhi's quote, "Be the change you wish to see in the world." This is a picture of the vehicle I use to go get groceries at the grocery store (figure 15).

HIS HOLINESS THE DALAI LAMA: This is wonderful. In classical Buddhist literature there is reference to four qualities that a teacher should try to embody, one of which is to not only share your wisdom with others but to actually live it.

JONATHAN PATZ: I live in a city that's very bikeable. I think we have an opportunity to design cities so this is possible. Many people to whom I give this presentation say, "This is not possible where I live." And that's the case in many cities around the world, so I think one of our missions could be to make cities more flexible like this.

THUPTEN JINPA: Diana, can you pick up on the question that His Holiness asked about the difference in impact from the ground-level versus high-altitude emissions from airplanes?

DIANA LIVERMAN: Yes, I will try. To begin, there is a difference between ozone at the ground level, where it's dangerous, and ozone in the stratosphere, where it's protective. I also think we could discuss the issue of aviation, which might be a source of concern for many of us.

HIS HOLINESS THE DALAI LAMA: I am wondering if there is a different impact on the environment from airplane emissions at high altitude?

DIANA LIVERMAN: There are a couple of very interesting, natural experiments that I will look at. One was when the Iceland volcano stopped airline activity for a few days. Another is following 9/11 when there were no flights. In both of these cases, scientists have studied the impact on the environment of those periods of no flights.

Figure 15. Jonathan's "vehicle"

Airplanes certainly produce a lot of greenhouse gas emissions that warm the atmosphere. On the other hand, one of the things that the planes do is help create clouds through their emissions. So it may be that aviation has a slightly cooling effect on the climate from the clouds they create; we have to look at the balance.

What Is an Intact Ecosystem?

JOHN DUNNE: You talked about the concept of the intact ecosystem. From a Buddhist perspective, from the notion of impermanence, intact sounds like static, meaning it doesn't change. I'm sure you don't mean that it is unchanging. I'm thinking of something I read about: ecosystems in which fire actually plays a role. Sometimes there are very large wildfires in the western United States, for example, where lots of acres are burned, and these are often a result of human activity. But in other cases, these could be natural cycles of burning and restoration of a forest that has been occurring long before humans were present in those areas, and long before the industrial age. So if you took a picture from a satellite you'd see a green forest one year, and then, because there was a fire in that area, you'd see it all burned down in the next. Isn't that still an intact ecosystem? I'm wondering if you could explain what you mean by "intact" exactly.

JONATHAN PATZ: First, ecosystems are defined in many, many different ways: through food webs and energy cycles, for example, and there's always a functioning interdependence of an ecosystem. As far as changing ecosystems through natural fires, for example, there are different issues at different periods of time and enormous complexities where even ecologists don't pretend to understand all of the interconnections. I wouldn't want you to think that ecosystems are unidirectional; if you preserve a forest and you don't change anything, it is not true that such preservation always leads in a certain direction and to less disease.

It's one of these issues of tradeoffs again. We have to clear some land for agriculture to feed ourselves. To some extent, for the benefit of society, we can change things a little bit for more direct benefits. But in other cases, if we were to clear whole areas and plant one crop, a monoculture, and have no wild biodiversity, if a pathogen came in, it could wipe out the crop and we would be vulnerable. This is where having some intact natural systems in agriculture has been shown to be very beneficial. But I don't pretend to know—and I don't think ecologists will tell you that they know—all of those interdependencies.

JOHN DUNNE: If I could follow up. Part of what I'm saying is it sounds like "intact" just means "not affected by humans," as if humans were not part of the ecosystem. So I'm curious how you're using the word "intact," so I can understand more clearly what effects you're pointing to. If nonhuman activity somehow changes an area, does that means it's still intact? Is it just the presence of humans that constitutes the loss of it being intact?

JONATHAN PATZ: Well, I'll first say that I'm not an ecologist, but I work with ecologists, and there is this issue of "humans as part of nature" versus "us and nature," and I think our latter speakers will get into that a little bit. I don't know of a definition that states "if humans cause it, it's always bad"; that's not necessarily true.

HIS HOLINESS THE DALAI LAMA: For example, changes occurring from the ice ages and other natural events have nothing to do with human actions; they are part of the natural cycles of change.

JONATHAN PATZ: Right. Getting back to Diana Liverman's talk, things are always changing. What we are observing with some human activity is the speed, or the rate, of change. We cut many square kilometers of forests every year, and in doing so we change the climate system faster than what would naturally occur. It's this rate of change that has the ecologists most concerned.

DIANA LIVERMAN: Forests, for example, have been affected by fire for centuries. But recent results suggest that we may have doubled the risk of fire, not just because humans are there and may be causing the fires, but because of global warming. We're affecting and increasing the damage to the ecosystem. Ecosystems are always fragmenting and changing, but it's the extra burden and the extra fragmentation that we're causing that's resulting in more mosquitoes, or increased risk of disease outbreaks. That's where deforestation is really very challenging in terms of the potential of interactions and interdependencies that could result in very serious diseases.

GREGORY NORRIS: I'd like to address two of the topics that came up around traffic. First, you asked, what would the economic impacts be of less driving? In the United States, people have been proposing to create zones in the center of cities where no driving is allowed. Initially, the businesses in the area tend to protest against this idea because they're worried that they'll have fewer customers. But in the cities that have tried this model, the majority of businesses find that they get more customers. It turns out that people like to have the experience of walking in the street with no cars. That's a win-win. Jonathan, in your research about traffic, when you took 20 percent of the cars off the road, did you include traffic modeling?

If you don't drive, maybe you bicycle and you might lose some time. But the other thing that happens when you stop driving is that all the other cars go a little bit faster because there's less traffic. So everyone else is saving a little bit of time and everyone else is also reducing emissions. Therefore, 20 percent fewer cars means more than 20 percent reduction in emissions, because now all the rest of the cars are moving more efficiently.

JONATHAN PATZ: This analysis was done by a very large team. The beginning of this analysis starts with a very sophisticated emissions model that calculates pollution from the tailpipes of automobiles based on location and census tract. We look at very specific locations, the type of road, the speed of traffic, and so forth. It's a high-resolution geographic spatial analysis of pollution coming out of the tailpipes of cars.

Something very interesting is that the most pollution from a car comes from short trips. A car's first emissions, when the engine is cold and before the catalytic converter and the pollution prevention mechanisms warm up, are the worst ones. We call this "cold start." So the short car trips are the worst. We've factored in that reducing these short trips is even more effective in reducing emissions. Then we take that model and we hand it over to a team of air pollution modelers, who give us back the air pollution scheme, and we put that into our health model. So it's a major linking model and the best analysis we have to date.

Climate Modeling and Projections

DANIEL GOLEMAN: We've been hearing many predictions about what's going to happen with climate change. How do you make those predictions, and how certain are you of those predictions?

DIANA LIVERMAN: Your question applies to both Jonathan's presentation and my own. A lot of the work that Jonathan is trying to do in terms of modeling the impacts of climate change on health depends on climate scientists modeling the change in the climate itself.

We input our basic understanding of how the climate works. Some of this is based on physics. For example, warm air holds more moisture and carbon dioxide traps heat. But the atmospheric system is so complicated that we can't input everything based on physics. So some of it is statistical correlations based on observations of past behavior. We've built computer models based both on our theory of how the atmosphere works and on past observations of how the atmosphere works. Then the first thing we have to do once we've built the computer models is run them to see if they can reproduce the observed climate of today. If a computer model can't reproduce what's happened in the past and what's happening now, we would have very little faith in its projections for the future.

So we test the model against observations. We also vary our assumptions to see if we've input something that produces unrealistic behavior. Only when we're confident that the model does a good job of reproducing the current atmosphere do we change assumptions, like the amount of greenhouse gases in the atmosphere or the warmth of the ocean. We then run the model for one year after another into the future and look at how the climate evolves. And so our predictions are very much based on our understanding of physics and our observation of past behavior.

But because we can't predict whether people are going to continue what they are doing now or change habits and begin reducing emissions, we have to work with what we call "scenarios," which are alternative futures. Climate modelers usually work with what they call "business as usual," which is continuation of current behavior. This is the one that tends to give us the very high temperatures. But we also look at scenarios that assume people will do half of what is needed, and those that assume people will do everything that is needed. Then we can actually provide helpful information: if we make one choice, we will have one climate future; if we make another choice, we would have a different climate future.

What's interesting for this discussion group is to imagine the different futures. Can we imagine a future in which we've done everything that we could do, or is the more realistic future that we do only some of what we can do? And for each of those futures, we get a different climate. The one thing we can't include in our models very well is what nature might do. For example, if there was a year with a lot of volcanic eruptions, we could put that into the model, but we don't know if that's going to happen again.

What we do to try to increase confidence in the climate models is run not only one prediction but hundreds and thousands. There are now fifteen different groups of scientists around the world in many different countries who are all working together, but using slightly different models, making these projections. Different scientists may have slightly different assumptions about the physics. One group might have placed more importance on clouds in their model, for example. But by having multiple groups working on models, and also having each group doing many projections, we compensate for the uncertain or random behavior in the atmosphere.

We use this kind of modeling to create results that say there's a certain chance of something happening. In the case of heat waves in a specific area such as Delhi, my colleagues will run a climate model that would produce thousands and thousands of results, a sort of picture of what might happen. Then I give all of this data to poor Jonathan, and then he has to make his estimates, based not only on all the complexity of the climate system but also the complexity of the behavior of the mosquito and the behavior of humans. So it's fascinating scientifically, but these layers of assumptions and testing make it very complicated.

JOHN DUNNE: Is it too early to know whether any of the models have successfully predicted certain outcomes?

DIANA LIVERMAN: No. The first computer models that were modeling climate and the impacts of global warming were actually being run when I was a student in the early 1980s. In fact, I was fortunate to study at the National Center for Atmospheric Research in the United States, where these models were just being developed. That was thirty years ago. Since then we have been improving the models, and one of the things we can do now is compare what the models said thirty years ago against what actually happened.

What we've seen is that computer models have accurately predicted, for the most part, the warming that we have observed, and also some of the changes in extreme temperatures. That's one reason we're much more confident in the projections of the models now than we were, say, thirty years ago. We've been able to compare them to what has actually happened.

The other big change in the models, which was always a challenge, and which links to Jonathan's work, is that the first models had very coarse, large-scale predictions. This was because we didn't have powerful comput-ers then. We were working with punch cards and not laptops. With today's computing power, and also with decades of knowledge and experience, we can produce much more detailed predictions of what might happen. This is what scientists like Jonathan need in order to give us more accu-rate predictions of the health impacts of climate change. The very first climate models didn't include the Himalayas; there were no mountains, and the oceans were just one foot deep. Now we have models that include the mountains of the world and real-sized oceans. We're constantly work-ing to improve the models in order to improve our understanding of the impacts, and hopefully to improve the solutions.

JONATHAN PATZ: And that's how the models that come from the clima-tologists are used in public health. It's not just at the local level that we need information, we also need to know how frequently we will have an extreme heat wave and how long will it last, for example. During the heat wave that hit Europe in 2003, an estimated seventy thousand people died in eleven days.

You can't say that heat wave was global warming, but the climatologists have looked at how hot the temperature was that summer, and what they found was that it was way outside the normal distribution of tempera-ture. As climatologists have looked at the probability of having such an extreme temperature again, they're able to say, based on climate science and the amount of greenhouse gases put into the atmosphere during the last thirty years, that changes in temperature won't simply steadily rise, rather, there will be extreme spikes with more frequency. Based on the data, that extreme heat wave that killed seventy thousand people had twice the normal probability of occurring.

And this is how we know that when the climate is at an average tem-perature and average moisture, we're doing well. But at the extremes of hot and cold, dry and flooding, we have concerns about the impacts on agriculture, ecology, and public health. And again, the predictions of cli-mate change from the climatologists say that things are not going to change gradually, but there will be an increase in the frequency of extreme events. That concerns me as a public health scientist.

Are There Benefits to Global Warming?

DANIEL GOLEMAN: Well, is there any good news about global warming? Are there any benefits?

JONATHAN PATZ: There will be a reduction in people dying from cold temperatures. Some diseases, such as those carried by ticks, will disappear. Places like the former Soviet Union will have better food production and better crops. So there will be winners and losers. When we've done assessments for the United Nations, the conclusion of our health chapter has typically been that there will be some decline in disease, and some increase, but on balance, there will be more adverse health effects than beneficial ones. That's been consistent in all of our assessments.

DANIEL GOLEMAN: What about the Tibetan Plateau?

DIANA LIVERMAN: There are a few studies suggesting that there might be benefits for some people on the Tibetan Plateau, because right now it's very cold in winter. There are suggestions that there could be some alleviation of respiratory problems and that people might be able to grow a wider range of crops with warmer temperatures. There's also an example that with the melting of the permafrost, the lakes are getting larger and that is allowing for an increase in the population of cranes and other birds that can migrate. But then, of course, there are many negatives as well.

It's a question of the geographic balance between places that benefit and places that lose. While some people might eat better, or be a little warmer in cold regions, it would be at the expense of millions of people in the river basins who will have less water. This is a big issue, since there are some countries that are less keen to negotiate an agreement on climate change because they think they could benefit. How do we get these countries to look at those that are going to lose?

Animals Don't Have the Same Choices

GREGORY NORRIS: To build on this: Your Holiness, you mentioned earlier today that as human beings, we can imagine the future and we can adapt, though certain populations of human beings will have much more difficulty than others. However, should we not also consider the natural world? For instance, animals, who don't have this same ability to predict climate change? In many cases, they can't adapt and can't relocate because we've cut off migration routes. The changes to the natural world could be much more rapid than the changes that nature has been dealing with historically.

DIANA LIVERMAN: Some of the strong indicators that the climate is changing are found in the thousands of studies about shifts in the distribution of birds. About 80 percent of the studies have found that birds are moving toward the poles or up mountain slopes. This is very consistent with a response to global warming. We can already see that birds, which have more mobility, are starting to respond to a changing climate. Many other species don't have the mobility, and the places they need to traverse to get to cooler regions are often occupied by humans. Dekila can talk about this, because the World Wildlife Fund (WWF) now has to think about it. They've invested money in protecting nature in particular places, but what happens if the climate changes and the species they are protecting can no longer survive in those habitats? I was recently in Australia, and they were talking about "assisted migration of species," where humans will actually have to help ecosystems move to a different place because of climate change. That model reflects what really is a human-dominated planet, where we're helping other species move and adapt.

DEKILA CHUNGYALPA: I could use the example of tigers. Most of the tigers in the India/Nepal area are in the Terai, which are the lowlands. But in the past three to four years, we've seen evidence from camera traps that tigers are starting to climb. Camera traps in Bhutan have found a tiger at 4,000 meters. This is unprecedented; we've never seen tigers this high before. What's happened is they're now in snow leopard territory. Tigers are quite large and snow leopards are very small. One of the things that we wildlife ecologists now worry about is the tension that's going to occur between the two predators, and which predator is going to dominate in this landscape.

Diana made the point that organizations such as the WWF have invested a lot of time and a lot of funding to protect areas. We thought we knew where tiger habitat was and we've done our best to protect it. Now we're finding out that the foliage and the trees are changing, and consequently, the animals are starting to move.

The first thing that happens is that the prey, not the predators, start to move out. Deer, for example, move and the predators follow. One of the solutions we're now looking into is wildlife corridors. But this gets very complex because, for example, the Terai is a very highly populated area; lots and lots of people live there. So how do we negotiate with the communities to get them to let a tiger, or a herd of elephants, go through their villages? Trying to figure out ways to get communities to think that protecting tigers is good for them and coming up with solutions is a very big challenge.

Another thing we have to take into consideration is how different species behave. A tiger is a solitary animal. It needs 5 kilometers of unoccupied space on either side before it will go through a forest. If, in a 5-kilometer radius, there's some kind of human activity, the tiger is not going to go through. It's not enough that we just protect the forest; we actually have to create a corridor that's quite wide. This is just one example of some of the impacts.

It's About Global Environmental Change

JONATHAN PATZ: As we are talking about changes in vegetation and animal migration patterns, we're really looking at global environmental change. As Diana has pointed out, climate change is a big topic but not the only topic. The Millennium Ecosystem Assessment reports explain how we have changed the landscape of Earth, especially for agriculture and land use. I just wanted to offer the reminder that it's really global environmental change and not just climate change that we are talking about.

Examples range from cutting forests for livestock and agriculture to simply building roads through a forested area—fragmenting it into pieces. All this completely changes the biodiversity of an area.

Lyme disease is a very interesting example of where a change in biodiversity in the number of species directly affects the risk of this disease. Lyme disease is transmitted by the tick that bites you, but the bacteria that causes Lyme disease comes from mice, which are the natural reservoir, or host—the place where the bacteria occurs in the environment. In a big expanse of forest, there are lots of animals: mice, raccoons, monkeys, a variety of species. Many of them may eat mice, and that reduces the number of mice to transmit the bacteria.

Also, ticks need blood, and they typically feed on different animals. If you have a big forest with lots of different animals, the ticks feed on all the animals and fewer ticks are likely to get the bacteria from mice. But if you chop up the forest into little pieces, that reduces the number of species. Foxes, monkeys, and other larger animals need more space. If you fragment the forest, the only animals left may be mice, because mice can live almost anywhere. In a chopped-up forest, because there are only mice, the probability that a tick will get infected with the bacteria increases. This is an example of how species diversity can actually reduce the risk of a disease, and how if you change the landscape, you change the biodiversity, and you can actually increase the risk of a particular disease.

ELKE WEBER: Your Holiness, you asked about economic impacts. I want to go back to climate change, and the question about the pros and cons of global warming from an industry perspective. Just as there are pros and cons for different countries—Canada probably would not mind global warming as much as Africa—there are also variances between industries.

For the shipping industry, for example, having access to the Northwest Passage, a shipping route around the top of Northern Canada, would be a huge economic advantage. It's currently blocked by ice. At the same time, companies in the insurance industry and the reinsurance industry, such as Lloyd's of London, are very concerned about climate change. Their business is based on the fact that catastrophes occur randomly and are not connected. But based on the interdependencies we've talked about, catastrophes are becoming larger and much more connected. With climate change, their current business model is disappearing. They are looking for new ways to forecast and react to these changes.

HIS HOLINESS THE DALAI LAMA: It appears that so much damage to the environment has been due to economic pursuits and, as I mentioned this morning, greed—and more specifically, lack of awareness and sense of responsibility. At the same time, we can't ignore the importance of the economy and the value of natural resources. The only approach is to find a working balance so that we don't go to the extremes. We have to do this with an increasing human population that will need more food and resources. This is a difficult task.

JONATHAN PATZ: This reminds me of a cartoon of a boat in a stormy sea. The back of the boat is sinking in the water while the bow is pointing up out of the water. In the bow, there are scores of tiny-sized people, some falling overboard. At the stern, there are a few very big people, sinking the boat, saying, "Hey you up in the bow, stop overpopulating!"

In reality, the people in the back are the Americans, Canadians, and Europeans. We have a very big environmental footprint. Our per-person consumption is enormous. Each of us is so big and we're sinking the boat.

Of course, population is also a key problem, and we can't ignore it. We can't just say the only problem is overconsumption, though reducing overconsumption is an area I think we are having very little if any progress in. We are not reducing per-person energy and resource consumption at the back of the boat.

Overpopulation is also a major problem, but I think through edu-cation and more opportunities for women, we are beginning to slow population growth. On balance, we are having more success at curbing population than in putting those big guys in the back of the boat on an energy diet.

HIS HOLINESS THE DALAI LAMA: So we have to think seriously about changing our lifestyle. But there seem to be a lot of contradictions. For example, generally, in the West, people value being fit; they talk about the importance of losing weight and being healthy, yet many eat to excess and are overweight. As you mentioned, with important issues, awareness is not sufficient, we must find a way to implement change.

JONATHAN PATZ: The Centers for Disease Control and Prevention has categorized overweight and obesity as our number-one health epidemic in the United States; 60 percent of Americans are overweight.

MATTHIEU RICARD: Thinking again about what is natural and what is intact, as His Holiness mentioned, in several billions of years, the sun will burn out, and this is natural. When we consider humans, our pres-ence here is completely natural. The issue is that we have developed technologies that make the impact of what we would otherwise naturally do thousands of times more powerful. That's not natural. And it is new in terms of geological and biological evolution, as is the issue of waste. In the past our waste was made of earth-based materials: stones, wood, leather. You throw them away and they decompose or integrate back into the earth. Now we are producing all kinds of toxic wastes, atomic waste, plastics, and other materials that don't break down and are poisonous. So we are facing two issues: one is the multiplying effect of our impact because of technology and the other is the amount of toxic waste we are producing.

But what's underlying the discussion of how to deal with these issues is a concern we all share: how to reduce suffering? How can we reduce suffering in terms of displacing populations due to climate change and severely affecting the poor even though they are not the cause of climate change? While we'll never stop the sun from burning out, we can certainly do whatever we can to reduce suffering. I think this is the most reasonable approach.

Also, someone was asking me about cremating corpses, and wondering if it wouldn't be better to bury them to reduce emissions.

HIS HOLINESS THE DALAI LAMA: There's a group near Nagpur, founded by Baba Amte, that has a tradition where, when anyone dies, instead of cremation the body is wrapped, buried, and a tree is planted on that spot. This is wonderful.

Collaboration and Cross-Industry Work Is the Key

HIS HOLINESS THE DALAI LAMA: I know people who have worked on wonderful initiatives, such as Baba Amte. I actually donated some of my Nobel Peace Prize award to him. There are many people and smaller organizations who are trying to make a difference. What seems to be lacking is an attempt to coordinate and bring them all together in an integrated way, to enhance the collective impact and effect. This would also give everyone an opportunity to share experience and support, possibly even implementation at both the global and local levels.

JONATHAN PATZ: That is exactly the way the international health community is trying to move forward. The WHO is now calling for something that they call "Health in All Policies." It's a new movement that seeks to address the health issue across work sectors and knowledge bases, including energy, agriculture, transportation, business, economics, and others. We have to work in this open and cross-sector way, embracing the complexity and the interdependence, or we won't be able to solve interdependent problems.

HIS HOLINESS THE DALAI LAMA: Yes, these are complicated problems that require education, awareness, a sense of responsibility, and a sense of community. It doesn't matter what our nationality is or whether we are believers or nonbelievers. We are all human beings and it is our responsibility to create a safer world for the next generation, at least, and perhaps for centuries and even millennia to come.

4 Footprint to Handprint: The Science of Measuring Impact and Making a Difference

PRESENTER: **Gregory Norris**
Harvard School of Public Health

Reevaluating Profit and the Value of the Environment

DANIEL GOLEMAN: An issue that's behind everything we've been discussing is profit motive. In fact, this meeting could have been called "Ecology, Ethics, and the Economy." Whenever a forest is cut up into roads for logging, whenever energy comes from a power plant that burns coal and releases greenhouse gases, someone is making money. It's the profit motive that's driving the vast majority of the destruction in the world's environment.

There is something we need to consider: these outcomes are not necessarily intentional. They are consequences of another dilemma of the Anthropocene age. Most of the systems and materials that manufacturers use—chemicals and processes—were developed in a time before we could measure their ecological impacts. Back then, people weren't aware there would be negative ecological outcomes from these choices. But now we can know. And with this knowledge, we can reinvent everything, to find ways to do things differently.

So the question is: What could be the engine that drives this change to finding alternative ways of making and transporting the things we need for our lives?

We're going to look at systems that may be very helpful in inspiring this change. There's a saying in business: "What gets measured, gets managed." If you don't measure it, then you don't know, and you can't tell if you're making a difference.

Similarly, in environmental science, there's a new field called "Industrial Ecology" that measures the impacts of manufacturing on the environment. This field has emerged within the last decade or two, and it brings methods from the hard sciences—physics, biology, chemistry, environmental science—together to work with people in industry, such as industrial engineers and industrial designers, who decide how they are going to make things. They are analyzing the actual ecological impacts of the manufacturing process.

Through the lens of industrial ecology, glass, for example, is not simply a product but a process. That process begins when sand is extracted from the earth, transported to a factory, combined with chemicals, heated at 2,000 degrees for twenty-four hours, then transported to a store where we purchase it as a glass. And someday that glass will break and be discarded. In other words, every object has a life history, just like a person, and if we look carefully through the lens of the life history of anything made, we can measure and manage the inputs and outcomes in a way never before possible.

Some of the things that are measured include obvious ones, such as carbon emissions and greenhouse gases. If you buy a bag of chips in the United Kingdom today, the packaging will tell you what its carbon footprint is, which hopefully helps people make better, ecologically minded buying decisions. Previously, we just didn't know what the impact was.

Another measure is called a "partially diminished fraction of an ecosystem." This tells us if damage was done to an ecosystem when an item was made. It's amazing that we now have this kind of insight into the impacts of manufacturing certain products.

Yet another measure that comes from public health is called a "disability-adjusted life year." For example, if there's a poisonous chemical used in a manufacturing process, and if people who work in the factory or who live in that neighborhood are exposed to the chemical, they could be at increased risk for cancer. This measure tells us how many years of life those people are likely to lose due to disability and disease because of this product and its manufacturing process. So this is a measure and view that, for the first time, takes the ethical implications Diana and Jonathan were discussing and brings them home such that we have information we can use to make better decisions about the things we buy. With this knowledge, we can be a deciding force for better outcomes.

Systemic Impacts

DANIEL GOLEMAN: While we've been talking implicitly about individual decisions and will continue to do so, we also need to look at business decisions. The reason is this: even though in the United States we have very good recycling programs, just recycling may be insufficient compared to the total impact of a product. For example, if you have yogurt in the morning in a plastic container, and as an ecologically minded person you recycle the container, that's good. But, if you look at the total carbon cost of that yogurt over its entire life cycle, recycling only offsets 5 percent of its carbon footprint. In fact, 95 percent of the yogurt's carbon footprint comes from other places or processes, such as the dairy farms that produce methane, manufacturing and transportation, and so on.

The individual can only do so much. We need to look at the entire system of industry and commerce. Many products are sold as "green," which is supposed to be ecologically superior. But we are going to learn that "green" is often a mirage.

For example, I bought a "green" T-shirt. They call it "green" because it's made from organic cotton. That's very good, because it's not grown with chemical fertilizers, which alleviates the challenges to earth systems from the nitrogen cycle that Diana explained. But the whole picture is more complicated than just fertilizer. Organic cotton requires more water and the fibers are shorter, so you need more cotton to make one T-shirt. Unfortunately, cotton is predominantly grown in areas of the world that have very little water. Also, it was a blue T-shirt, which means it was dyed. Many of the chemicals used to color our clothes are poisonous; they're toxic.

The question you may ask is, "Did the dye house that made this T-shirt blue take the poison out of the water before it released it back into the river?" Because if it didn't do that, and many don't, then the people who use that water get those poisons, and those poisons cause diseases.

There are tens of thousands of chemicals used in making products, and one of the problems with industrial chemicals is that very few of them have been studied for how poisonous they are, for their toxicity.

It's now been discovered that if you take tissue samples from anyone in the world you will find traces of toxic industrial chemicals. We all have what's called a "body burden": the amount of industrial chemicals we've absorbed in the natural course of breathing, eating, and just living. We all carry some amount of these toxic chemicals.

There's a theory now coming out of Harvard Medical School that suggests the buildup of these toxic chemicals causes inflammatory syndrome. This means that many organs in our body are in an inflamed state from exposure to chemicals, and because they're in an inflamed state we are more likely to get diabetes, heart disease, or cancer, and we are more susceptible to a whole range of diseases.

Environmental-Economic Value

DANIEL GOLEMAN: All of this means there's a lot of suffering caused as a side effect of standard business practices. And until now, those costs have not been seen as the responsibility of the companies, but rather the burden has been on the families and individuals who get sick.

But that seems about to change. This month there was an article in *Harvard Business Review*, a prestigious business journal, about sustainable business, which they describe as taking into account your own company's responsibility. This practice is becoming good business for several reasons. One reason is something that Diana mentioned: ecosystem valuation. We now have a way to measure the value of an intact ecosystem. For example, the World Bank has calculated that the plant-pollinating actions of insects living within an ecosystem has a business value of 200 billion dollars per year.

HIS HOLINESS THE DALAI LAMA: Can you explain that concept? How do you calculate that?

DANIEL GOLEMAN: The idea is that if you didn't have bees and other insects to pollinate plants, and you had to do that some other way, what would it cost you?

HIS HOLINESS THE DALAI LAMA: So this applies only to flowering plants?

DANIEL GOLEMAN: Mainly to agricultural plants, yes, including grains, vegetables, and fruits. And that's just one example. If you consider everything in nature and how we benefit economically, they estimate the total value at 44 trillion dollars. Two-thirds of that is in poor countries. One argument for the benefits of sustainable businesses is preserving this value in nature. A second is that there's a current trend to put more and more investment money into companies that are more sustainable.

And a third is what we're going to hear about this morning: ecological transparency. This is about creating public knowledge so that shoppers know what they are buying. There's an organization in the United States called GoodGuide, which has a website as well as mobile apps. You can use your smartphone to read the barcodes on products and get reports on ecological impacts as well as comparisons to competing products.

The same thing is going on within and between businesses, and that's where our speaker this morning comes in. We can now identify manufacturing processes, such as ways of making glass, that perhaps don't use as much energy, or use less toxic chemicals, or make other sustainable modifications in the supply chain.

With new data, at every point in the supply chain, we can determine which manufacturing choices are better and which are worse. This new information could drive what's called "a continuous upgrade," meaning that consumer awareness creates economic pressure to make products in a more sustainable way. This makes it more profitable to come up with better ways of manufacturing.

For example, Styrofoam was traditionally made from oil, and like plastic, oil never degrades; it never goes back to nature. Today, a better, sustainable Styrofoam can be made from rice hulls and mushroom roots. These ingredients biodegrade without causing harm to the environment or generating toxic outputs during manufacturing. Hopefully, these kinds of manufacturing changes are the wave of the future.

To learn more, let me introduce our speaker today, Gregory Norris, PhD. Greg is an industrial ecologist. He taught industrial ecology at MIT and he now teaches the same at the Harvard School of Public Health and the University of Arkansas. He has developed a system to help companies understand the environmental costs of everything they make, which suppliers are better and which are worse, and also to identify which factories, for example, use child labor or have terrible working conditions. So he is bringing supply-chain and humanitarian awareness to manufacturers. I'm happy to introduce Greg Norris.

Human Activity and the Indirect Causes
of Environmental Degradation

GREGORY NORRIS: Your Holiness, yesterday morning you taught us that when we want to look at an ecological problem, we need to start with science that asks, what is the situation? And then we need to look at the causes of the problems and their consequences. Diana did a nice job of explaining the alarming status of the current situation, and Jonathan began to look at the consequences. Both speakers also helped us understand the direct causes of global environmental changes, which I would summarize here as a combination of emissions (or air, water, and land pollution from human activity) and extraction (or other impacts on natural resources such as taking water from the ground, taking minerals from the earth, changing the landscape, changing a forest to a field, and so forth). Those are the direct causes of global environmental change.

What I'll try to do this morning is share with you the science and the art that we're using, as Dan says, to try and understand the indirect causes. We're looking at what, in terms of human activity, specifically causes these emissions and these extractions, which are in turn causing the global change.

As a quick way to refer to the environmental impact of the activities that cause change, we speak of the environmental "footprint." And by looking at and understanding our individual, personal footprints, we can make choices that lead to reductions in our impact.

So what I'd like to share first is how we practice this science and art of footprinting. I call it "a science and an art" because we can build models with data and scientific principles, but we can't exactly observe and test the results, so there's an art to this, too.

After I share how we do footprinting, I'll then share seven lessons I've learned from doing this work over the past twenty years.

And, finally, I'll talk about life-cycle assessment. As Dan explained, life-cycle assessment is the methodology we use to calculate these footprints.

We're focusing on a large subset of human activity: the chain of production, distribution, use, and disposal. If we want to know the impacts, we need to know information for each of those steps, each part of the life cycle. And to do that, we have to break each one of those down into little steps.

I'll use a very specific example here today, a cell phone, which most people can relate to. I just downloaded information from the web about how Apple makes a cell phone, and I'll use that information to build an analysis of the impact, the footprint, of a cell phone.

The Ripple Effects of the Manufacturing Supply Chain

GREGORY NORRIS: Dan mentioned manufacturing glass. For that we would need energy, sand, and chemicals. And for a cell phone, we need some glass, but we also need a battery, plastic, and metal. And most importantly, we need integrated circuits, which are like the brain of the cell phone. It turns out that those integrated circuits are very lightweight, but they carry by far the biggest impact when making a cell phone.

Footprinting teaches us some interesting things about how we create impacts. Figure 16 almost looks like a mandala, but it's actually a portrait of the supply chain for making a product, such as a cell phone.

Each one of the little dots is a step somewhere in the world, somewhere in the economy, that's making something that will be used in the next step in the manufacturing process. Cell phone manufacturing is right in the middle, and all of the supplies and all the pieces needed to make the cell phone are the dots leading to the middle. For example, to make an integrated circuit, we need a lot of pieces, energy, and transportation. We actually need gold to help make the components of the integrated circuits, so there's gold mining, and there's manufacturing of equipment and energy to mine the gold. When you look at the whole chain, you can really see the ripple effects buying a cell phone sends out across the world and the economy.

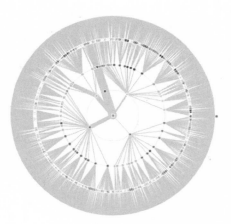

Figure 16. Portrait of a supply chain

Seven Lessons on Environmental Impacts

GREGORY NORRIS: One lesson that I've learned from this research is that when you buy from any one sector, you're touching almost the whole economy; you're actually buying from many sectors. If I buy a cell phone, I'm actually buying a little bit of gold, for example.

Another lesson is that when we buy from one country we're really touching many countries on Earth. I use a database that studies the linkages between countries and production. I asked, Which countries have workers participating in the supply chain, the life cycle, of making electronics that are assembled in Mexico?

In figure 17, the darkest sections represent the most worker hours, the most worker activity. In this case the most worker activity is happening in Mexico, where they assemble the cell phone or the electronics. But there are other areas providing inputs to that activity, too. You'll notice that China is pretty dark, and what's really striking to me is more than half of the countries on Earth are being touched by my decision to buy

Figure 17. The international supply chain

electronics from Mexico. So when we buy from one country, we're really buying from many areas in the world.

A third lesson is this: because of those first two facts, when we buy one product, we're really touching the planet in many different ways. We're influencing climate change, we're influencing water use, we're influencing toxic chemicals, and we're influencing land use. Even one product has at least a small impact on every environmental issue that you could think of. So you really touch the whole planet with each purchase.

That brings me my fourth lesson. When we purchase one product, we're touching millions of people on Earth. This database helps us understand how well they're paid, how long they're working, whether they're forced to work too long, and so on. So we can have a social footprint alongside our environmental footprint.

The fifth lesson is that not everything has the same impact. And we can use this information to prioritize our actions. Here is an example that is sometimes controversial but a good wake-up call for people: Many of my friends and most people in this room probably worry about plastic bags that we get from shopping and think that they are a really bad problem, that they contribute to litter and pollution. However, from the perspective of climate change, just one round-trip flight from India to the United States will have the same environmental impact as manufacturing one million plastic bags. So we can use life-cycle assessment to help us focus on the activities that have the greatest impact and find the changes in our lives that will bring the biggest benefits.

The sixth lesson that I'd like to share this morning I call "the smile," because it's a happy lesson; the seventh lesson I call "the tear," because it's not such a happy lesson.

The smile is the interdependence that we see occurring. When one business makes a strong innovation and uses its human creativity to reduce the impact of its products, that actually makes everybody's footprint smaller. Here are two brief examples: First, Caterpillar, which makes bulldozers, recently redesigned their bulldozers to be much less energy-consuming and polluting. That changed everybody's footprint, because there are bulldozers involved in building roads and mining the coal we use for electricity. And second, Hewlett-Packard and other companies now make printers so we can print on both sides of the paper, and that means each of us uses fewer trees for paper every year.

In this way, through an appreciation of interdependence, one smart choice by a company helps each of us reduce our footprint.

But the tear is that at the end of teaching life-cycle assessment class, I ask my students, "Now that you've learned all of this and you've studied these data, and you know that everything we do, each day, has a footprint, how many of you feel that the planet would be better off if you had never been born?" And they all say they feel that the planet would be better without them.

Handprints

GREGORY NORRIS: I think what my students are expressing is that they feel a sense of guilt, that every day they're causing pollution; this is not something that we do on purpose, but now we know that we're doing it. With life-cycle assessment, it becomes very clear to us that we're having this impact.

When I saw my students respond in this way, I asked, "How can we make this not true; how can we make the planet better; how can we reduce suffering and bring happiness to all beings if we're causing these footprints?"

Well, footprints are only part of the story. We have feet, but we also have hands, with which we create. We have imagination; we can change things. So we introduced the idea of "handprints" to quantify the positive impacts of our creative activity. And in fact, if our handprints are bigger than our footprints, then we're healing the earth.

We can create these handprints by making changes in our own lives: setting the heat a little lower at night, driving less, using telephone and video conferencing instead of flying, and many more beneficial choices. We can also influence our friends into making better decisions.

HIS HOLINESS THE DALAI LAMA: Is there any way of evaluating and assessing the environmental impact of human activity before the industrial age? For example, for a long time, on the Tibetan Plateau, nomads have been herding yaks, which probably releases methane gas similar to cattle. So even though that was a simpler lifestyle, did it also have some impact on the environment?

GREGORY NORRIS: Yes, they have an effect, but it's a very small footprint. The impact of their traditional herds was thousands of times smaller than what we are seeing today.

Every living being has an impact, but if we can minimize our impact and maximize the benefits we bring, the net result will be beneficial.

HIS HOLINESS THE DALAI LAMA: Yes, that's the only choice. We must do things similar to what Matthieu mentioned about the national parks program in Bhutan, which has increased the number of trees in that country.

GREGORY NORRIS: Exactly. I think it's also helpful to think back to the science we saw yesterday and remember all the graphs that showed that the earth was very stable for thousands of years and now the impacts are spiking. So while it's always been true that every animal has an impact on the planet and other life forms, previously these impacts weren't out of control. That's why I think it's important to use this framework to find out where the major impacts are happening and both reduce those and balance them with beneficial actions. With the data we have, we can calculate footprints and handprints for individuals, organizations, communities, and even events, and then we can make better choices. For example, I've done some calculations to see what the footprint of this wonderful meeting this week will be.

We have the good fortune to be together this week, and we hope and intend that this can bring benefits to the planet, but let's also look at the footprint. We have roughly a hundred people who have flown here and are staying in hotels while here. Just calculating with a few inputs, I estimate that we are creating roughly 400 tons of greenhouse gases. And we also have to consider our use of water and other resources. So the question is, how can the benefits of this workshop to the planet be larger than this footprint that we are creating?

Diego Hangartner has said the Mind and Life Institute is committed to planting enough trees, if necessary, to more than offset our carbon footprint. But there's another way we can address this. That would be for each one of us to look for actions that we can take in our own lives as a result of the things we learn here, implement them, calculate the benefits, and add up the total.

For example, some of us, especially after we hear from Matthieu, might consider eating less meat. We can set our thermostats back, we can drive a little bit less, and so on. We can make changes in our own lives, and we can encourage our friends to make changes, and they can encourage their friends—and the effects ripple.

So that's the message: by understanding our own impacts and committing to being beneficial, we can make a difference.

How Can Companies Use Data to Improve Manufacturing and Help the Environment?

DANIEL GOLEMAN: Some people have been asking Professor Norris for more details on the information he presented. How can we use it, or how could a company use it? I wondered if you could talk about the cost and the benefits a little bit more.

GREGORY NORRIS: Yes. Life-cycle assessment is sort of an interesting enterprise; we have to look at the details for each and every product. To show how we look at the details, let's look at one particular product, the cell phone.

What I've done is collected information on the cell phone, a product that many of us can relate to, and linked it to databases that tell us how the various components and electronics are made. These databases have thousands of different supply-chain steps recorded that we can access.

Someone asked, "How can companies use this?" The answer is that companies are already using this data to analyze their manufacturing, study their impacts, and make reductions where they can. Let's pretend we're working for Apple and we just modeled our iPhone using life-cycle assessment. The first thing that we see is that there are many different kinds of impacts. Remember, every single product has impacts on climate, human health, ecosystems, water, and so on. So as we're designing the cell phone, we can look at what's causing ecosystem impacts: what's causing the loss of biodiversity through land use, the loss of biodiversity through toxic emissions in the air, water, and land.

By looking at the data, the answer is very clear: it's the integrated circuit, the brain of the cell phone, that accounts for about 80 percent of the impacts, even though it is a fraction of the total weight of the product. The next most impactful component is the battery. And if we can find ways to make these two components less impactful, we can create a more environmentally friendly phone.

One of the main drivers of impacts on the ecosystem is gold mining in countries like Papua New Guinea and Chile. While gold is needed to make the integrated circuits for cell phones, the mining is highly destructive to the environment, extremely energy intensive, and uses a tremendous amount of water. Companies seeking to make a change can use all of this information to prioritize materials and suppliers, and some companies are starting to ask suppliers to reduce impacts or switching to suppliers that have a lower impact.

DANIEL GOLEMAN: Perhaps you can address how we can compel companies to make changes. Often information on toxins and hazardous emissions is kept from the public, and even if it is available, how do we create awareness and then encourage companies to change their practices?

GREGORY NORRIS: Yes, that is the core issue here, so I'll try to address that. First, we're now in an age of radical transparency, meaning there is more information available than ever before. And with that, everyone should be able to begin to understand the greater impacts for each product.

We work with two different kinds of information. One is called "average information," such as the average production inputs for a cell phone battery, which allows us to calculate average impacts for parts of and whole products. Already many retailers are requiring manufacturers to report the impacts of their products, because customers want to know. The second kind of information is "actual information," gathered through a web portal through which people all over the world can report into the system actual impacts in areas and communities.

We heard yesterday that one-third of the carbon footprint from China is associated with production of products to be sold in the United States. If that's the case, then the companies in the United States who are being pressured to provide impact information to their customers will, in turn, pressure the supply chains in China and other countries where this data is not yet as available to increase the transparency, requiring them to report the impacts of their activities.

DANIEL GOLEMAN: For example, 20 percent of the factories in China make products for the biggest company in America, Walmart. And Walmart has said, "If you don't report this data, we will not buy what you make."

HIS HOLINESS THE DALAI LAMA: That's good, very good.

GREGORY NORRIS: So we are starting to collect more and more information, in part due to an increase in researchers and companies reporting, so the databases are getting more and more comprehensive.

DANIEL GOLEMAN: Greg, you mentioned that there's a cost and a benefit when we do things that are beneficial. Can you give the example of a cost-benefit analysis for the Netherlands power grid?

GREGORY NORRIS: Dan is referring to a study I did. While every purchase we make stimulates production all over the earth as well as pollution all over the earth, buying a product also distributes money to companies all over the earth. I wanted to find out how much of the money was getting to workers and helping to raise people out of poverty, and compare that to the environmental impacts of production.

Because I had access to the data, I looked at the Netherlands power grid and asked, "If we produce electricity in the Netherlands, what are the pollution consequences, where does the money go, and what's the potential to improve lives economically?" We found that most of the pollution, in this case, occurs in wealthier countries because that is where the production happens. But about 10 percent of the supply chain results in money flowing back to poorer countries, and if the economic development is managed well—in that it increases income to the poor—the economic benefits could be a thousand times greater than the impacts of the pollution generated. But that's only in the case of properly managed economic development that favors supporting people out of poverty.

The interesting part is, when we consider life-cycle assessment, if we only focus on pollution, we're potentially missing something else that's very important: the benefits from economic development. The other important point is that in order to determine beneficial outcomes, we need detailed data from each location to prove that the activities in a particular area are raising incomes for the poor and money coming back through the supply chain is being invested in public infrastructure for education and health.

The Cost of Pro-Environmental Business

JOHN DUNNE: When I spoke to His Holiness the Karmapa, one of our distinguished guests, about these issues, he raised questions about the role that costs and profits play in all this. For example, one reason that so many products in the United States come from China, where we have factories that are quite problematic, is that they're cheap. This is a symptom of a driving, fundamental interest in having low costs and high profits, which pushes a certain amount of the manufacturing to places where you can't get reliable information about environmental or social impacts.

It seems like part of the problem that's built into this system is that there's not enough appreciation for that fundamental mechanism, the fundamental expectation of low costs and high profits by US consumers and companies, which is driving manufacturing in China, for example, and enabling the lack of information transparency.

GREGORY NORRIS: There are really two sides to a response to that point, and it's good news in two ways. First, there have been studies in the past few years which show that if you treat workers well—in other words, pay them livable wages and respect their human rights—you save money. It's actually economically beneficial in the supply chains, because the workers are not as sick, they're more productive, and they stay with the company longer.

That's one thing, but there's a second pressure. Dan mentioned Walmart; they're requiring the major companies that sell to them to report on the environmental and social impacts in the supply chains of those products. Further, for years companies have been collecting data on working conditions in individual factories. That information has not yet been brought into this kind of analysis, but it's now starting to become publicly available. We know, for example, where the high-risk sectors and countries are for many different worker issues, community impact issues, and social issues.

There now exists something called the Social Hotspots Database, which has been compiled by researchers with more than a hundred different data resources. It's free and available to the public, and it offers a portrait of worker treatment, risks, and opportunities in global supply chains. And there are progressive, leading companies using that tool to help guide data collection to report to customers, and to demonstrate that the manufacturing of their products is happening under good conditions.

DANIEL GOLEMAN: We make the assumption that it will be more expensive to be environmentally positive, that it will cost more to do the right thing. Can you speak to that concern?

GREGORY NORRIS: Right, we make that assumption perhaps more on the social side. As consumers, we might make the assumption that we have to pay more for green, but companies have known for a long time that they can save money being green.

Looking at Walmart again, they love to save money in their supply chains; that's what they're all about—low cost. Walmart's vice president for strategy uses these kinds of tools to identify major costs. And they've studied and seen that there's a positive correlation between environmental performance and lower costs, or, you could say, between eco-efficiency and economic efficiency.

These correlate many times. Frequently more pollution is associated with greater energy and waste costs. Doing things smarter often actually saves money. So we need to have this information in order to put the pressure on the companies to spend money to reduce the pollution and impacts.

Social Responsibility

JOHN DUNNE: There's another observation that's implicit: it sounds like the only values here are profit and cost. And I'm wondering if there's value in the equation besides how much something costs to produce and how much you can sell it for. What's being brought into this analysis besides the traditional economic perspectives?

DANIEL GOLEMAN: I can speak to that. There's an ethical debate happening in business today. Some argue that their only responsibility to shareholders is to keep costs down; that only money counts. Another group asserts that we have a responsibility to everybody we impact; to communities, to customers, to people who work in the factories, and so on. The term for this position is called "social responsibility."

Today, there's a movement toward social responsibility. More money is being invested in socially responsible companies, and there's evidence that socially responsible companies do better in the long run.

JONATHAN PATZ: We have also made advances in workplace safety. We now have requirements such as the "worker right-to-know," where workers have a legal right to know about the materials they are working with. Along those lines, companies are required to publish material safety data sheets listing the chemicals they use and the associated hazards. Now sometimes they are published in the wrong language, or there may be other obstacles to worker safety, but we are creating legal instruments designed to protect workers.

Another comment, going back to the tradeoff considerations, is about a recent analysis by two economists, Bill Nordhaus and Robert Mendelsohn, from Yale University. They looked at the costs and benefits of electricity. We all benefit from electricity; it runs our computers, lights, air conditioning, and so on. Electricity is very valuable for development. But when they looked at the way electricity is generated, which is primarily through burning coal, they found that the environmental and health costs of burning coal outweigh the benefits of electricity. So it does more harm than good.

Buying Local: Not Always the Environmental Choice

DIANA LIVERMAN: Greg, I want to ask you a couple of questions that I think are interesting in light of what you talked about. The first is that in many countries people who wish to reduce their environmental impact are trying to buy local rather than buy products that are imported from other parts of the world. I wonder if you could talk about that; is asking consumers to buy from local companies better than asking them to buy from elsewhere in the world?

The second is in regard to the effectiveness of industry and corporations becoming aware of their environmental impacts versus informing individual consumers about the impacts of everything they buy. I know from the experiments in carbon labeling that it can be very confusing and perhaps overwhelming to a consumer, who is already reading labels for nutrition and calorie information. So do we really need every individual consumer to know the impacts, or do we just need the companies to know, along with a few environmental activists who can call them out if they don't behave?

GREGORY NORRIS: Great questions. For a while, we embraced the idea of "buy local" because we assumed that since local vegetables aren't transported as far, they don't have the same environmental impact. But the reality is actually more complicated. For example, produce that has to be flown in, perishables such as soft fruits and berries, yields a huge footprint, and the impacts of those products are large. But produce such as potatoes or apples that can travel slower on boat or rail often carry smaller impacts than the impacts created by managing a local farm. Even produce from far away, such as apples from New Zealand, can have a lower impact than produce from local farms.

To take it a step further, if the potatoes are grown in the right place, say, Idaho, where the fertilizer, energy, and water requirements to grow such produce are naturally minimized, you have efficient farming. On the other hand, a potato grown in Massachusetts, a less favorable environment for that vegetable, would take a lot of energy. Somebody living in Boston might have a smaller impact by buying an Idaho potato versus a local potato.

So the answer is that it is very dependent on each product and situation. Now, does that mean we need to be glued to our iPhones while shopping, to analyze carbon data and impacts? No.

My vision for the consumer is a few forms of extremely simple information. One could be a store guarantee that everything sold there is produced as greenly as possible, or even better that the products and their business yield a net benefit to the environment. That would be a simple consumer choice: buying products that have a net benefit. However, this does put a lot of pressure on companies to collect and analyze their production data and demonstrate that their products offer a net benefit.

JONATHAN PATZ: Can you give an example of how a company could offer a net benefit?

GREGORY NORRIS: One way could be that a manufacturer redesigns the product so that over the life cycle it would have a benefit it didn't previously have. For example, as I mentioned earlier, Caterpillar, using life-cycle assessment, found that 90 percent of the impacts of their bulldozers were not in the manufacturing of the product but in its use of fuel. They redesigned the bulldozer to be more efficient and now, over the lifetime of the item, its "handprint" impact is less than the footprint it created when it was built. So innovative companies can look at the life cycle of products for benefits in addition to the manufacturing processes.

Ecological Vision: Mindprint

MATTHIEU RICARD: I have a good story about chocolate. There's a company that most of you know, Mars, which makes chocolate, among other things. They are a family company with plenty of money, and it happens that one of their heirs, who is also a Buddhist practitioner, is also their CEO.

A few years ago, this CEO of Mars developed what's called a triple bottom line: people, planet, profit. This reduced their profit but improved the impact on the planet as well as the conditions for the workers in Ghana growing the chocolate. They even have Joseph Stiglitz, the Nobel Prize–winning economist, advising them, and they are going to expand this approach into other product lines. This is a good example of a company that has the capacity and the vision to do something with the goal of bringing benefit.

Also, you mentioned "footprint" and "handprint," and I want to add "mindprint" to that list. The mindprint would be the motivation and the vision. The people at Mars were visionaries. They said, "We have to reduce our profit in order to have a quality of life and protect the environment." It takes a lot of mindprint to do that.

As Sallie McFague often says, ideas have power. In Buddhism we say that if you are content, it is like having treasure in the palm of your hand. If every morning you recite the mantra "I need nothing, I need nothing," you are less likely to be a big consumer during the day. I see mindprint at the root of handprint, which in turn reduces our footprint. So let's change our minds and change the world for the better.

HIS HOLINESS THE DALAI LAMA: This discussion is getting complicated, but from a broader perspective, one could say that capitalism and its focus on profit, its greed, is causing a lot of problems. If we were to consider other socioeconomic theories, such as Marxism or socialism, at least ideologically they are more holistic and more concerned with the well-being of society.

On the other hand, the Communist movement in the Soviet Union failed, and today we have capitalist communists and capitalist socialists in places like China, for example. And despite ideologies, I'm not sure these countries have better ecological records. In fact, I wouldn't even consider many of these places genuine socialist or communist countries. Ideology has more to do with political control in such places, while the issues of public health and pollution are just as bad or worse than other areas in the world.

SALLIE MCFAGUE: Yes. I want to follow up a little bit on what Matthieu said about vision. That is, it depends in part on what vision we have for our economics. People talk about economics as if there's only one kind—market capitalism—but that is just one model.

We could have ecological economics, which would put more emphasis on distribution and sustainability rather than on the single individual, as in market capitalism. In other words, our current model is built upon the premise that the individuals with the most power get the most resources—Adam Smith's classic insatiable individual.

But what if we start with another premise, such as distribution—to ensure that everyone gets enough basic food, and further that all life forms that are part of the system get their necessary essentials? From there we could also look at sustainability of the whole, and those could become our economic goals.

Working within one system of economics limits us. And I think the Occupy Wall Street protests questioned this system at a deeper level, saying that there's something wrong with the way that we're putting our economics together.

HIS HOLINESS THE DALAI LAMA: I think that ultimately, as you mentioned, a sense of concern and responsibility for the well-being of others is the key. Otherwise, no matter how good of an economic system you have, it will be vulnerable to the human motivations of the people running it, and if their motivations are not altruistic, the system will be ineffective at addressing these concerns.

That's the key factor, and that's something that can't be created on a computer or taken out and replaced by brain surgeons.

SALLIE MCFAGUE: Your Holiness, I agree with what you're saying. You talked about Bhutan and Estonia as being examples of different visions of how we might live. So perhaps it's more than just the system, but rather the vision that we have and live within that system. And what we have been learning is that an effective vision has to include interdependence and interrelatedness.

That's not the way market capitalism works, which is more or less every person for themselves. But if we have a vision, as Bhutan does, that enables individuals to deepen their awareness and rise to the challenge of supporting the greater good, the vision itself supports people in being this way.

The Need for Individual Responsibility

HIS HOLINESS THE DALAI LAMA: It's the vision of "me, me, me" that's creating difficulties. Despite that, the truth is that we are social animals and we depend on each other for our well-being and the well-being of society. Now there are 7 billion whose futures depend on this awareness.

Whether we are talking about economics, religion, or politics, I think a sense of responsibility for the well-being of others, in each of us, is the key factor.

For example, I once met an Indian Parliament member, and we were talking about how many poor people there are in India, especially in rural areas. He agreed and told me that the government recognized the problem and was making efforts to institute assistance programs for these people. But then he said that one of the important people involved in the programs was not implementing them properly; he was actually misusing the money.

So even if we have good systems in place, ultimately it's up to the moral ethics and individual sense of responsibility of the people involved to make those systems effective.

GREGORY NORRIS: Your Holiness, you have taught me and millions of others that compassion—being compassionate to others and caring about their well-being—is a source of happiness for us. You've also shared that once our basic needs are met, rarely do more material possessions lead to greater happiness. In other words, income is poorly correlated with happiness.

For the first time now, with the technological tools we have, not only can we show people the environmental impact they are having on the world, but we can also give them tools to track their well-being over time based on what they are doing.

And as this kind of information gets shared socially and publicly, people will see examples of individuals who have reduced income and spending and are happier. Perhaps this kind of awareness is part of the solution.

CLARE PALMER: My question for Greg is that the data and projections seem to rely a lot on market forces and not so much on regulation. But given the tendency for people and business toward corruption, do you think there is a role for regulation in managing emissions and other environmental impacts?

GREGORY NORRIS: I think so. I'm very disappointed by the progress in the United States over the last ten years, as well as most other First World countries, to sufficiently regulate to address climate change. It's not the only issue, but if we look at climate change as an example, regulations are often fought and defeated by very powerful economic interests. As a result, we don't get effective regulation.

On the other hand, consumer behavior and purchasing is a language that is already being spoken to companies every day, and consumer sentiment is a strong influencer of change. So while I certainly think we need effective regulation for environmental pollution, good working conditions, and so forth, I also feel that we have to do more through voluntary mechanisms to get the results we need, as fast as we can. Not to say that voluntary mechanisms or consumer pressure are the only solutions, but I think we've learned that regulation is not sufficient either.

DANIEL GOLEMAN: There was an interesting implicit question in what Clare said, which is, what would keep the system's integrity? In other words, how would you keep it from being corrupted? I think you were alluding to that.

GREGORY NORRIS: Well, validation of the data would do that. And we're proposing a new realm where every producer reports on impacts, and those reports need to be verified locally to avoid cheating.

DANIEL GOLEMAN: Do you mean independently verified by someone who hasn't worked for the company?

GREGORY NORRIS: That's right. And as His Holiness said, the ethical compass of the individual overseeing the program is what's going to make the difference. You could have great programs and regulations, but if the implementation isn't done with integrity, they won't be effective. Remember, we are talking about people. I've never met anyone who wants to pollute, but people don't always have options.

One company that I'm starting to work with is the seventh largest employer in the world. They have programs where employees are not only encouraged to reduce the impacts of the business at work but also encouraged to reduce their impacts at home. Again, I think it comes back to finding ways to really make it clear to people that their actions at home and work are ultimately the only things that are causing environmental impacts. And if the heart of the people overseeing change programs is in the right place, I think our progress can be very deep and rapid.

JOHN DUNNE: So far, we've essentially been talking about manufacturing and business responsibility. But as consumers, for example here in Dharamsala, we go shopping in areas where there are busy streets and lots of pollution, and that's because either we drive there or it's convenient. Factor that in with the underlying demand for low prices, and one can ask if consumers are yet sincerely generating interest for impact data and change. Or do consumers themselves need a change of heart first?

DANIEL GOLEMAN: I have some data that speaks directly to that. There have been market surveys that ask shoppers, "Do you really care about how sustainable your products are?" In the West, about 10 percent say, "Yes, I care a lot," and around 30 percent say, "No, I don't care at all." The middle 60 percent say, "If it were easy and convenient, I would make the better decision." That's particularly true for the current generations of shoppers. But if you ask younger people, the ratio changes. Because they have grown up with constant exposure to bad news about the environment, they are much more motivated to pay attention and make different choices.

Companies are looking at this data and incorporating it into their long-term strategies. They know that no company lasts forever. In the history of America, no more than a few companies have survived more than a hundred years. So they are looking ahead and strategizing for survival.

In addition to the consumer, another key player in this is the brand manager, the person who makes the product. We also need to get the attention of brand managers, because they're making decisions on whether or not to make changes based on the kinds of data that Greg is producing.

HIS HOLINESS THE DALAI LAMA: While my knowledge of trends and business is limited, I do think about human ways of being. And it seems that we need to get more realistic. Even if we are only thinking of our own interests, we need to be realistic about what will preserve them.

I think generating awareness is critical. We need to get more convincing information out about the roles and impacts of individuals, the community, the economy, the environment, and all of the factors. When you look at it, the whole conglomeration is really one interdependent entity. I think the best people to stimulate awareness about what's happening and what needs to be done are not the politicians or leaders but the scientists. They are the real gurus in these matters.

Over the course of the twentieth century, humanity's way of thinking changed considerably. For example, early in the twentieth century, war was more of an accepted event. Later in the twentieth century, we began seriously questioning war and violence, and even expressing intense opposition to war. I think this is an indicator that we are becoming more realistic about the impact of what we are doing.

The same holds with the environment, and even the brain. One hundred years ago, we weren't worried about the environment and didn't really understand the brain. Now these issues are current and we are talking about them more and more. They are of real interest to many, not just a few individuals.

So if we look at it from this point of view, there have been positive changes, which can inspire the individual who otherwise might feel like he or she can't do anything and it's better to turn away from the issues.

Even in my personal life experience, which I often share, sometimes tragedy happens, as well as sadness and frustration, but we need to find ways to transform that into more enthusiasm and determination to do what's right.

Our discussion today has outlined a lot of problems—not just one person's problems or one country's problems, but the whole world's problems. And these are very serious problems. But in order to survive and be happy, we have to be realistic, take responsibility, and make the necessary efforts. And change is a real possibility. We've seen, throughout the twentieth century, a tremendous amount of change just through increased awareness. I think this can continue into the twenty-first century with the information and guidance from our scientific gurus.

DANIEL GOLEMAN: Your Holiness, thank you very much. That's a wonderful note to end on, and a good starting point for the rest of our conversation, which will now shift from discussing awareness to talking about action.

5 Ethics and the Environment

PRESENTER: Clare Palmer, *Texas A&M University*

JOHN DUNNE: Two years ago, Dan Goleman and I began planning this meeting with the Mind and Life Institute. We started by considering what the elements essential to understanding the environmental crisis might be. Soon we were joined by Jonathan Patz, and it became evident, in part because of Jonathan's work, that ethics are a crucial component in understanding the environmental crisis. One very important role of ethics is to guide our actions once science gives us a clear understanding of the reality we face. But ethics can also precede science. And values are also connected to ethics.

For example, as we discussed previously, if we only value profit, we might not care about the environment or the impact our actions have on others. Some may even use political and economic power to block environmental science, because it's an obstacle to profit. So ethics are important factors, even before we see the scientific evidence. They are crucial to understanding how we have found ourselves in this environmental crisis.

With that in mind, we connected with Dr. Clare Palmer, professor of philosophy at Texas A&M University. She completed her graduate work at the University of Oxford, and she has a background not only in philosophy but also in religion. Much of her work occurs at the intersection of philosophy, religion, and the environment. She has focused on ethics related to the treatment of animals.

Dr. Palmer was the president of the International Society for Environmental Ethics from 2007 to 2010. She founded an important journal in this new area of philosophy, called *Worldviews: Environment, Culture, Religion*, and is the author of *Animal Ethics in Context* (Columbia University, 2010). She has also coedited a number of volumes, including the five-volume collection titled *Environmental Philosophy* (Routledge, 2005).

As I was doing my research, I came across an article that Dr. Palmer had written that was amazingly clear. It laid out the various positions within environmental ethics and the way that philosophers throughout the world are thinking about environmental ethics today. That's part of what Dr. Palmer will do today: introduce us to some of the key positions in environmental ethics and then raise some interesting questions for us to consider.

CLARE PALMER: Thank you. I am honored to be able to meet you and to talk to you today. I'll say something about the key positions in environmental ethics, and then I'll talk about three fundamental problems environmental ethicists continue to debate.

Environmental Ethics: A Nascent Field

CLARE PALMER: Diana, Jonathan, and Greg have introduced us to different kinds of impacts that we have on the environment. What environmental philosophers do is to pick up on that work, and then consider what values are at stake, what kinds of ethical issues environmental impacts raise, and how we should behave in response to these particular problems.

Before we explore the issues, let's look at the field of environmental ethics. The field is relatively new, with beginnings in the late 1970s and early 1980s. Since then, it has grown significantly, and now there are many universities throughout Europe, the United States, and Australasia that teach environmental ethics. However, because it's such a young field, or possibly because of the nature of what it looks at, it is very contested and there is often little consensus about basic positions in the field: about the fundamental questions and how to answer them. As they say, wherever there are two philosophers in a room, there will be at least three opinions. The same is true for environmental ethicists.

HIS HOLINESS THE DALAI LAMA: This is why we need to listen to the scientists, who bring us the many, varied aspects of realty. In fact, it's impossible for one word, or the concepts derived from one word, to fully capture reality.

In Buddhist philosophy, as well as classical Indian philosophy, a distinction is made between the direct experience of reality and conceptual thoughts about reality. Thoughts tend to be very selective, typically picking up only a facet of reality, whereas direct experience can engage with reality in a much more comprehensive way. And when the philosopher, using conceptual thoughts, says, "This is the truth," that's a mistake. In fact, it's a perception of reality from one angle or perspective.

CLARE PALMER: There is one idea on which most environmental ethicists do agree, however. We are all looking for reasons and explanations for the values that people hold. So when people make claims that something should be protected, or something is important, philosophers are asking, "Well, why do you say that? What reasons do you give for that?" That inquiry has been one of the jobs that environmental ethicists have undertaken.

The Key Views

CLARE PALMER: Figure 18 outlines some of the basic positions in the field of environmental ethics. As you can see, there's a fundamental divide between two concerns: one concern is human centered, the other nonhuman centered. This divide has been a great source of debate in environmental ethics. Of course, not all human and nonhuman concerns are necessarily in opposition to each another. Rather, some concerns could benefit both humans and nonhumans at the same time, or have cobenefits, to use the term that Jonathan introduced yesterday. However, with the potential for co-benefits, you also have the possibility of co-harms, where one action affects both human and nonhuman concerns.

Starting with the human concerns, or human-centered positions in environmental ethics, let's look at "ecosystem services." We talked about this concept previously as the free services that nature provides to human beings. Environmental ethicists are interested in ecosystem services. These are very important for our own well-being, and in many ways we are dependent on the natural world. While that can be denied in our practices and actions, to be prudent, and for our own well-being, we need to think about this relationship.

A second position explores the ideas of "Beauty" and "Place." While these ideas are sometimes included in ecosystem services, I wanted to separate them for our discussion, because I think the language of "services" does not easily capture interest in beauty and the value of place. These are really things that we value, rather than services that are provided to us.

So some philosophers argue that natural beauty has some kind of intrinsic value for us, and certainly beauty has been something that has underpinned the protection of the natural world in many places, especially in the United States, where the national parks were formed initially in beautiful places.

However, there are some concerns about weighting natural beauty too heavily. Notions about what's beautiful have changed over the centuries, and a place that was once protected may lose value over time. Additionally, ugly things or places may be very ecologically valuable. A corpse full of maggots may not be very beautiful, but it will be very environmentally significant for other reasons. Further, there could be something very beautiful with a cause that may be problematic, like a beautiful sunset that we later discover was caused by pollution.

Place is also very important to people. People become rooted in particular places, come to value the places where they live, and will try very hard to protect those places. The value of place has been important in environmental protection. This, too, can be problematic when the value of place conflicts with environmental values. For example, people may

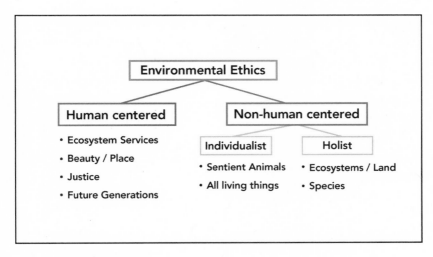

Figure 18. Environmental ethics

protect some land against windmills and miss the opportunity to generate wind power.

The third human-centered concern is concern for "justice." Here, the concerns look at the ways the environment can be a cause of injustice between different groups of people. For instance, one group of people might control a natural resource and prevent other people from accessing it without consulting them and without compensating them. This might happen, for example, if a dam is built, and to do so people are pushed off the land, people who don't benefit from the electricity that's generated and didn't cause their own relocation but end up suffering disproportionately. There are many cases like this, and environmental ethicists have spent considerable time thinking about these justice issues.

The fourth area of debate considers future generations and the impacts on people that don't yet exist. This is one of the main topics I want to address later.

Now let's look at the nonhuman-centered issues and talk about these views. Here, again, there's a dispute. The divide occurs between those who argue that individual, sentient organisms are what matter, and those who argue that all parts of ecosystems are important as a whole, and each piece or species is morally important as well. The first group is the individualists, and the latter is the holists.

The individualists argue that what matters are beings that can have experiences, that have lives that can go well or badly, that can suffer pain and pleasure. In particular, they are referring to animals and mammals, including human beings, as well as fish and reptiles. There is some discussion about whether all those beings can feel pain; the scientific evidence is unclear.

The second group says, "Thinking about individuals and sentient animals is not going far enough. What matters are beings that are alive, not only whether or not they can feel pain or pleasure. So all living things are morally important, and we need to take them into account."

There are disagreements about whether all living things are equally significant, or whether some beings are more significant than others because of their capacity to feel pain, or for some other reason. So there are lots of arguments even within each category.

Further, there's a debate about the moral significance of ecosystems. Those who adopt this view argue that we should see the land as being morally important itself, arguing that individual species should be thought of as morally significant units. They contend that extinction is a very bad scenario, and that losing the last of a species is far worse than losing an individual member of a species. For instance, there's something far worse about the loss of the last tiger than the loss of a pet cat, because the species itself is valuable. Not just because it matters to us, or because it's bad for all the individuals of that species, but the species itself is a unit that we need to take into account. So that is a summary that sets up the different kinds of views that environmental ethicists debate.

Ethicists' Critical Questions

CLARE PALMER: The first problem I want to address is "future people." It seems clear, and others have raised this point already, that we can harm future generations in various ways. We can leave a legacy of nuclear waste, we can change the climate, we can cause pollution, we can cause climate change, we can make species extinct—and many other negative impacts. But how to think about this ethically has been very troubling for environmental ethicists, and even more so for Western ethicists. Some philosophers argue that we shouldn't take future people into account at all; they're not morally relevant. Certain human rights theorists take this view. Not all of them, but some of them. These philosophers argue that to have rights you must exist, and since future people do not exist they are not able to claim rights; they can't recognize rights, and for that reason they can't have rights. Their conclusion is that we should discount future people, not think about them.

HIS HOLINESS THE DALAI LAMA: Is it not true that our own future lives do not yet exist as well? Yet we still need to seriously consider our own futures, as well as those of our children and grandchildren. And these theorists, who argue that future generations are not relevant, will they, in their own lives, ever complain or appreciate the actions of their ancestors, experience loss or benefit as a result of their parents' or ancestors' actions?

CLARE PALMER: That is a consideration I am curious about, too. As it turns out, most philosophers argue that future people do matter, though for varied reasons. Some say, "We can harm future individuals." Others argue, "There will be more suffering in the future if we behave in particular kinds of ways." There are many arguments for the impacts we could have on future people.

Yet even from this point of view, there are difficulties in deciding how to factor future people into current decision making. There may be cases where the interests of present people and future people conflict with one another. For example, development that supports present people may harm future people. Another pervasive problem is that the motivation for present people to take future people into account is very weak. One of the main reasons for this is that many people believe that to resolve some of our current environmental problems, we need collective agreements that benefit all of the parties in the agreement, and that everyone needs to keep the agreement. However, future people can't join in collective agreements, so they can't be represented. We don't necessarily benefit from an agreement with them, and consequently we are not as motivated to include them. We can harm them, but they can't benefit us; it's a one-way relationship.

Another reason why we're weakly motivated to consider future people is that it's very difficult to feel compassion for beings that don't yet exist. While we can feel compassion for a distant person, in part because we can often see a picture of their suffering, for beings that are nonexistent, that kind of compassion is difficult to achieve.

HIS HOLINESS THE DALAI LAMA: There's a classical Indian Buddhist philosophical school that argues that everything that exists must exist in the present, which seems to be a similar line of thinking.

CLARE PALMER: Yes, and it would be very demanding if we had to take into account everything that would ever exist in the future now, in the present.

HIS HOLINESS THE DALAI LAMA: And yet even in the case of these classical Buddhist philosophers, who insist that to be real is to be real now, they, too, worry about what will happen to them tomorrow, and a day after. As a matter of fact, they are often talking about nirvana as something that will happen in the future.

Where Do Systems and Species Fit?

CLARE PALMER: The second issue I want to talk about is how to consider systems and species, since this is a big problem for environmental ethics. It seems accurate to surmise that when we think about environmental problems, we're not just thinking about groups of individual species and the impact on them, but also the relative value of those species or systems. For example, we don't regard a tree plantation and an old-growth forest the same, even if they have exactly the same number of species. The plantation might be thought of more as a collection of species, the forest as a system, perhaps. And while we think of these differently, it's very hard to identify what, exactly, it is about a system that has moral significance or value.

One guidepost was offered by a very famous American philosopher and forester named Aldo Leopold, who said we should follow a land ethic that states, "A thing is right when it tends to preserve the integrity, stability, and beauty of the biotic community. It is wrong when it tends otherwise."

However, individualists don't agree with this view. They say, "Well, ecosystems don't really exist in the way Leopold thought they did. There are, in fact, not coherent areas with integrity and stability out there. We can't clearly identify the boundaries of ecosystems; we can't pick them out. They're much more chaotic than Leopold thought that they were. Organisms arrive randomly, they have relationships with one another, but they're not systematic in any way. And even if they were, why would we think that the integrity of a system mattered morally anyway?"

Instead, individualists say that what matters would be whether or not ecosystems could suffer, and they claim to know that ecosystems don't suffer. Some individuals or species might suffer, but not the ecosystem as a unit.

Similar arguments are made about species as well. Those who think that species are morally significant argue that individual species have interests that aren't the same as the interests of the members of the species. For instance, imagine if we had a species with only fifty remaining members, so in order to keep the species going we bred all of the remaining individuals of the species in captivity, and all fifty had horrible lives because we were doing horrible things to them in order to make them breed. The species then might flourish, but the individuals would have a terrible life. You might say that was in the interest of the species as a whole but not in the interest of the individual members of the species. That's an interesting distinction.

However, an individualist could retort, "That's the wrong interpretation of what's happening. All that's really going on is that you're sacrificing the interest of present individuals for the benefit of future individuals, and because there will be more of them over time, ultimately you benefit more individuals, and that's all you mean when you say the species is flourishing."

As you can see, this is a very important debate, one that will affect environmental policy, because there are many cases where individuals are sacrificed for systems. As another example, let's say hunting of certain species is permitted to manage population growth. In this case, individuals suffer to benefit systems. But if systems are not morally important themselves, that action is problematic.

Creating Future Environments

CLARE PALMER: The last point I want to consider brings the issues together and addresses what kinds of future environments we want to create. Some ethicists say that's an overreaching question, that ethics should really only address issues such as not harming, or not infringing upon rights, and not consider farther-reaching ideas such as trying to create better worlds. On the other hand, many philosophers say that we are already creating a world, and given that, we need to create the best world possible, or at least a better environment than we are currently creating.

So if there is a goal to create better future environments, then the question is, what would they look like? What is a better future environment? And since there are many different views about what matters, as we've seen, what would constitute a good future environment is problematic. A further complication is that while an issue such as climate change, as we have seen, will produce various kinds of harms, it will also create a new environment with new systems and new individual organisms, and many of those new organisms will then be as valuable as the other organisms. From some philosophical points of view it's very difficult even to say there is a problem with climate change. For instance, we know that one current effect of climate change is that there is less tundra in Siberia, that the forest is expanding in that region. Is that bad? Is that a harm? Does it matter that there will be more forest and less tundra? Has an ecosystem been harmed? Has the tundra been harmed?

One characteristic of the vision of a future environment that many people think is important is that it should contain less suffering. But ethicists find this problematic, too. For example, that might suggest that it would be better to have a world that contains fewer organisms with the capacity to suffer, such as more trees and fewer sentient animals. Or it might mean eliminating predators, such as tigers, because they kill other organisms and cause suffering. Maybe a world with no tigers would be better than a world with tigers, but obviously that would conflict with other environmental values about protecting species. So this question about what kind of future environment we should create is very probing.

Three Important Questions

CLARE PALMER: In closing, I'd like to offer three questions for consideration. I would be honored to hear views from the perspective of the Buddhist tradition to help us in environmental ethics think through these problems in new ways we may not have previously considered.

1. How do we think about and value future people? How should we factor future people into our ethical decision making?
2. Can species or ecosystems be ethically significant in themselves, above and beyond the individuals that compose them?
3. What kind of environment should humans be trying to create, if they should be trying to create environments at all?

HIS HOLINESS THE DALAI LAMA: Broadly speaking, ethics seems to relate directly to organisms that can experience pain and pleasure, that want pleasure and happiness, that do not want suffering. It's interesting to consider animals that don't have the same kind of intelligence as us.

However, most animals take care of their offspring. They have some sense of responsibility to look after their young. Perhaps even if it is only on a biological level, they also have instincts about the cycles of life, the seasons, where and when to find food. So, to some extent, they are thinking about the future as well, not just the present. They also remember past experiences to some extent. Perhaps not past generations, but they recall their own lifetimes. But even so, I do not think that the animal world has its own sense of ethics. Ethics, as we understand it, seems to be more directly related to human intelligence, our experiences of pleasure and pain, and our long-term future interests.

To that point, referring to those who emphasize that only present beings have rights, what do they consider the present? A year, a month, an hour, one second before or after, a decade, a century? The very basis of that view is challenging because we cannot find the collective definition of "present."

Further, ethics seems to be socially dependent. When you look at early communism, the Marxists sought a classless society in which everyone was equal and had equal access to the things they needed. In that case, maybe ethics wouldn't apply the same way. That system may have worked for a smaller population, but as the population grew, injustices and unhealthy balances occurred, and they needed to appoint a leader to manage society. Then ethics entered the conversation in order to prevent injustice and protect the weaker members of society.

In today's societies, nobody denies they have feelings of pain or pleasure, and we have to have concern for their well-being, so ethics apply. This is my overall view of the evolution of ethics.

So how should we factor in future people? We need to first acknowledge that our present experience is very much related to the past, and we need to think about what we can learn from the past. Then it follows that our present behavior will affect the future.

For example, the twentieth century was filled with violence, and even in the beginning of this century there is continuing violence despite the fact that people everywhere are calling for peace. This is, in part, a result of our behavior in the past century. It's quite logical that many future problems will be largely dependent on how we act today.

Another issue is that specialists and philosophers often pick a focused area of study and go very deep without paying much attention to the holistic system, to the big picture. They may only look at the small details and may lack understanding of relativity and interdependence. From this pointed perspective, things are often considered absolute and taken for reality. This usually leads to the problem of trying to uphold a position that is not really a position, because it is not taking into account all the factors.

The reality is that all things are relative. From one angle, an event could seem to be a good thing; from another angle it's a horrible event. My essential view is that everything is relative. Perhaps my view is influenced by Buddhist Madhyamaka philosophical thinking. And, at the same time, there is a demarcation between what is true and what is untrue. At least at the level of everyday experience, we have to make distinctions between what is true and what is untrue.

Are Certain Points of View Absurd?

TENZIN PRIYADARSHI: I think part of the concern with modern ethics is that it's more philosophical than practical. If you took a survey of how many students in the United States, for example, would willingly want to enroll in an Ethics 101 class, it's a very small percentage. The reason being that ethics, for some reason, is being taught in a manner that is not very appealing. Ethics often has been taught as a restraining mechanism— don't do this, don't do that, such is the value of this thing or that thing. Thus, to a large degree, ethics is more of a theoretical approach than an application.

However, when Buddhists engage with ethics, they're looking from the point of view of optimization. How do we, by virtue of exercising ethical behavior, become more optimal human beings, or become more optimal people? That is why certain aspects of ethics, such as the problems that you raise about future people, at times appear to be a bit absurd. It's odd to think of a scenario, such as our concern for the environment, arising in a human being's mind without accounting for future people, future generations. From the Buddhist point of view, in my opinion, taking that proposition as an ethical consideration is an absurdity.

JOHN DUNNE: I want to make this a little more concrete, because this actually has very important ramifications in the context of moving environmental policy forward. It may seem absurd, but what's important to recall is that the policies that will be made on the basis of science are going to restrict what others can do. One famous example that occurred in the northwestern United States was the case of the spotted owl. The spotted owl was an endangered species that was losing its habitat and facing extinction from logging. However, a community was making its living by cutting down trees, and they objected very strongly to a new law that required them to stop cutting these trees down, or at least limit the cutting a great deal, in order to protect the owl. A certain kind of ethical choice was made there to value not just the individual owl but the species over the individual people.

We're doing the same thing with future people. For example, if we decide now that we're going to make it illegal to hunt, then we are not only restricting the rights of the people today who want to hunt but also the hunting rights of their children and cultures that depend on hunting. I'm not saying that hunting is good, but we are making a choice that has future impact.

If we say we're going to make it illegal to raise the temperature more than 70 degrees in your house, then we are making a choice that affects not just us but our future generations. So there's a way in which we are forcing future people to abide by our ethical standards. We think we know what is right and wrong, and we say, "It has to be this way. They have no choice." That's really the issue: how do we make those choices? How are we going to decide what is good and bad for these people? It's as if we are deciding what is good and bad for others around us. I think that's really the concrete issue in many ways.

MATTHIEU RICARD: I think the question of whether this is an absurd notion or not is rooted in self-grasping. Tenzin Priyadarshi may find it absurd because his concept of "in group/out group" is vast enough that he has genuine concern for all; he values future generations. Some have made the opposite statement. Steve Forbes, an American billionaire, said on Fox News that to change our behavior now because the ocean might rise in a hundred years is absurd. He was strictly and only concerned about now and himself. So if our self-grasping is narrow, it's all about us right now. If we extend it a little bit, it's still about us and we'll also care about what happens to us next year, and in ten years. If we extend further, we will care about our friends, about our family, possibly about our ethnic group, or our nation. The ultimate challenge in concern for others, and altruism, is to extend that "in group" out until we include all sentient beings. So it's actually a measure of our self-grasping.

CLARE PALMER: It seems to me that we've been presented two different kinds of views. One where people think the alternative to their own view is absurd, that it's absurd to think that we wouldn't include future people, and another that it's absurd to think we should restrain our behavior now to prevent something happening in a hundred years. In my understanding, in environmental ethics, to say that something is absurd is not a valid reason. We need to provide reasons to support these kinds of intuitions that something is absurd or not. What you subsequently said, Matthieu, provided a reason for that kind of view.

MATTHIEU RICARD: The Buddhist reason is "I don't want to suffer, no one wants to suffer, future sentient beings do not want to suffer." It involves recognition and value of all sentient beings.

Western versus Buddhist Ethics

THUPTEN JINPA: Let me step out of my role as His Holiness's interpreter and speak in my own voice. One of the things that is being brought very sharply into focus in your presentation is the problem of thinking through these questions, because what all of these competing positions show is that there are competing values that we hold dear. When it comes to the nitty-gritty of figuring out the best way to behave, sometimes these values are in conflict. For example, how we factor future generations into our decision making is a very important consideration, and I think the key phrase that you're using in all of this is "moral significance." What is the moral significance of future generations in our consideration of ethical responsibility? What is the moral significance of ecosystems?

The difference between the Western philosophical style of ethical thinking and the Buddhist style of ethical thinking is that in the Western style of thinking, there seems to be an assumption that somehow reason can take you all the way through to the answer, that somehow we can find the right rules, and then everything will be fine. Although Buddhism emphasizes the use of reason extensively, it does not argue for a set of absolute rules that apply in all contexts. Buddhism's emphasis is on relativity, that everything is complex and interrelated, that you should look at things from a contextual point of view, that something might seem to be valuable in one context and not in another.

I suppose the closest that classical Buddhism comes to rule-based ethics is in the area of monastic codes, the precepts by which monastic members live their lives. These are very clearly spelled out—you should not do this, you should not do that—and all of these precepts govern the physical and verbal behavior of a monastic. Yet even though these rules are clearly spelled out, there are more important ones and layers that lead to subsequent rules, so even in the case of monastic codes exceptions are made.

Even the Buddha was known to prohibit something under one circumstance and then allow it under another. Our approach is very context-sensitive. The ultimate aim of the Buddhist approach is to avoid harm and to bring benefit. To achieve this, we operate from key principles, such as compassion, versus strict rules.

I think this is where the tension is coming from—the contrast between classical Buddhist ethical thinking versus the Western style of ethical thinking. The Western approach is primarily focused on action and discovering hidden rules. The Buddhist approach focuses on the development of character, the cultivation of the right kinds of motivation and value, and is context-sensitive as to the specifics of how to act.

CLARE PALMER: Traditionally in Western ethics, there have been three theoretical approaches: one is focused on bringing about the best consequences and avoiding the worst consequences; a second that's essentially been rule-oriented—it sounds like that's the one that you think is the dominant one in Western ethics—and a third is a theory of virtue ethics, which is close to what you're saying the Buddhist tradition is.

When the focus is more on thinking about yourself as a person, action is not primary; rather, it's being a good person that would be important. Virtue ethics is also particularly context-sensitive. The idea that it's right to do one thing in one circumstance and wrong to do the same thing in a different context would comfortably fit into Western virtue-ethics traditions.

That sounds closer to the Buddhist view than the rule-oriented traditions, but it also seems as though you were saying there is both a virtue tradition and an idea of trying to maximize pleasure and minimize pain. It sounds as if both those traditions exist at the same time.

THUPTEN JINPA: Yes, both elements are there.

Do We Need Reasons to Be Ethical?

DIANA LIVERMAN: His Holiness expressed his opinions about some of the ethical positions that you described, Clare, including comments on whether or not future generations count, but you were very careful not to give your own position in your presentation. I'm wondering if you would like to tell us what your position is?

CLARE PALMER: With respect to all these issues, or future generations in particular?

THUPTEN JINPA: I think on ecosystems as well. That's probably the more challenging one.

CLARE PALMER: I think we must take future generations into account in moral decision making. I'm just not sure what the best way of doing that is, or how to weigh them, or how to deal with conflicts of interest. For instance, while I think compassion is very important, I'm not sure how you deal with cases where compassion for one may conflict with compassion for others, and so I'm less clear on that issue. In the case of species and ecosystems, while I would like to find good arguments that support the idea that either species or ecosystems are significant units in themselves, I have not found those arguments. Most of my work has focused on sentient animals, because I think the case there is very clear: we need to change the ways that we treat animals. That is very difficult to argue against.

But I can't find good arguments, though I have tried to construct them and failed, for why we should think that species and ecosystems are important as units themselves. Even so, they are very important to us. Any policy that takes our long-term interests into consideration, including future generations, is likely to protect species and ecosystems for human-centered reasons, and for sentient animals. You don't necessarily need arguments to say that these things are important in themselves. Now there are some cases where those concerns come apart, but generally speaking, you get protection for species or ecosystems by being concerned about animals, future generations, and human well-being.

JOHN DUNNE: I find it interesting that you can't find any arguments for taking an ecosystem, or species as a whole, as kind of an object of concern in understanding whether something is virtuous or unvirtuous. That may be the case in Buddhism too, but I wonder, Your Holiness, would you say that is true?

HIS HOLINESS THE DALAI LAMA: In a way, it's true. If you don't take into consideration the notion of suffering and happiness, then the whole basis of thinking about morality and ethics, as well as justice and injustice, disappears. The premise for considering ethics is just not there.

But this is complicated. As humans, we tend to emphasize the long-term benefits over short-term suffering or temporary comfort. For example, athletes train hard, feel pain, and sweat to see a long-term benefit. Even students prefer the holidays and the breaks but are encouraged to stay focused on studies for the long-term benefit. In most every society, individuals make sacrifices in the present to achieve long-term goals. But when we consider society as a whole, how do we determine which group's interests to sacrifice for the benefit of the majority?

This is why the democratic system is necessary. It's not 100 percent perfect, but generally speaking, it's much better than other decision-making models. I always say that the world belongs to humanity, not to governments, kings or queens, or religious leaders. In order for people to govern their own country, the democratic system is the best. That does not mean everyone's interests are met, but it's the best approach for meeting the needs of the majority. In ethical considerations, if there is a choice, all participants should have their needs met. But if we are left without that choice, and some needs have to be sacrificed, then we must meet the needs of the majority.

JOHN DUNNE: That's a very productive answer, Your Holiness. Thank you.

6 The Uncomfortable Truth: On the Treatment of Animals

PRESENTER: Matthieu Ricard, *Shechen Monastery, Kathmandu*

JOHN DUNNE: At this point, we need to make a slight transition. We've been talking about, in part, the rights of nonhuman beings, especially animals. In fact, one of Clare's main areas of expertise is the treatment of animals. That's very appropriate now, because we're going to ask the Venerable Matthieu Ricard to make a few comments about the treatment of animals. As it turns out, the way in which we treat animals has major ethical considerations and can have a tremendous impact on our environment as well.

HIS HOLINESS THE DALAI LAMA: When Buddhists say "human rights," sometimes there's an implication that human beings have a special right to use other animals. But this is false. As far as the right to a peaceful life, all sentient being have equal rights. Basically, all beings have the same feelings of pain and pleasure, so all have the same right to exist.

MATTHIEU RICARD: If we were to reduce ethics to one single right, it would be the right to not suffer. That's the overarching, fundamental right. Your Holiness, you often say that Buddhist philosophy can be summarized in the view of interdependence of all phenomena and the behavior of nonviolence. And when we say nonviolence, we mean nonviolence toward human beings, toward animals, and toward the environment.

Interdependence is the wisdom of understanding reality, and nonviolence is compassion.

You may remember Al Gore's documentary on the environment, *An Inconvenient Truth*. Similarly, the way we exploit and treat animals is a very "uncomfortable truth." It's uncomfortable because while we may have some compassion for animals, we feel a very strong resistance to objectively see the reality of our treatment of animals.

To begin, we can add to our discussion of our own ethical interests by reviewing some data on the environmental impact of our industrial use of animals. I am not a climatologist, but I have been very motivated by that question, and I have done research, which I verified with scientists.

The Environmental Impact of Meat

MATTHIEU RICARD: First, 99 percent of meat production is not from field-grazing animals, it's from industrial farming. That's consistent for all livestock animals. This practice contributes 18 percent of the greenhouse emissions that are leading to global warming. These emissions come from methane as well as CO_2 generated from transporting and processing feeds and meat products. The methane produced through industrial farming is 25 times more active in terms of the greenhouse effects it produces than CO_2, although it does dissipate in about ten years, whereas the CO_2 lasts for about one hundred years.

Because of these facts, the IPCC stressed in their United Nations report that one of the fastest and easiest ways to quickly reduce the greenhouse effect would be simply to reduce our consumption of meat.

To illustrate this further, producing 1 kilo of meat, including the use of the land, feed, and the methane produced, creates 50 times more greenhouse gases than producing 1 kilo of wheat. Waste from meat production is a major cause of pollution, impacting the air and rivers, creating dead zones in the ocean, and more. In the United States alone, industrial farming produces 130 times more waste than the country's human population does. That's a huge difference.

The Feed Dilemma

MATTHIEU RICARD: A deeper consideration, which we addressed during Jonathan's presentation, is the ethical impact on different communities. Generally, the poorest nations are suffering from the actions of the richest nations. It takes 10 kilos of vegetable protein, which could be used to feed poorer nations, to produce 1 kilo of meat for those who can afford it. With one acre of land, you can feed one meat eater or twenty vegans. And the disparity will likely increase as worldwide meat production is predicted to double by 2050.

The ethical impact is that the nations that are contributing most to global warming, the richer nations, are causing the poorer nations that contribute less to global warming greater suffering. In poorer countries, water is scarcer, and often polluted. Sometimes women wake at four o'clock in the morning and walk 10 or 20 kilometers just to get water. It requires 50 times more water to produce 1 kilo of meat than 1 kilo of wheat.

Currently, livestock and meat production takes up about two-thirds of available agricultural lands. But who is eating the meat? It's the people in the richest countries. Individuals in India average a couple kilos of meat per year; those in the United States consume 120 kilos per year. That's about 60 times more meat per person.

Looking at health issues, in the United States, 60 percent of all antibiotics are used to keep industrial farm animals alive until the moment they are slaughtered. Those medicines could be used for medical purposes in poorer nations.

Part of the reason for this use of antibiotics is that industrial farming does not allow for the care of individual animals. In one case, a farm had ninety thousand chickens that were overseen by three people. To manage disease, they used mass antibiotics in the entire population rather than treat individual animals. As a result, new pathogens and antibiotic resistances are often developed, and the antibiotic waste goes into the land and rivers and contributes to pollution and negative ecological impacts.

In fact, if we reallocated the 775 million tons of grain we currently use to feed livestock each year, we could feed 1.4 billion people in the poorest countries, simply by stopping our consumption of meat. If North Americans all chose to stop eating meat for one day, the grain used to raise that meat could feed 25 million poor people for an entire year.

But even if we aren't concerned with the poor countries, there are self-interest benefits to not eating meat. A study of more than five hundred thousand people found a 20 percent increase in the risk of colon cancer from eating meat. I estimate that the cancer-related deaths of 11 percent of men and 16 percent of women worldwide could be avoided by reducing meat consumption. That's a significant health consideration.

Species and Environmental Deterioration

MATTHIEU RICARD: Worldwide, 120 billion land animals and 1.5 trillion sea animals are killed every year for human consumption. Tyson Foods kills 10 million chickens per week. Also, overfishing is gradually leading to the extinction of many species of fish, a huge impact on biodiversity. Commercial fisheries are going deeper and deeper into the oceans. First, they exhausted the species that lived closest to the surface—many of those that were plentiful a hundred years ago are gone. Then they fished deeper, and now they are scraping the ocean floor to harvest fish for human and pet-food consumption. This practice has a terrible effect on biodiversity throughout the oceans. About 95 percent of the original whale population has disappeared.

Worse, the amount of waste and collateral destruction is immense. For example, because of regulations, shrimp fishermen are not allowed to keep other species they catch. But to catch shrimp they must trawl, so they wind up catching and killing all kinds of ocean life. For every 0.5 kilos of shrimp that are caught, another 13 kilos of ocean life is caught in the nets, dies, and is then thrown back into the water.

Perhaps one of the main issues is our general attitude that, beyond food and meat, animals have no value for human beings. The manager of Wall's meat company was quoted saying, "The breeding sow should be treated as a valuable piece of machinery, whose function is to pump out baby pigs like a sausage machine." That's a very powerful statement about other sentient beings.

Here are some facts: 99 percent of animals raised for meat are in industrial farms. They live about one sixteenth of their normal life expectancy in horrible conditions before they are slaughtered. A cow that would normally live for ten to fifteen years lives six months. A typical chicken lives a similarly shortened life in an area smaller than a sheet of paper. Baby cows raised for veal are put in constraining boxes where they can't even turn around, so that we can have softer, better-looking meat. The list could go on. Once you look into it, it's unbelievable what industrial farms do.

Why Do We Treat Animals This Way?

MATTHIEU RICARD: The question is, why do we do this? Is it because we think that human beings are so superior? If so, then how do we define altruism, which usually means valuing other sentient beings, having concern for them?

We have witnessed genocides, such as in Rwanda, where human beings are devalued and treated as impure, as vermin. With animals, we go one step further: we treat them as objects, commodities, and farm products. This is reflected in the vocabulary. Instead of killing, they speak of "harvesting" animals, as if they were objects.

I think this stems from the idea that man feels superior. We say, "Human beings are so intelligent, so clever. They have long-term value, they can have wonderful lives; animals don't have that." But the pertinent consideration is found in a question that Western philosopher Jeremy Bentham posed: the question is not "Can they reason?" or "Can they talk?" but "Can they suffer?" From this perspective, if you are getting your throat slit by a knife, it doesn't matter if you are a cow or a professor at a university; neither desires that form of suffering.

So I think the attitude of superiority is one of the main reasons we treat animals this way. There are many counterarguments, such as, "Nature is like that; animals eat each other." But what's the point of having higher intelligence if we cannot have more compassion? And in reality, animals only eat what they need; they don't continuously increase their consumption. Also, people used to say, until recently, that animals don't suffer. Now it has been found that fish have neurotransmitters that signal pain. It has been found that lobsters, when they are put in boiling water, suffer a lot. These are more recent findings.

The idea that we are so superior that we can do anything we want is ethically wrong. Here is a quote from a Nobel Prize of Literature recipient, Isaac Bashevis Singer, whose entire family was killed in concentration camps. He was so struck by the similarity of his family's experience and our treatment of animals that he said man has convinced himself that "all other creatures were created merely to provide him with food, pelts, to be tormented, exterminated. In relation to them, all people are Nazis; for the animals, it is an eternal Treblinka." The difference with animals is that we do it again and again, year after year, everywhere, all the time. Reflecting on this situation, it is sometimes said that the greatness of a nation and its moral progress can be judged by the way its animals are treated.

Here we have a problem that is vast, that is immense, but the solution is so simple. It doesn't require us to stop traveling; it doesn't require us to stop many of our normal activities. It only requires one simple decision: stop eating meat. It's so simple, and everything else in your life can essentially remain the same.

One final quote from George Bernard Shaw: "Animals are my friends, and I don't eat my friends."

HIS HOLINESS THE DALAI LAMA: During my first visit to Japan, the guide showed me a large poultry farm, where they held about two hundred thousand chickens in very small cages. It was like an egg-laying prison, and after about two years, the chickens no longer laid eggs and were killed.

MATTHIEU RICARD: It's often even worse. Large farms cannot treat individual animals, so when the production of eggs goes down a little, it's usually cheaper to kill ninety thousand chickens and start from scratch than to find other means of increasing production.

HIS HOLINESS THE DALAI LAMA: I think your presentation is really convincing. Thank you. Another consideration is that many people, from childhood, learn to fish and hunt with no sense of concern for animals' lives or their pain. And sometimes this attitude is later directed toward human beings. We often see behavior with no concern for others' pain, such as shootings and beatings.

Our sense of compassion, our concern, must start with the smallest of animals and insects—although my relationship with mosquitoes is not very good. In Tibetan society, we learn, from childhood, the habit of not killing even the smallest or seemingly insignificant animal or insect. Nowadays, we hear about a hundred thousand animals being killed and we barely react. I think that's a very serious matter. Our love and compassion, our respect for all animals, from the smallest insects, is the basis for building a genuinely compassionate world.

When I was about thirteen, the Tibetan government decided that all official functions would be vegetarian, which saved more than ten thousand animals from the butchers.

In the 1960s, in India, at a Tibetan refugee camp, a poultry farm was started as a source of income. They said it was only for the eggs, not for killing the chickens. We tried that, but we would not allow any other animal farming. When I asked them what happened to the chickens when they could no longer lay eggs, I was told they were killed. So I pleaded with them, saying that if egg farming was essential for economic well-being, I have no right to say anything, but if it's not crucial, they should stop. They've since all closed, and today all of the kitchens in our monasteries and institutions are vegetarian.

And while this is very important, I myself am not vegetarian. In 1965, I became completely vegetarian—no eggs, nothing. But instead, I was eating lots of cream and nuts, and after twenty months, I had trouble with my gallbladder and got jaundice. My skin, eyes, nails—everything—turned yellow. An Ayurvedic physician advised me that I should go back to my original diet. So I am a little bit of a contradiction, telling people to be vegetarian as a nonvegetarian myself.

JOHN DUNNE: As we heard from Greg Norris, even if one is not able to become a strict vegetarian, a reduction in one's consumption of meat can have a tremendous impact, not only on the maltreatment of animals, but also on the environment.

And because reducing consumption is one of the easiest ways to have a positive impact, we've asked the viewers of this conference to consider reducing meat consumption, just a little bit, to help offset the environmental cost of this conference. One doesn't have to become a strict vegetarian to make a difference.

HIS HOLINESS THE DALAI LAMA: Yes, in my kitchen we cook once a week nonvegetarian; otherwise it's all vegetarian.

7 Religion's Responsibility

PRESENTER: Sallie McFague, *University of British Columbia*

JOHN DUNNE: We wanted to bring at least one voice from another religious tradition into this conversation, and one colleague said, "Well, if you could get Sallie McFague, she's what we call 'the source of it all' within Christian theology." I have to say, I think that my colleague was right.

Dr. Sallie McFague was educated at Smith College and at Yale University and for many years taught at Vanderbilt University Divinity School in Nashville, as the E. Rhodes and Leona B. Carpenter Professor of Theology. She has also taught at Yale Divinity School and Harvard Divinity School. Currently, she's a Distinguished Theologian in Residence at Vancouver School of Theology in British Columbia. She has authored ten books and many articles.

In one of her most important books, *Models of God: Theology for an Ecological, Nuclear Age* (Fortress Press, 1987), she presents an alternative model, a challenging model to our notion of how we think about God. One way that she reconceptualizes God is as the body of the world, or more precisely, she argues that the world can be seen as God's body. Her latest book is *Blessed Are the Consumers: Climate Change and the Practice of Restraint* (Fortress Press, 2013), in which she analyzes the concept of *kenosis* (restraint or self-emptying) as one important action to deal with climate change.

SALLIE MCFAGUE: Your Holiness, you have said that the religions are part of the problem. They're supporting the status quo; they're not fighting greed and laziness and shortsightedness. Now the question is, can the religions be part of the solution? You also said that we need to put knowledge into action. We need deep awareness; we need dedication, simplicity, and contentment. We need to do all this on a daily basis, to practice mindfulness at all levels, and we need a different lifestyle and a different worldview. About 20 percent of the population is now into the consumer lifestyle that's ruining our planet, and the other 80 percent would like to live the way the 20 percent now live. The problem is going global; the consumer view is going global.

You pointed to the solution: a different vision. You mentioned Bhutan and Estonia, and I would add also the lives of the saints, people who had deep awareness. People have been able to express in themselves joy, confidence, and the sense of responsibility that we need. So the question becomes, how can religions help bring about this deep awareness? Science has told us we need a worldview of radical interdependence and interrelationship. What should the religions do?

Over the years when people have asked me what I do, I answer that I'm a theologian who investigates the connections between religion and economics and ecology. They usually give me a funny look, saying, "What does religion have to do with financial and environmental matters? Isn't religion about such things as God, sin, and salvation?" Times have changed.

The 2010 State of the World report suggested that the religions must be major players in the most important issues of our day, the ones we have been discussing: the economic and ecological crises. The report applauds religions for doing such things as turning off lights to save energy in their churches and finding scriptures that support environmental behavior, but it bemoans the fact the religions haven't paid the same attention to economics.

Increasingly, however, we're becoming aware that these apparently different fields, economics and ecology, are tightly interlocked, primarily through the use of energy, which creates both a consumer paradise and global warming. So consumerism is a major problem in well-off Western countries, and it's increasingly becoming a major problem everywhere.

To put it as simply as possible, it's not sufficient to simply consume less, to consume in a so-called "green" fashion. While quantity still matters, the fact is that we are at such a level of consumption in relation to the carrying capacity of our planet that reduction is a major responsibility. But no one wants to face this fact. No one wants to buy less, have less. Really, we want more and more.

What if we had to give up the use of cars? What a thought! It makes us gasp. How could we live without automobiles? What about reducing or not taking airplane trips? The shock that we feel when we imagine this causes us to realize how far we have to go in our attitudes and our practices. We human beings are so embedded in the culture of consumerism that being asked to consume less makes us almost gasp. And we do; we stop for a moment, and then we have to inhale and take another breath, and get back in our cars and our airplanes, and continue on.

But it's important to take this very seriously. The culture of consumerism is not just a form of life that we can accept or reject. It has now become like the air we breathe, and this is the nature of culture. Culture becomes nature; it becomes natural. It becomes the way things are; it becomes the world in which we live. Consumerism is a cultural pattern that leads people to find meaning and fulfillment through the consumption of goods and services.

Given this, consumerism is the newest, the latest, and the most successful religion. Every month we pay handsomely into this new religion when we pay our credit card bills. We support this religion very well.

If consumerism is like a religion, then the task of changing our culture from consumerism to sustainability is a huge problem. I think the religions are being handed a very significant and difficult challenge here. They're being asked to take on what no other field wants to take on: a wholesale transformation of dominant cultural patterns, particularly at the level of consumerism. The State of the World report says there are three causes of environmental impact: population, consumerism, and technology.

The secular institutions have had the least success in dealing with restraining our consumer desires. However, restraint at all levels, summed up by the golden rule "Do unto others as you would have them do unto you," is a major practice of most religions.

It's needed now, and I believe it's both a gift from the religions and a challenge to them. So far, religions have not been doing this. They've been going along with the status quo. They've been doing what everybody else is doing. So I think this challenge of restraint could be a sort of "coming home" for religions, as well as their greatest contribution to this economic and ecological crisis that we face.

Religion's Special Gift

SALLIE MCFAGUE: Religion's special gift is urgently needed now. What is this gift? It is the age-old paradoxical insight that happiness is found in self-emptying. Satisfaction is found more in relationships than in things, and simplicity can lead to a fuller life. I consider these words to be marching orders for the religions, and they're also the central theme of what I want to share with you this morning. However, as the report points out, advocating this kind of position—restraint—could make religions very unpopular. No one wants to hear that. People don't want to go to church if the sermon is going to be about sharing with your neighbor. But such a position would not only serve the planet; I think it would return the religions to their original roots, to their spiritual foundations.

The message that the purpose of human life is to consume is a heresy, and it should be condemned as such. The religious traditions may well find such a return to their basic insight of restraint, neither for the sake of ascetic denial, nor in order to flagellate oneself, but rather because abundant life for all is only possible if some of us restrain our desires.

Moving from Belief to Action

SALLIE MCFAGUE: My contribution to our discussion is to condemn the heresy of consumerism by taking a look at what I call kenosis, or self-emptying, which is in Buddhism in certain forms and also in Christianity. In a nutshell, we have reached the point in the public discussion about the planet's two crises (the monetary and the ecological) where we have one major thing we need to do. We need to move into action. And I want to look at this process of moving from belief to action.

While there's no one solution to this big problem that we have, we need to ask whether religions can make some contribution by sharing their profound countercultural and unpopular message: the abundant life, at both personal and public levels, is not found by satisfying one's ego in a market-oriented, individualistic culture, but is found by losing one's ego in service to others. Can we see that this much-neglected aspect of many world religions, the countercultural self-emptying, is one important perspective that needs to be added to the sciences?

Who Are We and What Should We Do?

SALLIE MCFAGUE: Increasingly, the issue of how to live well has become one of changing how we are living now to living in a different way, and as the crises become worse, more and more people are questioning the reigning culture of insatiable greed; it's not making them happy. They're coming to the conclusion that the rewards of the consumer culture have been greatly overrated, and that serious change needs to happen at a fundamental level, which is the most fundamental level of who we think we are in the scheme of things. Where do we fit into the big picture as human beings? And once we decide who we are in the scheme of things, what should we be doing? Change at this level is very, very difficult, and in fact, most people find it impossible.

HIS HOLINESS THE DALAI LAMA: When you say the fundamental change, the concept of who we are as human beings, are you talking about the notion of "self" and "I"?

Nowadays, many people have the belief that if material progress continues, then everything will be okay. That way of thinking is a mistake. We have our physical existence as well as our mind. Material goods provide comfort for the body, but not for the mind. So we need another way to bring peace and satisfaction to the mind, and that can come through some form of religion or spirituality.

There are the theistic religions, such as Christianity, that have made tremendous contributions to the planet, as well as nontheistic religions such as Buddhism and Jainism where we ourselves are the creators. Both bring a kind of inner peace and inner strength.

But we need a third religion, one without scriptures, that is based simply on common sense, our common experience, our inner experience, warm-heartedness, a sense of concern for others' well-being, and respect for the rights of others. This would be a spirituality without religious faith, not centered around Jesus or Buddha, God, or heaven and hell. It would be a way where nobody can deny our experience of inner peace and satisfaction, and it would be based on rest. Rest in the sense of mental rest, peace, and calm. Even when we still the physical body through sleep, often the mind remains busy, not calm and not peaceful. We awake the next day and are unhappy. So cultivating mental rest even during sleep is very important.

It's clear that just taking care of physical comforts is insufficient; it's just half of the task. The other half is taking care of our mental health. This is very important, and it doesn't necessitate becoming religious-minded or a person of faith, although having religious faith can be very powerful.

Every religion talks about inner peace and has some kind of message of love and compassion as the source of inner strength. And with inner strength comes confidence and more peace. Suspicion and anger are based on fear and distrust, and with them there is no possibility for inner peace.

Total faith in God is a very powerful method to find inner strength. Even when we experience difficulties, with full faith in God, these experiences are also God's creation, so there must be something meaningful, even good, to them.

The Nature of Self and Selfishness

SALLIE MCFAGUE: We are talking about the same thing—who we are, the nature of the self.

HIS HOLINESS THE DALAI LAMA: That is very complicated. For thousands of years people have been discussing and investigating this to understand what truly is the nature of self, and it's still not very clear. Each person seems to have his or her own view. Even the great scientists can't clearly pinpoint the self. It's as if the more we investigate, the more elusive it becomes.

SALLIE MCFAGUE: Yes. And one thing that science is showing us is that we cannot be selfish and greedy; the world cannot live well in this way. The nature of reality, and the world, is rooted in interdependence and interrelationship, so we need to change our understanding of who we are in order for us to act differently. Currently, we're caught in this bubble of consumerism and we don't think we're doing anything wrong, but the subconscious assumption of who we think we are is this insatiable individual. As Erich Heller once said, "Be careful how you interpret the world; it is like that."

So we live inside our views, our interpretations of who we think we are, and we're profoundly, deeply, and often subconsciously influenced by them. For instance, if one holds the view that God, the world, and human beings exist in a dualistic and individualistic state, then we may decide that climate change is not a serious matter. Let God—who is the supernatural, all-powerful being up there, somewhere in the sky—take care of the problem; we don't have to do it.

If we see everything, including God, as interrelated and interdependent, then we will also see the self as interrelated and interdependent, and we will see that we are, in fact, responsible for the whole, including less fortunate beings. This is a worldview that's supported by science and the wisdom of many religious traditions, such as dependent co-origination, for example.

So we need to change our ideas about God—from seeing God as king and master *over* the world, off there, up there, where the world is held within God's hands, to seeing God as *with* the world, imagining the world almost within God, like a baby in the womb. We live and move and have our being in God. God is not some far-off, distant being.

We need to wake up to the lie held in the current worldview of individualistic, selfish fulfillment. This is a lie. The religions say it's a lie; science says it's a lie. We need to wake up to a different worldview, one that shares all our resources with our fellow creatures. And I think that the religions can help us here through their understandings of limitation, of detachment, self-emptying, and compassion. The Christian notion of self-emptying and the Buddhist understanding of compassion are two of the major contributions that religions can make.

We need to move from the narrow, individualist, and greedy worldview of ourselves to a worldview that has an understanding of the self as universal, a self that includes everything that is. Your Holiness, you have said that we ought to think of the needs of strangers in the same way a mother responds to the needs of her child. Christians say the same thing with the phrase "love your neighbor as yourself." One could say, in both of these cases, that one sees the world as one's body. One's body doesn't just end with the skin; it includes everything in the world. The world is my body, and this includes everything, even the smallest insect.

We have to start from loving every single creature. Only a radical change in who we think we are is going to be able to make the deep changes that we need. As Your Holiness has said, we need to put awareness into action, but in order to do this, there has to be deep awareness. That is the difficulty: how do we get to deep awareness? The change has to happen at all levels of our life: personal, what we eat, how we get to work, taxes, car emissions, everything.

Self-Emptying for Others

SALLIE MCFAGUE: I want to share about the life of a contemporary saint, Dorothy Day. She was a contemporary Christian saint who lived in a very poor neighborhood in New York City for forty years, serving soup to home-less people and organizing strikes for workers' rights.

Her worldview came from trying to follow the Jesus of the Gospels, whose whole life, message, and death on a cross was a way of total self-giving for others. He emptied himself of all selfish desires, so as to bring his will into line with God's will; he emptied his own will, so that God's will could take him over completely. Dorothy Day understood Jesus to be the visible face of the invisible God.

Jesus tells us who God is, and who we are. God is love itself; God is total self-emptying, whose power lay not in controlling the world, but in giving it life. And likewise, Jesus can be seen in the face of the neighbor; when we love the neighbor, we are loving Jesus, we are loving God.

HIS HOLINESS THE DALAI LAMA: Yes. Similarly, I have a Muslim friend who said a genuine Muslim practitioner should extend love to all creatures. Buddhists may not use the word *creator*, but we also believe in extending love and compassion toward all sentient beings.

SALLIE MCFAGUE: That's the heart of the matter. That is the under-standing of the self that we need, of who we are in the scheme of things. We need to include the whole world so the world becomes one's body. Dorothy Day was a middle-class, well-off American journalist. She chose voluntary poverty. I'm not talking about destitution—she could eat and she had money—but she chose voluntary poverty, because she needed to move out of her bubble of middle-class consumerism; she needed to think differently, she needed to be upset and disoriented.

HIS HOLINESS THE DALAI LAMA: There are similar practices in the Buddhist tradition. We speak of the twelve cultivated qualities. These are all aimed at adopting a deliberately simple life. Some of the disci-plines include not living in a house, rather seeking shelter without a roof, such as under a tree, even during the monsoon season; only wear-ing very simple clothes, ideally some that have been discarded by some-one else; and eating only once a day, if possible on alms. Altogether there are twelve that cultivate a reduction in desire and the practice of contentment.

SALLIE MCFAGUE: Yes. This is exactly what Dorothy Day lived. She said, "Being poor is smelly and noisy and dirty; it's not fun." She didn't want to live that way, but she forced herself to live that way so she could identify with people who had nothing, so that she could stand in their shoes and feel what they were feeling. A middle-class person often doesn't feel that. We have everything, so we don't feel that the poor are deprived. She did this in order to change the way she thought about herself, from this consumer idea to the universal self. So she found no limit to her compassion.

I'm suggesting that the religions of the world have a major role to play in the climate-change crisis. As the glaciers melt on the Third Pole, the Himalayas, along with at the other two poles, religions should answer the call to return to the deepest roots of the traditions: the roots of restraint, of limitation, of sharing, and of self-emptying. They should not do this to flagellate the self, but rather to allow enough resources for other people and for other life forms. This is especially critical to First World people, like myself, who are well-off consumers, but it's also important for all of those who aspire to be well-off. Most of the world now wants that kind of lifestyle.

This process of change that I'm talking about is difficult. How do we change? We know that we should live differently. We have all the information, but we don't change. How can we do this?

A Fourfold Process of Change

Step 1: Voluntary Poverty

SALLIE MCFAGUE: I'm suggesting a fourfold practice that begins with the experience of voluntary poverty for people like me. This will open our eyes so that we can pay attention to something other than our desires and ourselves. It will help us pay attention to the other, to the neighbor, near and far, and to do so at the most basic levels—not just feeling sympathy, but actually sharing food. Unless we share the things that people need to live, we haven't really walked the walk. The insights from Dorothy Day's story and other people and saints like her show that such a practice is not spiritual or religious; it's not about God and sin, but about sharing basic necessities. Some people, like Dorothy Day, see the world as their body, and they pay with a total price of self-emptying. Saints are like that. They are the people who do extraordinary things that none of the rest of us can do, but they make us see differently. They wake us up to our own lives of indulgence.

With the fourfold process of change, it needs to start with middle-class consumer people and experiences of voluntary poverty. Those in the middle class need a jolt; they need to wake up; they need something different in their lives. I call the move away from the model of possessions toward self-emptying a journey toward "wild space." Wild space is the space where you can begin to think differently. And for middle-class people, who have a lot of money, the one thing that can cause them to think differently is not to have so much money.

This also includes millionaires and billionaires, but it isn't just the superrich. It's also people like us, the 20 percent who have enough food and have air conditioning, and so forth. We need some wild space; we need to wake up, even if only cutting out simple things in our lives. Not driving our car or eating differently helps us to experience a little bit of poverty, a little bit of deprivation, a little bit of what it's like to be poor. Once one experiences this change, and wants to change, and sees things differently, one becomes open to a different model of living. From this view, we can begin to imagine an alternative. We can see that the current model is a lie, it's harmful to the planet, and we need to have a different model.

Step 2: The Needs of Others

SALLIE MCFAGUE: The second point in the fourfold process is to focus one's attention on the needs of others, especially other people's most basic needs. Once we're freed from the narcissistic obsession with ourselves, we are able to do a rare thing: to really pay attention to others, not as objects to use for our own goals, but as subjects in their own right.

These subjects include other human beings as well as other life forms, all sentient beings, and even the processes that support life: the rivers, the trees, the climate. Realize that every breath we take and every mouthful we eat depends on others.

We begin to realize that just, sustainable planetary living is both personal and public. One has to give up the old selfish, narcissistic self in order to get the new self, which is able to live for others and in service of others. Real abundance in life doesn't come from getting more and more things, it comes from giving up those things when others need them and living differently.

Step 3: Cultivating the Universal Self

SALLIE MCFAGUE: The third point in the fourfold process is that if we start doing this, we gradually develop a universal self, the self that includes everything, the dependent co-origination self. The line between one's concern for oneself and concern for others shifts and gets wider and wider. First you care only about yourself, then maybe you care about your family, then you care about your relatives and your friends, and then your nation, and even other human beings, and eventually you care even for the caterpillars and other insects. Paradoxically, this journey, rather than diminishing the self, increases its delight; we become bigger when we include everything.

Instead of being narrow and tiny and turned in upon ourselves, we turn out to the world; we fall in love with the world itself. This may seem like an impossible ideal, this universal self. We see the lives of the saints, people like Dorothy Day, and we say, "I can't be like Dorothy Day." But we can be better than we are; we can be different. We don't have to be the narcissistic, selfish consumer self; we can go in a different direction. That's why Bhutan and Estonia, places where they've tried to do things differently, are good ideals.

HIS HOLINESS THE DALAI LAMA: Yes, and the question still remains, regarding those communities, whether they are doing things differently because they don't have the opportunity to follow a consumer model or because they do have the opportunity and they choose to do otherwise. We will have to watch for ten or twenty years, and then we will know for sure.

SALLIE MCFAGUE: Yes, and it's not that any one of us, or any community, is going to achieve everything; there's no perfection. Everything is relative. We live within the models that our culture creates for us, and that we create for our culture. It doesn't mean that we're going to live perfectly within them, but when we say yes to a new, universal model, we will try to live differently.

Step 4: Bringing It to the World

SALLIE MCFAGUE: The last step in this fourfold-process model is to operate at a public level. This means every individual has to change, but we also need different laws; we have to have a different public system.

I talk about planetary house rules. If you live in a house together, you put up house rules, such as take only your share, clean up after yourself, and keep the house in good repair for others. These rules work at the individual level and they work at the whole planet level: take only your share of the planet, clean up after yourself, recycle, and keep the planet sustainable, in good shape for others to come in the future.

Some other fields make a contribution in the form of a statement of what needs to change. Religions need to acknowledge the facts and then help enable a process that can create the change, that can take us from understanding and belief to action. I'm suggesting four steps: voluntary poverty; paying attention to the needs of others; gradually developing a deeper, broader view of the self; and then applying this at all levels, personal and public.

HIS HOLINESS THE DALAI LAMA: Wonderful, thank you. As we have heard, different religions and fields of philosophy may have varying views, but as far as the real practical message, they all speak to the elements of love, compassion, forgiveness, tolerance, contentment, self-discipline, honesty, and justice.

SALLIE MCFAGUE: Different religions disagree about a lot of things. Some of them have ideas of God, some don't; they disagree about what is sinful and what is not. But they don't disagree that the goal of human life is to live in a different way than the culture is living. And if all our societies are living in greedy, selfish ways, the religions should stand up and say, "No, that's wrong; that's a lie. We should be living differently."

HIS HOLINESS THE DALAI LAMA: About twenty years ago, I visited the monastery at Montserrat and met a Catholic monk who had been in hermitage for the past five years. He had spent the time in isolation with little food, just bread and water, I believe. I asked him about this practice; what was he contemplating? "Love," he said, and as he spoke there was a clarity in his eyes that reflected the beauty of becoming a wonderful person by working on what you truly believe.

I think that in modern times our Christian brothers and sisters have made such a great contribution regarding educating people about these values. We Buddhists, not as much; nor the Hindus and Muslims—perhaps more so in ancient times. So I always admire our Christian brothers and sisters for their total dedication. Many of them are interested in the well-being of others, though some are perhaps more interested in the impressiveness of their costumes!

The same is true with Buddhists. There was a custom in Tibet for the high lamas to wear sleeveless jackets made of silk brocade. When I came to India, I gave up all that in favor of the monastic way of life. In fact, one of our precepts is no solid meals after noon. About forty years ago, when I came to India, I received full ordination. But that ceremony went until about two in the afternoon, and we missed lunch. So when the dinner was served, I thought I had a good excuse to eat. It smelled good and my mouth was watering. I thought about it for a moment and then decided, "I follow the Buddha as a monastic and this is one of our precepts, so I am going to observe that," and I did not eat. So in that small way I can relate to your advice of restraining our desires.

I wish many different churches and religions would give talks like yours in addition to speaking about the importance of praying to God. Even in Buddhism, there is perhaps too much reliance on praying to Buddha. That is important, but not sufficient. We must also implement these intentions in our day-to-day lives. Teachings should be integrated into our lives, not just be the focus of our attention for the few minutes we sit in front of the Buddha.

SALLIE MCFAGUE: Another Christian saint, Teresa of Avila, said that if you don't feel confident about your relationship with God, don't think about that, forget that. Love your neighbor and the relationship with God will take care of itself. It's the same thing. And God isn't up there, anyway, God is all around us.

The Names of God

DEKILA CHUNGYALPA: I was very struck by the suggestion that we see the world as a baby in God's womb. It is such a feminine way of describing the earth, and it brings into question the nature of God in Christian theology. I wanted to hear more about that. It's so different from the way I understand Christianity.

SALLIE MCFAGUE: One of the most important things when talking about God is that no one has seen God. We don't know how to talk about God, so we use images from our own experience to talk about God. Traditionally, in Christianity, one of the words that people have used is to say that God is "father." Some people think that's a good name or description for God. But really, it's an interpretation. Talking about God with one set of images sees God as father, lord, king, and master. This suggests that God is way off there, and we're way down here. There's no connection, and God is the king and the master over us.

But what if we understood the world as within God, within God's hands, or within like a baby in the womb? This would be a different understanding of God, and it would mean God is everywhere. We don't have to only meet God when we pray or after we die. God is present with us right here and now in this room. God is in the atmosphere. And so the baby in the womb is not just a feminine image, it's another interpretation that everybody can use. Similarly, in the same way people talk about God as the father, you could also talk about God as the mother.

Taking Only Your Share

DIANA LIVERMAN: Sallie, I love your planetary house rules. As you talked about them, I was trying to think whether they cover all of my planetary boundaries; do they cover all of the trends that I was describing? And I think they do, but I have two questions about them. One is relative to "take only your share." How would you apply that to how many children each person should have? Is that share two children, or 1.8, or can we have as many as we want? And my second question is about "keeping the house in good repair for future generations." Why do you just have "good repair"; why don't we improve the house for future generations?

SALLIE MCFAGUE: Let me start with the second one first. Indeed, we should improve the house; that would be wonderful. I guess I wasn't that much of an optimist. I thought we would be doing pretty well if we could keep the house in as good repair as we got it. If we could improve it, that would be even more wonderful. Human beings, as we have seen, haven't been too good at managing the planet. Most of the things we've done have had negative impacts, so we have to be careful that we don't think we're going to suddenly get control and manage the planet.

Regarding "taking only your share," I wasn't thinking about families. Rather, I was thinking about all of the billions of life forms that need nourishment. So it's not just taking only your share as a human being, but also as a species, and this is not easy. That's why I say applying the planetary house rules at an individual level is easier than applying them at a planetary level, but the concept should still be basically the same: that we should have the same share.

One of the reasons why I wanted to focus on the 20 percent of human beings like us, the consumers, is because we are taking much more than our share. No matter how you calculate it, it's way out of proportion. We need to cut way back. When His Holiness shared that one of the disciplines that he adopted was to give up eating in the afternoon, he exemplified that even the smallest thing that we do becomes a lesson in restraint. If we're able to say no to a dish of food, then maybe we can say no to a new car, or a trip to Paris. That is a whole different mindset and foundation for action. Rather than "I have enough money, and I can buy more and more," it becomes, "I'm going to go into voluntary poverty; I'm going to go into my 'wild space,' and I'm going to live differently."

There are lots of different ways to practice this. You don't have to do what Dorothy Day did, which is spend her life living in a smelly, noisy tenement with bad food. You don't have to do that. But she showed us a direction to go toward, which is to begin to cut down and limit our consumption.

What About Fate?

JONATHAN PATZ: This month we had our holiest day of the year in the Jewish religion, Yom Kippur, the "Day of Atonement." We fast and ask for forgiveness. What we are told is that you can pray to God as much as you want, but it's useless until you apologize to the person you harmed, wronged, or lied to. It's very similar to what we've been talking about, that the compassion from human to human is the most important priority. Given the importance of human relationships and interactions, I'm curious about the many people who believe in fate—that there's nothing we can do, that the big picture is all in God's hands. In the context of our conversation, this is paralyzing, but what would your approach be to talking to people who believe in fate?

JOHN DUNNE: His Holiness also pointed out a similar Buddhist attitude, which is, "Oh well, it's just karma; there's nothing we can do." So how does one respond to that sense of resignation?

SALLIE MCFAGUE: I'll attempt to answer this difficult question. Before our awareness of climate change, some people thought floods, droughts, and other natural disasters had nothing to do with us. They were fate,

God's doing, something outside of our control. But what we've realized is that a lot of things that we thought were fate actually require our participation. Some of the floods and droughts that are happening are because of climate change, not just natural factors. Of course there are things that happen that are out of our control. You could walk under a ladder at the wrong moment and be hit on the head by a pail of water, and you can't do anything about it. On the other hand, there's so much that we can change, and yet we don't. I don't think fate should ever be used as an excuse for doing nothing. It is sometimes used that way by religious people who say, "Oh well, that's just God's will, I can't do anything about it." Some things we can't do anything about, but for many things, we can do something.

HIS HOLINESS THE DALAI LAMA: One time, a Jewish rabbi was visiting and he said that the creation of the world was one-half God's blessing and the other half our participation—a combination of God's blessing and our activities.

But the idea of fate, of something fixed and out of our control, is interesting. In the purer forms of Buddhism and Jainism, there is no notion of a creator. Everything is subject to the law of causality, of cause and effect. And among the causes are our current actions, our karma. Some of these are of our own volition, and some are natural. Shantideva, in *A Guide to the Bodhisattva's Way of Life* (Snow Lion Publications, 1997), distinguishes this, explaining that some causal processes are purely natural, similar to Darwinian theory, where there are multiple natural factors producing an outcome.

If we consider all the scientific exploration and investigation, ultimately it traces back to the Big Bang, before which scientists don't see anything. But even here, we have to accept that there was some cause that stimulated that immense release of energy. So the deeper question is, what was the cause of that?

Shantideva then explained that karma comes into play when it relates to questions about the origin of human suffering, sentient beings' experience of suffering and happiness and of pain and pleasure. And in this case, karma means action. This action is entirely dependent on the individual and the motivations of the individual; it was not created by God, or Buddha, or by nature, but by our own motivation and intention. And the actions driven by intention and motivation produce specific results.

Now, Buddhists, Jains, and many Hindus believe in the continuation of mind, no beginning or end of consciousness. In this context, actions from previous lives can influence this life, in particular how we are incarnated.

I heard a story about the oldest woman in the world who, at the time, was 115 years old. Researchers suggested that there was a genetic disposition toward longevity, even from birth. In this case, the causes and conditions of her karma trace back to her parents, and their parents, and so forth.

Some people believe we cannot change fundamentally. For example, if you have done something bad in your life, cultivated negative karma, that imprints and continues in the mind. However, if you take a positive action with the right intention that is stronger than the previous negative action, the effects of the previous negative action will be neutralized or possibly eliminated.

So, due to some karma, you have a certain destiny, but as new karma unfolds, that destiny changes. Therefore, we cannot say anything is fixed. In fact, resignation is often a sign of laziness. We must make effort to change, even if we are dealing with negative karma.

JOHN DUNNE: Your Holiness, in Sallie's talk there was an important role for restraint and self-discipline. Does that also play a role in this context? In thinking about negative karma, could it be that we develop emotional habits that are negative, and one approach to that might be restraint and self-discipline, to resist those states and change our destiny?

HIS HOLINESS THE DALAI LAMA: Definitely. Most action is automatic, like scratching an itch without even thinking about it. But with serious and important considerations, there must be motivation. And in order to change or adopt right motivation, you must know the consequences of different actions. Since we do not want suffering, rather we want happiness, we must restrain from actions that bring unhappiness, pain, or suffering to others. These actions ultimately bring suffering upon us. Conversely, any positive actions that bring benefit or happiness to others ultimately benefit us, too. That's the law of causality.

We can even work with the law of causality for selfish reasons, for our own benefit, without bringing in Buddha or God. As far as pain and suffering are concerned, they're very much connected to the cause, the karma, of one's own actions.

The key factor, motivation, depends on awareness, how causes and conditions give rise to certain consequences, and their dependent relationships.

8 The Dalai Lama Responds

Group Discussion

JOHN DUNNE: One of the unique and important aspects of Sallie McFague's work is that a religious tradition, in this case Christianity, is encountering a very new situation: the environmental crisis. Our understanding of what is happening to us in the environment and our roles and responsibilities accordingly are going to be important questions for Christians and for other religions. We're also looking for secular answers to these questions, and it's important to hear both sides to see where the religious and secular overlap.

I'm wondering if something could be said about this situation from a Buddhist perspective, as I think the environmental crisis is new for Buddhism as well. What are our responsibilities? How do we understand this from a Buddhist standpoint?

HIS HOLINESS THE DALAI LAMA: At the time of Buddha, or Jesus Christ, or Muhammad, the environment was not really an issue. In some of the traditional Buddhist texts, Buddha talked about trees and plants. But that was more in relation to the fact that monks did not stay in one place—they planted things and then moved on—so they would leave instructions for the new arriving monks to care for those plants.

On a playful note, Buddha preferred open spaces. He left the palace to sit under a tree, and then when he reached final enlightenment, it was under a tree. And when he died—it was under a tree. So if he were in politics, he might create the Green party.

But getting back to the point, we religious people are supposed to practice love and compassion—not just for oneself, but also toward others and animals. And naturally that extends to nature: plants and grasses and so forth. One of the things Buddha said about the precept of avoiding taking life was to not dig the earth or cut plants unnecessarily. Particularly during the rainy season, we shouldn't cut plants or pull leaves off of them. So there was some indication of caring for the environment in the early days. Also, plants and trees are the home and source of life for many birds, insects, and other animals; they depend entirely on them. Out of our commitment and respect for the right of animals and insects to exist, we have to take care of plants.

I think our basic human disposition includes a love for nature. Even in big cities, we grow plants and trees; we even use fake flowers sometimes to remind us of the beauty of nature. We love our technology, which is very new. But our relationship with plants and nature is very old and very deep.

And as we discussed, for religious people, our main practice is love for others. So we must respect all different forms of life, particularly life that holds experience and feeling. We might have less of a tendency to practice this toward animals than people. With humans, we get some benefit from showing love, something in return. But with animals, to love them often offers no selfish benefit, as with a mosquito. So loving every living being is really a genuine kind of selfless love.

Expanding that idea to ecology and ethics, shouldn't the believers of these ideals practice this in service to humanity? This earth is our only home; we must take care of it. And the religious people should be the ones who demonstrate the value of ethics and lead others toward caring for our home.

For example, Archbishop Tutu embodies the principles of taking care of others and of practicing forgiveness. He actually implements the process of reconciliation, so I would consider him a man of God. In this way, people who believe in God should be examples to others.

JOHN DUNNE: One important issue that Sallie presented is how one motivates a group of people in this regard. In her case, what notion of responsibility or plan of action can be presented to her fellow Christians to encourage them to feel like they must do something? Do you have any encouragement or guidance for Buddhists who are seeking to become more involved in these issues?

HIS HOLINESS THE DALAI LAMA: Over the past few decades at monasteries in India and Tibet we have been cultivating tree plantations. This brings in the action of serving others and of creating a better environment and a happier place. And to truly acquire a sense of responsibility for community, one has to first feel responsible for one's own place or home.

In the classical concept of Buddhist karma, there is the notion that the effects of karma are not necessarily confined to an individual's experience. They can also have a collective effect, including in the environment where you live. If an environment where you live is not hospitable, not pleasant, that is considered, in part, to be an effect of karma. One could say, "Well, this is my karmic effect, I can do nothing." On the other hand, one could actually improve the area where one lives to make it more hospitable and pleasant by planting trees and making it cleaner.

The trees are homes to birds, butterflies, and other beautiful natural ornaments. These are often missing in cities, but when you spend time in the country, in a place where there are a lot of trees and birds singing, you feel good inside. You are part of nature.

Instinctively, we love nature. When we are surrounded by artificial things, it's harder to be peaceful. It's as if we begin to be artificial; we develop hypocrisy, suspicion, and distrust. In that state it's hard to develop genuine, warm-hearted friendship. We are social animals, and without nature, it's hard to be a truly happy person. If we just think of ourselves as a composition of organic material and neurotransmitters, we cannot get a clear understanding of the nature of mind and consciousness.

SALLIE MCFAGUE: You spoke about seeing our planet as a home. This is such an important idea, because not only do we need to know that our home is good, we also need to *feel* it. Some people treat the planet like a hotel— use the water and the towels and leave them for someone else to clean up. But we don't have this option with the planet; we only have one home.

Children are amazing because of their fascination with real-life things, like caterpillars. We should never outgrow our so-called childish love for natural beings. We should think of our planet as a home, rather than a hotel, and encourage the deep feelings that children naturally have for caterpillars and all other animals.

In response to your earlier comment about how one is more motivated to love when there is a reward, we need to be able to love even when we don't get a reward. That's part of self-emptying. People who sacrifice, and are self-emptying, love because it's the right thing to do. And when they do this, they feel the love of the divine coming through them. We have to be able to love without return, and so we have to include the mosquito.

HIS HOLINESS THE DALAI LAMA: Yes, and that kind of genuine love and genuine compassion is unbiased. That kind of love can be extended toward your enemies or the people who harm you. Mostly people try to get rid of or avoid the ones that harm us. But the genuine practitioner of love must keep genuine compassion and concern for their well-being as well.

Even in the case of caring for or reaching out to an enemy, if the motivation comes from the hope that the enemy may eventually come to love me, then there is a self-benefit. While that could be present in genuine compassion, if it's the primary motivation, then the action is not one of pure love.

JONATHAN PATZ: I would disagree. I think mosquitoes love us too much; that's the problem.

HIS HOLINESS THE DALAI LAMA: I have some experience with this. Usually, during my public talks, if I'm in a good mood and I know I'm not in an area of malaria risk, I offer a little blood to mosquitoes. Their bodies swell and turn red, and then they just fly off with no sign of appreciation.

So, out of curiosity, I asked some professors at the University of Oxford how big the brain of an animal would have to be for it to have the ability to experience appreciation. I didn't get an answer. But I'm still curious. Mosquitoes have a mind—they know when it's time to feed, how to move—so perhaps there are emotions there as well. Dogs, cats, even birds exhibit genuine love and respond with appreciation, but what about butterflies, mosquitoes, lice, and fleas?

JONATHAN PATZ: I can address what is known about the difference between human appreciation for the environment and what Harvard ecologist E. O. Wilson calls "ecophilia," or love for nature. There have been experiments done in hospital patients recovering from surgery. One group sees a brick wall outside their window while the other sees trees and nature. The ones that see nature tend to have a much faster recovery.

JOHN DUNNE: Along those lines, Scott Atran, author of *Cognitive Foundations of Natural History: Towards an Anthropology of Science* (Cambridge University Press, 1996), has demonstrated that certain cognitive abilities, such as the ability to orient within location and space, are prevalent in country dwellers and lost by city dwellers. People in the countryside and in forested areas have the capacity to know their environment in a way that we who were raised in cities no longer have.

DIANA LIVERMAN: I wanted to add one more thing in favor of the mosquito. We talked about the beauty of the birds and how they are inspirational to us. Well, the mosquito sacrifices itself for the birds, so they show their appreciation indirectly. They bite us, and then they fly off and feed the birds, and the birds return the favor with their songs.

HIS HOLINESS THE DALAI LAMA: That reminds me of a Sakya scholar who talks about his experiences living in the central plains of India, in the Varanasi region. He talks about the heat and about being pestered by mosquitoes, yet he gives them a beautiful name: those flies that sing with a flute. In that way he recognizes their beauty.

SALLIE MCFAGUE: To follow up on Diana's point, in nature, there's no true altruism. Animals don't decide to be self-sacrificing; they are sacrificed involuntarily. And that's the pattern we are trying to get humans to adopt voluntarily—to make sacrifices for other life forms and for the planet. The scientific view says that sacrifice, limitation, sharing, and give-and-take are all part of the natural world, part of the way reality works. Yet humans are the only creatures that purposefully do not do this.

HIS HOLINESS THE DALAI LAMA: Let's talk about compassion, or the sense of love and caring. Our sense of caring for another's well-being exists at two levels. The first level is biological. You will see mother birds that will, if necessary, sacrifice their own life in order to save their offspring. That is a purely biological motivation, and we humans have that same capacity at a biological level.

The next level is based on religious faith and intelligence. This is something we cultivate by believing in a deeper meaning or reality. Already possessing the biological seed of compassion, with the help of intelligence and faith we can develop our unbiased compassion. Perhaps on a limited basis at first, but ultimately we could strive to hold this infinitely.

So when you talked about children naturally possessing empathy and love for nature, and how adults may dismiss this and even suggest they grow out of it, that points to our responsibility in the education of our youth.

Looking at the foundations of the modern education system, going back, say, a thousand years, the concepts of moral ethics, love and kindness, were the domain of the church. Over the centuries, the influence of religion in education has diminished, and with that so did teachings about caring and responsibility for others. As science and technology has developed over the last century, the foundations of our educational system have become mostly scientific and materialistic.

People who grow up in this system don't learn the importance of inner values, but rather tend to think that progress, money, and material values are more important. So how can we bring balance to this?

I feel that religion itself is not sufficient because no one religion can have universal appeal. However, these inner values we are talking about, love and compassion, are universal. So without involving religion, we can rely on common sense as well as some of the new science that is showing that health and peace of mind are very much connected to a sense of concern for the well-being of others. With these concrete facts, conviction in the importance of cultivating inner values can be acquired. Further, this is a way in which we can address the need to bring inner values back into our secular education system.

I've mentioned this before, and people seem to agree, but to date nobody has developed a concrete plan to implement this idea. Some ways in which this is moving forward, for example, are with the mindfulness studies that Richie Davidson and his contemporaries are doing, which are showing positive results. We need to let more people know about these, not in religious circles but in educational circles.

More evidence can be found in the millionaires and billionaires who embrace technology and money and yet still feel like something is lacking, who are unhappy.

The drive for materialism is strong. When I talk about inner values to a poorer Indian audience, they don't respond so much. With American, Japanese, and European audiences, who have already reached a certain material level for the most part, they seem to understand the necessity for these inner values. In that way, I feel like things are shifting a little.

This is catching on in the area of faith and religion. It's important that we are practical and do not simply perform rote ceremonies and rituals, but rather are connected to real, underlying values.

There's a Tibetan expression that sums up how a religious person can become complacent: "If it matters to you, Buddha, then I will refrain from engaging in negative acts"—as if you are doing the Buddha a favor. But this is absolutely wrong, and the same holds true for that kind of attitude toward God. The true practice is love for yourself, for your future, for the future of humanity and the world, whether there is a God or not, whether there is a Buddha or not.

So I think that the cultivation of these inner values has to come practically through education, not through superstition or belief.

JOHN DUNNE: Your Holiness, you said that sometimes we need a secular approach that does not involve religion, and at Emory University, we've heard you offer similar advice. It's had a big impact at Emory, where there is an emphasis on educating not just the mind, but also the heart. My colleague Geshe Lobsang Tenzin is developing a program in Secular Ethics that aims to take your advice and put it into practice.

MATTHIEU RICARD: Stepping back to follow up on the hospital study, the scientist Eric Lambin used another approach to explore the effect of nature on people. He showed all kinds of people pictures of different landscapes and discovered that people from all parts of the world, even Eskimos, who have only ever seen snow, found that the most pleasant pictures were ones with a lot of open space, green, water, and some trees. He deduced that part of this was survival instinct, the innate knowledge that the green spaces could provide food and water and shelter from the trees. He also found that jails where the windows offered a view of a natural setting, versus brick walls, had a lower incidence of violence.

And to the point of altruism, I don't think it came out of nowhere, but rather developed across millions of years of evolution. One of our friends, Frans de Waal, told me a beautiful short story about chimpanzees. There was an elder mother chimpanzee who had a very hard time walking to the water hole. Some young female chimpanzees who were not related to her noticed this, and when they would see the mother chimpanzee going to the water, they would run ahead, fill their mouths with water, and run back to share the water with the elder mother. That occurs to me as a case of genuine altruism.

And finally, a comment about mosquitoes. In Buddhism, we talk about pain and suffering, but it's not only the subjective pain—the expression of pain and the cognitive realization that we are in pain—but also the tendency to avoid what is harmful and go toward what is beneficial. So I'm curious: on this basis, wouldn't that tendency to avoid pain be the most basic example of sentience?

HIS HOLINESS THE DALAI LAMA: This relates to the Buddhist attitude toward other sentient beings, including animals. There's a very influential text, *The Eight Verses on Training the Mind*, in which there is a verse that says, from the point of view of the practitioner, "Whomever I may interact with or associate with, I shall always view myself as the lower."

So genuine compassion is not to look down on someone, or an animal, as if you are superior, but to approach with respect. This is so even in the case of the mosquito. We humans are too clever; we can lie and cheat. But mosquitoes are more honest; once they feed, they are full and content, not greedy. They don't harbor negative emotions. Also, mosquitoes' actions are innocent—their wrongdoing or ignorance is innocent—whereas usually our human wrongdoing is done with knowledge and awareness, which is much worse. So, from that viewpoint, we are lower than the mosquito.

Yesterday, we talked about how language and concepts tend to guide our view of the world selectively, through the act of focusing on one facet of reality. So a statement such as "I am a human being" or "I am a Buddhist monk" has certain implications, but from another perspective, I am worse than a mosquito. Both are selective views.

So, as a Buddhist practitioner, one needs to develop the ability to have a holistic, comprehensive perspective on reality. This holistic view is very important early in our practice. Once we have acquired that, then we can focus on specific aspects of mind training.

Then when we look at our relationship with the mosquito, we can see it from different angles, one being where we are actually lower than the mosquito.

CLARE PALMER: It seems as though many scientists would argue that mosquitoes don't feel pleasure, and yet as Matthieu said, there are other behaviors mosquitoes engage in that relate to avoiding suffering. So I wonder how far the idea of sentience extends in Buddhism, and what kinds of creatures would be considered sentient.

HIS HOLINESS THE DALAI LAMA: Many years ago, in a talk with Francisco Varela, we discussed the idea of sentient beings and nonsentient beings, and we agreed that as far as sentience, we are talking about embodied beings. From the Buddhist viewpoint, as well as the Christian view, there are different forms of existence, such as angels and others that we cannot see but can sense. That phenomenon is quite mysterious. Also, scientists have been curious how the bodies of certain advanced tantric practitioners remain fresh and intact after death, at times for weeks.

But given all these considerations, in that discussion, we agreed that a sentient being was any embodied living being that has the capacity to move autonomously from one place to another. This implies that there is some kind of intrinsic motivation, and with motivation, there is desire and some quality of emotion and consciousness. For example, with insects, if we try to touch them, they fly away or play dead; there's a desire to protect themselves.

This view has important implications. If you go to the market nowadays, you see lots of chickens hanging everywhere. People treat them not as sentient beings but more like vegetables. They're not appreciated as sentient beings, but rather only for their monetary value.

If you follow that view, then beings that don't have worth within our society's current value system could be eliminated. And if we took that to the extreme, that would mean getting rid of all the old people, too.

GREGORY NORRIS: Back to the hospital example, studies have also found that if someone is given a plant in their room and told that the hospital will care for the plant, the patient will heal a little better than he or she would have otherwise. But if someone is given a plant and asked to care for the plant, they heal and recover much faster. I'm also curious about the early comment that if we perform a negative action, and then we later perform a stronger, positive action, we cancel the negative karma.

HIS HOLINESS THE DALAI LAMA: Think about a physical example, such as getting an infection. That's harmful. But if we take a stronger antibiotic, that can reduce the harm caused by the infection. The potency of the harm is reduced. The same process is true in the realm of action. A negative action has impacts and consequences, some of which continue and grow over time. But a stronger, positive action can reduce the potency and impact of the negative action. This can occur in different ways. In some cases, the negative action will be overridden or neutralized, and possibly replaced. It depends on the potency of the positive action.

This applies to thought, too. If you become irritated with someone, that can develop into anger and very strong negative feelings. Not only is that unfavorable for the person, but it also hurts your own health and won't solve the problem. So to first develop forgiveness and then respect and even appreciation can ameliorate the impact that was caused by the original negative thoughts.

As a practitioner, I need to practice forgiveness, so someone must provide me with the opportunity to practice forgiveness. My enemies do this for me by agitating me, and then in my practice I can observe if I have genuine compassion or not.

There's a saying in Tibetan that in some cases religious practitioners have the outward form of being holy people, which holds when everything is fine—when the sun is shining and the belly is full. But when they are confronted with a real challenge or crisis, then they become just like everyone else. You hear religious people and even politicians calling for peace, and then as soon as a crisis hits, they forget about peace and nonviolence.

The point is, we need antagonists to help us in our practice of cultivating compassion and, instead of reacting, developing appreciation and respect for them.

I often tell a story I heard in 1967 from a great master of compassion, Khunu Lama Rinpoche, which really transformed my thinking. He said there was a man meditating in a cave, and another person walked by and asked, "What are you doing in that cave?"

"I'm meditating," the man responded.

"What are you meditating on?" the passerby asked.

"I'm meditating on patience and forbearance."

"In that case, you can go to hell!" the passerby said.

"You go to hell!" the meditator retorted.

This sums up the gap between how we look and our real, present ability to act with compassion.

DEKILA CHUNGYALPA: I wanted to follow up on what Matthieu said about altruism among chimpanzees and other animals. My colleagues and I who work in the field see this all the time. We see animals, especially herds of animals that live in very large families, self-sacrifice. For example, if there is a predator present, the animals will help push a weaker animal out of the way even if they're not related.

Elephants, especially, are very intelligent. We've observed rituals where, if an elephant dies, the other elephants mourn. You can see them exhibit their sadness. They have rituals where they will use their foreleg to pat the ground, and each one of them in the herd will do it before leaving. I think there is a lot to be said about altruism not just being a human condition.

We've also been talking about the inherent value of nature. If you look at the poorest people in the world, most of them depend on nature for their survival. In fact, we could consider nature their grocery store or pharmacy. It's where they go to get food, medicine, and wood for fuel. And there are many studies that show if we harm nature, we essentially make poor people poorer; harming nature contributes to poverty.

And this is where I am not clear if just education is enough. We take these studies to decision makers, to policymakers, in governments and corporations. On an individual level, most of them agree with us, or at least they will feel bad. They agree that the facts are accurate and the science is real, but they almost always end up saying that, for the greater good, they have to make the difficult decision to go ahead with industrial development.

I think they do this because they no longer factor the individual human into their decisions. Rather, they are thinking about an entire system. I'm wondering if this can change. If the leaders and decision makers would consider the fate of one person, of individuals, perhaps that would have an effect on their decision making and policy. And how can we decide what good leadership is? Should being compassionate to people and nature be part of the criteria for good leadership, and can religions play a role in making that part of the criteria?

HIS HOLINESS THE DALAI LAMA: If we consider the biological motivations of social animals, we see them living together, working together, eating together. There is some sort of emotional quality to that, a love or sense of caring for each other's well-being. That's basic to their nature. They are interdependent. Their individual survival depends on the rest of the herd or group. But then I think about turtles, for example, where the mother lays the eggs and then leaves. The mother and the youngster never meet, and once hatched, the youngsters' survival depends on them alone, not their mothers. With these animals, I doubt if you put the youngster and the mother together that they would have the ability to show affection to each other.

But humans are not in that category. Our survival depends entirely on someone else's care. Biologically, we already have a level of compassion given to us by nature.

But we can't blame the leaders who are saying one thing and doing something else—even if they believe the facts, they can't implement effective policy. That's an outcome of today's social reality: through our modern education we are conditioned to only think about money. We don't emphasize moral principles in education. The underlying foundation is that if you have money and power, everything will be okay. Naturally, our leaders are a product of this system and have that same way of thinking.

Just a few people talking and educating about the needed changes is not sufficient. We need to have a movement and a real method, a revolution in modern education. New ideas and new thinking, derived from reality, can be greatly helped and supported by the scientists.

This is different from serving God or serving Buddha, or preparing for the next life. It's simply how to build a healthy human mind, and therefore a healthy human being. All of the awful events and circumstances—such as the gap between rich and poor, hypocrisy and corruption—stem from a lack of moral ethics. Even religious people suffer from this. They often think moral ethics mean serving God. No. Ethics are what create the basis of a happy human society.

In economics, we develop five-year and ten-year plans for change and growth. That's fine. But we need similar plans to cultivate warmheartedness and compassion. Even in our religious circles, we don't pay sufficient attention to the real meaning and implications of guidance, such as the four noble truths. We just focus on our offerings and don't understand the underlying meaning.

Last year, I was visiting a Buddhist community. During lunch we were sitting and talking and I asked one of the members, "What is Buddhism?" He said, "Taking refuge," and recited some verses. I said, "Good, now what is Buddha?" And he said, "I don't know."

Another time, I was in a school and there were students in yellow robes, and again I asked, "What is Buddha?" They responded, "No idea."

In another instance, a Buddhist monastic leader was doing some very nice chanting, and after my lecture, he asked me whether we Buddhists really believe in reincarnation or not. If a person does not believe in the continuation of life, then the Buddha just becomes a fairy tale.

It's sad, but it's an indication that people are not paying attention to what Buddhism really is. We have more than three hundred volumes of texts, and some are about ritual but most are the philosophy of living. Yet people aren't studying the essence of these; rather they are putting the texts aside and just looking to the Buddha as an object of worship.

I see the same with my Hindu friends who wake up early and make offerings of flowers and incense and recite verses in Sanskrit, and yet don't understand the real meaning of these verses. And we can see this in people who have a very serious practice of worshiping God but do not hesitate to get involved in corruption.

What I am saying today is that there is no third way. If you accept religion, then cease practicing wrong things like corruption, injustice, lying, and hypocrisy. Be honest and transparent. And if you feel compelled to do wrong things, then stop worshiping God—forget God, forget Buddha, and just take refuge in money and power.

JONATHAN PATZ: Following up on Dekila's important question about the nature of leadership, and bringing in Diana's comments about tipping points and boundaries, if we don't act soon, there may be irreversible consequences. If we were at the Earth Summit meeting with the world's leaders giving key messages about the environment, what, specifically, would you say to them to inspire them to embrace environmental sustainability?

HIS HOLINESS THE DALAI LAMA: I would speak bluntly. But just my presence or my words now won't make the difference that needs to be made. No single person can change the world. Jesus Christ tried and didn't succeed entirely. Now we are in a modern era, with democracy, so it's really the voice of the people together, the collective, that will make a difference. And that's where the power of education plays a big role.

At the Earth Summit, many of the leaders are from Christian backgrounds, so perhaps a sincere practitioner from that belief such as Sallie McFague would be the best person to carry the message.

We should speak about these things without elaborate dress, fame, or political influence, just telling the truth as a human being. When people in their human sincerity speak clearly, I think the leaders will be more inclined to listen.

I say this to the media. I tell them that in this modern time they have a special responsibility to bring awareness to the people—not just report on bad news, but bring people hope. We must make public these ideas we are discussing and share them with other people. The most important idea is the promotion of human value, and the second is religious harmony. I tell people in the media that they need to have a long nose so they can smell not only what is on the surface but also what is underneath what they are reporting. Then they need to be clear with the public and provide honest and unbiased reporting about what is really happening in the background, not just the sensational story. On the surface, generally people behave and try to look good, to practice restraint. But underneath there may be other things happening. We've had scandals involving Buddhist teachers who weren't following the precepts. By being transparent and public, it made them a little embarrassed and they reconsidered their roles. Transparency acts as a deterrence to wrong motives.

In free countries, at least, the media has a huge role to play and can make a big difference. It's a different matter in countries with heavy censorship. For the time being that is a difficult situation.

JONATHAN PATZ: What about when the media intentionally tries to misinform the public?

HIS HOLINESS THE DALAI LAMA: There are newspapers and media outlets that are heavily funded by special interests that do not report objectively. In that case, I think there should be peaceful demonstrations led by reputable people like you, the scientists and professors. That is the only way. We cannot use the stick, but we must make the truth clear. We can do this though demonstrations and perhaps fasting, if necessary. The important thing is we need to bring awareness to the truth and to the environmental issues.

ELKE WEBER: There's an interesting psychological effect that when people do something that causes harm, they feel bad about it; they feel responsible. On the other hand, when we don't do anything and our inaction causes harm, we don't feel bad, a least not as responsible. I'm curious if there is a distinction in Buddhist philosophy between mistakes of action and mistakes of inaction? Should we feel more responsible for the things we fail to do?

HIS HOLINESS THE DALAI LAMA: In the Buddhist tradition, a vow, or precept, contains both elements. We should avoid causing harm by doing something we are not supposed to do *and* by not doing something we should. This is a relevant point. When we practice forgiveness, it doesn't mean we just tolerate the wrongdoing. We must distinguish between the actor and the act. Toward the actor, we practice forgiveness and relinquish negative feelings and anger. But where the act is concerned, a measure or countermeasure may be required.

It's like God who doesn't forget our sins but forgives us as sinners. That's a very special kind of love. Similarly, we must offer compassion toward the actor, even if their actions are very destructive. We must have love and a sense of concern for their well-being, and that practice usually leads to a desire to stop their wrongdoing. And if you have the ability, you must stop the wrongdoing. To not act if you can is a sin, a negative act. In the bodhisattva practice, one of the precepts is that you do not respond to harm in a way that causes more harm, but you take counteraction when it is appropriate.

In the case of the Tibetan crisis, we are against the wrongdoing, but we don't allow negative feelings toward these people. For example, after the March 2008 crisis in Tibet, where there were riots and Chinese officials were shooting people, I engaged in a special practice. I visualized the Chinese officials, and took their anger, suspicion, and negative feelings, and offered in their place my love, my compassion, and my forgiveness. That's a practice called *tonglen*. It won't solve the problem necessarily, but it was an immense help at keeping my mind calm. On an intellectual level I recognized how bad the situation was, but on a deeper emotional level, I could stay calm and maintain peace.

That practice helps immensely to keep the mind calm and healthy, and with a calm mind, you can be more effective with solutions or countermeasures. If you lose your peace of mind, your solutions could go the wrong way. With anger, you may strike someone. With a peaceful mind, you may want to strike, but you will hesitate and "strike" with a smile instead. In order to be wise in your response, you must have a calm mind. Anger destroys a calm mind; you cannot judge properly or see reality.

In leadership, the original motivation for making a policy may be good, but the methods may be wrong. For example, consider President George W. Bush's policy regarding Afghanistan and Iraq. I love President Bush as a human being. He is a very nice person and we have a friendship. Since I first met him, I saw him as a good human being, even though he did not always act like a great leader of a great nation. On one occasion I told him, "I love you, I respect you, but I have some reservations about some of your policies." He just laughed and smiled.

His was a case where the motivation was good—to bring freedom—but the method was wrong. In part it's due to the lack of a holistic view and an understanding of the whole reality. If people had that view, they may have foreseen the years of consequences and not taken that action. The narrow attitude that by removing one person, Saddam Hussein, everything would be okay was a skewed view. The reality was much more complex—an economic crisis, billions of dollars spent, and an enormous amount of useless effort wasted. It's quite terrible.

America can make a big difference. They have individual freedom and innovation. And now science and technology are making discoveries and innovations in mental awareness. Where mental health is concerned, America should lead the world. But many Americans believe, sadly, that their weapons and military force can solve anything. That's unrealistic.

Look at Communist China. Mao Zedong once said, "Power comes from the barrel of a gun." That is shortsighted. The truth is the source of real power, and the power of truth never diminishes. The power of a gun often creates more problems. But this is not a political meeting.

ROSHI JOAN HALIFAX: In a way, it's a very political meeting. I want to reflect on one thread of Buddhism that is present here but hasn't been identified, and that is engaged Buddhism. Engaged Buddhism has two ways in which it can interact with the world. One of those ways is service. How can we help others—for example, in the prison system, or in the hospital system? The other is social action: How can we speak truth to power?

This is very present for me, as after this meeting, I am going to

Bodhgaya for the annual conference of the International Network of Engaged Buddhists. And one of the people by whom I feel we in the Buddhist world are influenced is a man called Gary Snyder.

Gary Snyder is a wonderful poet, who in the '50s and '60s was a kind of hippie. He was in a tower looking for fires in the forest when he read poetry that was written a thousand years ago during the Tang dynasty by a poet called Hanshan: the Cold Mountain poems. I do not believe that Hanshan ever had the intention of influencing anyone a thousand years in the future. With this poetry, Gary lived in a fire tower and rejected civil life, as did Wu Wei and Li Bai, and various other poets from the Tang dynasty.

They moved away from culture and society into what Sallie called wild space. That is the thing that Gary Snyder recognized, wild space. And suddenly he put it together in a very interesting way that became a domain in the environmental movement called "deep ecology." This is a view of ecology that is a little different than the environment. It separates the human from the natural world. In fact the natural world became, from the point of view of Gary Snyder's insight, a source of tremendous wisdom, and also a source of compassion. Snyder, along with Stephanie Kaza and Joanna Macy, has had a tremendous influence on Western Buddhism. They have sensitized us to what you call a universal self. Macy called it the ecological self: a vision of us being in a continuous weave with the natural world.

I wanted to bring this forward, since this relates very much to a question of how to teach about the natural world in a secular way. How can we take into account the vision of Indra's net—or interconnectedness, interdependence, and interpenetration—in a secular way in the school system? I wanted to pose that question, knowing that we're at a very odd moment in terms of education, where so much of our education is happening virtually and through technology.

Looking at Sallie's wild space, that wild space is an internal space, it's a space about the unconditioned, but it's also about the natural world. It's about, if you will, the places in the world that aren't civilized, aren't turned into parking lots and shopping malls, but in fact have this unconditioned dimension. How can we share this in a classroom? How can we bring this vision forward in the classroom?

JOHN DUNNE: Richie Davidson has suggested that Buddhist practices could help children develop this kind of ecological awareness of their interdependence with the environment.

HIS HOLINESS THE DALAI LAMA: This is something that we have touched upon before. It's for the experts to really think through and see what kind of programs can be developed.

THUPTEN JINPA: Your Holiness, I deeply believe that your strategy of reaching out to the children and trying to impact their education really is one of the most effective approaches. I can share with you from my own personal experience how children's natural and intuitive understanding of the environment seems to be so different from adults. One day my younger daughter said to me, "Daddy, I need to look at the rubbish bin in the kitchen." I said, "Why do you need to look at the rubbish bin in the kitchen?" She said, "It's for my school project." It was a school project on the environment, which involved looking through the rubbish and listing all the things in the kitchen rubbish bin to determine the percentage of recyclable materials that were thrown away. I immediately imagined millions of children doing the same thing in their homes. Imagine the impact this could have on parents' behavior. It's small things like this that I think will have a huge impact.

ROSHI JOAN HALIFAX: It's like Hanshan's Cold Mountain poems, written a thousand years ago. One small poem opened up a whole domain of the environmental movement a thousand years later. Who knows, but this small meeting might have some kind of outcome that we can't even begin to imagine.

9 The Influencers of Choice and Decision Making

PRESENTER: Elke Weber, *Columbia University*

ROSHI JOAN HALIFAX: At this point in our exploration, Elke Weber will help us understand why we don't act on global environmental problems. What holds us back? What are the cognitive and motivational challenges that we face, both as individuals and as collectives? And what about the role of attention? She also wants to address our motivational deficits, what primes action, and the role of fear.

Elke works at the intersection of psychology and economics. She's an expert on behavioral models of judgment and decision making in conditions of risk and uncertainty. She studies how attention, emotion, and memory, and their representations in the brain, influence preference and choice. She holds many different seats at Columbia University: she's the Jerome A. Chazen Professor of International Business at Columbia School of Business; she's a professor of psychology; she's also a professor at the Earth Institute; and she's the founder and codirector of the Center for Decision Sciences and the Center for Research on Environmental Decisions.

ELKE WEBER: The psychology of action and behavior change is a very active area of behavioral and neuroscience research, with hundreds of publications. I won't be talking about the methods or specific studies, but everything I say is actually based on many careful investigations. Let me give you an overview of where we will go. I will address two questions. First, I will ask, "Why don't we act on environmental problems?" and provide you with some diagnoses. Then I will take those diagnoses and turn them into treatments, asking, "What can we do about the problem; how can we help people take more environmental actions?"

The Public-Goods Dilemma

ELKE WEBER: Let's start with the first question: Why don't we act on these very important environmental problems that Diana, Jonathan, and others have told us about? To answer this, I will explore four different types of causes. The first one comes from a very famous paper published in *Science* in 1968 by the ecologist Garrett Hardin, titled "The Tragedy of the Commons." He compared global public goods that we have, such as clean air and water, to the grass in a meadow in the middle of a village that is freely accessible to villagers. He predicted that every villager would bring as many cows as possible to graze, and in a short period of time the grass would be gone; the commons would be gone. That's a tragedy because although it's a rational thing to do from the capitalist, economic view of human nature, it drives destruction. One can say self-interest is a legitimate motivation; everybody takes as much as possible because if they don't their neighbor will. We all know that greed is an important part of this problem. We will also see that this view of human nature is incomplete. It's true that greed is there, but many other motivations coexist at the same time.

HIS HOLINESS THE DALAI LAMA: Why would you call this a public-goods dilemma?

ELKE WEBER: It's a dilemma because we all have an interest in maintaining the public goods; without clean air, without water, we're all doomed. We can't continue to exist on Earth without public goods, and yet we deplete and destroy them. We know we shouldn't, but we can't help ourselves. And the problem, seen from the economic perspective, is that it's a tragedy because depletion is inevitable; it is our human nature.

Information and Cognitive Barriers

ELKE WEBER: The second problem has to do with information. There are two types of informational barriers; one of them is that we might not know what the problem is. Scientists like Diana and Jonathan have done a lot of careful work, as have other people, and we have had the privilege of learning from them what the causes and consequences of our environmental problems are. But not everybody is aware of these, and we have to make the causes and consequences more known.

There's also the informational barrier of not knowing what to do. You might know what the problem is but not have a solution. I think we, as scientists, have not done a good at job at mapping out for the public and for policymakers an effective set of relatively comprehensive solutions.

Going deeper into barriers, I would like to explore cognitive barriers, which are barriers to action, as well as motivational, or emotional, barriers.

Some of you may remember a video of young people playing basketball. Some of the players were wearing white T-shirts, others black T-shirts, and they were all throwing the ball back and forth. We were asked to count the number of times that the people in the white T-shirts threw the ball back and forth, and to ignore the people in the black T-shirts. It was a very difficult task. What happens is this: as viewers pay attention to the people in the white T-shirts, they tune out the others. When you watch the video afterward, you see that at one point a big black gorilla walks right through the middle of the group, but while you are paying attention to the people in the white T-shirts, you do not see the gorilla; it's a real blind spot. And afterward, when you're not paying attention to the people in the white T-shirts, you can't believe that you did not see the gorilla.

It's a great illustration of how limited our attention is. When we focus on one thing, we don't see everything. Matthieu talked about the blind spot that many of us have around the consumption of meat, but it's also true that vegetarians have other blind spots. We all have blind spots; there are many things we do not see.

HIS HOLINESS THE DALAI LAMA: In Buddhist epistemology we speak of a particular type of perceptions, which at the sensory level you do see but at the cognitive level you're not able to recall. The moment you're able to consciously bring attention, thoughts play a role. That's why a distinction is made between nonconceptual perceptual processes and thought processes.

So in order for a perceptual event to occur, there needs to be at least three principal conditions present: one is the object on which you're focusing, the second is a functioning sensory organ, and the third is some kind of immediately preceding attentiveness to the object.

Attention: We Tend to Focus on Ourselves

ELKE WEBER: It is true, we have very little attentiveness, so we have to be very careful how we allocate it. In fact there are many forces out there that are constantly trying to get attention from us. And so the question is, how do we focus our attention?

From an evolutionary perspective, it makes sense that our immediate attentiveness will be on ourselves and on the present, because if we don't pay attention to the present, to the dangers around us, we won't survive. While that type of attention is good for evolution, it's not so good for farsighted goals: for the future, for the environment, for other people. Naturally, farsighted attention is not as active. In some sense, focusing on the future can be thought about as a luxury for people whose immediate needs are taken care of. In other words, the focus on ourselves and on the present is good for survival, but it's bad for environmental action. When our attention is focused on the present, the immediate costs of environmental action, how our comfort will be reduced, loom large, but the benefits are far in the future and somewhat uncertain.

Limited attention is only one barrier. There are also emotional barriers to environmental action. It's not enough for us to know the dangers in our heads, we also have to have an emotional connection to the danger, and it is physical fear that motivates action. The challenge with many environmental problems is that at this point in time, to nonscientists, they're not very visible and scary; they're abstract, they're statistics. Diana talked about the fact that we probably would be more scared about global warming if those greenhouse gases that come out of the tailpipes of cars were purple, and the sky started filling up with purple smog. Further, although we continuously hear bad news and scientific evidence of serious environmental dangers, the news usually comes without any concrete actions that we can take. That makes us feel powerless and out of control. Your Holiness, you said yesterday that if one hears all this bad news, it's natural to just turn away and go on with your normal day, because if you can't do anything about it, why worry about it?

On top of that, and especially in the United States, there's a great distrust of science, and in particular environmental science. One of the reasons for this distrust is that the message environmental scientists bring is very uncomfortable and negative, so we question their motives rather than paying attention to the message.

HIS HOLINESS THE DALAI LAMA: When I have traveled, often scientists have approached me to say that the fact that someone from a contemplative or religious background is showing interest and respect for science is very helpful, that it may help raise the regard for science among the general public. I'm curious about the nature of the distrust for environmental science; are there reasons besides profit?

ELKE WEBER: In addition to economic motivations, there's also very little respect for education in the United States. The religious right in the United States also is antiscience; they often take the Bible quite literally.

HIS HOLINESS THE DALAI LAMA: That reminds me of a time years ago in Australia when I was approached by someone from the media who asked me if I believe in dinosaurs. I said, of course; we can see the fossils and other evidence. I was puzzled as to why someone would ask me the question, and later I found out that he was part of a religious group that felt that these kinds of beliefs contradict the idea that the world was created in seven days and just a few thousand years old.

ELKE WEBER: Yes. That is a good example and one of the areas of distrust of science. So now that we've talked about the problems, the obstacles to action, let's turn to some solutions.

Many Goals Can Mean Conflicting Goals

ELKE WEBER: What can we take away from what we've learned about what keeps us from acting, and what lessons does this teach us about how we can help people engage in more meaningful action with respect to the environment?

While we have very little attention, we're rich in goals and intentions. We have a wide variety of goals that coexist. We have many material goals: we need food, safety, and shelter. But we also have other goals, such as spiritual goals: we worry about meaning, and we need beauty. We have psychological goals: we need connection with other people, to feel respected, loved, in control, and to feel that we make a difference and affect our environment in a good way.

Many of these goals are contradictory; they conflict with each other. We want to save for the future, but we also want to buy a gift for our loved one today. Often we're not even aware of these conflicts. One reason why we aren't keenly aware of the conflicts is that in any given decision or situation, there's only a subset of the goals that are active, and the active goals are the ones that influence our decision. So an important question is, what makes goals active?

Some goals, such as our focus on ourselves, are always active. But it's the long-term forward-looking goals for others and for the environment that need to be activated. Our upbringing plays a role in this. The formal and informal ways in which we learn what is important, as a function of our culture, make a huge difference on which types of goals are more continuously active. A monk from Dharamsala will have a very different set of active goals than a banker on Wall Street because of different experiences and a different environment.

There's an interesting study that was done in a wine store in Belgium. They were selling German wines and French wines. On Mondays, Wednesdays, and Fridays, they would play German music, and on Tuesdays, Thursdays, and Saturdays, they would play French music. On the days with German music, they sold more German wine, and on the days with French music, more French wines. When customers were asked, "Why did you buy this wine?" they didn't have a clear notion, but it was the music that, at least in part, triggered the purchase.

HIS HOLINESS THE DALAI LAMA: Wouldn't this susceptibility to environmental influences vary from person to person? One with a very strong standpoint would be less susceptible and another might be easily swayed. Wouldn't there also be a difference from individual to individual, depending on how rooted they are in their own cultural values and tradition?

ELKE WEBER: Absolutely. It depends on the person, and it depends on how strong existing values and preferences are, and it depends on the type of decision, but it also depends on the environment. We know that Europeans are much more environmentally active than Americans, and I think one reason for that is the higher population density in Europe versus in America. In Europe, you cannot go anywhere without constantly seeing other people, and that reminds you of the fact that we are not alone in the world, that we are all interconnected, and that other people matter. In this sense, our physical environment really influences our values, because seeing other people primes collective values and collective concerns.

Inspiring Environmental Action

ELKE WEBER: Let's talk about a few other ways in which we can enable environmental action. We've talked about the importance of reminding ourselves of important, long-term goals by putting reminders in the psychological or physical space around us. Also, as Greg shared, quantifying the environmental impact of our actions and the goods we purchase is very important. He provided us with some measures for these actions, including his website that allows us to track our progress and goals.

Earlier Dan noted that "what gets measured, gets managed." I would add that what we measure, we pay attention to. Measures introduce new goals into our mind and into our motivation. And one of the psychological needs we have is to feel effective and to feel that we're making progress.

Another strength we can bring to decision making is having multiple perspectives. Naming things differently and looking from different angles or perspectives can be a resource for problem solving. It matters, for example, whether I call someone a terrorist or a freedom fighter. It matters whether I describe insecticide as a mosquito killer or a malaria preventive. These labels suggest different goals and impacts.

Your Holiness gave the example yesterday of shifting perspective when someone makes you angry. It's good to rethink, to reframe the situation as an opportunity for compassion. It's the same physical situation looked at from a different angle. In the same way, we can use multiple perspectives to encourage environmental action. As Sallie said, we don't necessarily have to think about consuming less as a loss of pleasure, but rather as a gain in fulfillment, or a gain in health. We can reframe, we can think about these actions as co-benefits in a positive way.

Making Decisions by Head, Heart, or Rules

ELKE WEBER: Let me end by saying something about three different ways in which we make decisions, any kind of decisions, including forward-looking environmental decisions. These ways of making decisions are associated with different processes that are located in different parts of the brain. They're not necessarily separate—often they all operate in parallel—but we may pay more or less attention to the recommendation that one process makes for how we should act. Sometimes we make decisions with our head, and sometimes we make decisions with our heart when we follow feelings, motivations, and emotions. And sometimes we follow rules. Let me say a little bit more about each one of those.

HIS HOLINESS THE DALAI LAMA: Could you clarify the distinction between the head and the heart?

ELKE WEBER: When I say making decisions with our head, it's a metaphor. What I mean is that we make, either consciously or unconsciously, a calculation. We think about what the costs and benefits of an action are, and then we pick the one that has the highest benefit-to-cost ratio. It's a very rational process, and because of our proclivity to focus on our own needs, it is not always the best method for making environmentally responsible decisions. If you're asked to give up energy or meat consumption, the costs occur right now. They loom large; they appear as a loss. The benefits are in the future or perhaps in other areas of the world. We don't even know whether the benefits will actually occur. We might be dead by the time they unfold. Because they are outside our immediate needs, we value them less. The economists say we discount them a lot. And so making decisions that way is often not effective for environmental action, unless we can reframe the costs as benefits.

Making decisions with our heart means that we pay more attention to how we feel about the options than to the calculations we could be making. It's more emotional. When something feels good, we approach and embrace it. If something is scary or makes us feel anxious, we withdraw.

When we make decisions with our heart, or when we try to use emotions to motivate environmental action, I think we have to be very careful that we focus on positive emotions and compassion, rather than focusing on fear or guilt. It's very tempting to use fear or guilt. In fact, this is the technique that the media and even scientists often use. For example, in trying to protect polar bears, we show images of them losing their homes, which elicit negative emotions. It's a great tactic for getting attention quickly.

HIS HOLINESS THE DALAI LAMA: In some sense, you cannot avoid the negative message. Even if we reframe it in positive terms, the negative consequences are still part of the situation.

ELKE WEBER: Yes, but whether the negative message is in the background or foreground is important. Here's an example based on medical decision making. When people have cancer, they can choose between different types of therapy. You can get radiation or you can have surgery. And different things happen with the different treatments. With surgery, you may die during surgery, but you also have a good chance to live longer. However, no one dies right away from radiation, though the five- and ten-year survival rates vary and may not be as good as for surgery. When you tell patients the probabilities of surviving the two treatments at different points in time, they tend to choose surgery, because of the higher survival rates. When you switch that to the probabilities of dying, patients tend to choose radiation, because nobody dies from it right away. But it's the same information in both cases. A 10 percent chance of survival is the same as a 90 percent chance of dying. What's different is where the attention is focused.

Negative emotions are good for getting attention, because they scare us. When we pay attention, we might actually do one thing to fix the problem. But we don't keep this kind of attention very long because it's a negative experience. We don't like to be in a negative state. So as soon as we have done one thing to address the issue, we are likely to turn away from the problem to distance ourselves from the negative emotion.

Conversely, when you motivate with positive emotions, the incentive is to stay with it, because it feels good. If you focus on positive, meaningful benefits, for example, that you are helping a species to survive, it might not be as gripping immediately, but it lasts longer.

The third way of making decisions is by following rules. This is probably the best way to encourage people to engage in a plan of environmental action. There are different kinds of rules that we follow. There are ethical rules, such as the Ten Commandments, or Sallie's planetary house rules, which tell us what's good. In fact, they discourage us from making calculations about costs and benefits and encourage acting out of principle.

There are also social rules. We do some things because we are a teacher or because we are a parent, and these actions are part of our role. We know the rules well and we know exactly what to do.

And then there are practical rules, or rules of efficiency that reduce the amount of conscious attention needed to act. For example, we might do what we did last time, or what we always do. These can be characterized as habits, and we usually don't even realize that we are making a decision. An extension of this would be a rule based on social norms, such as doing what everyone else does. This is good if the social norm is an environmentally responsible one. It's bad when it's not. When this is the case, we need to ask, how do we change social norms?

Benefits of the Passive Decision

ELKE WEBER: Another rule might be to do nothing as long as possible. Your Holiness, you talked about laziness. Laziness can actually be quite adaptive, because whatever resources we don't use for a given decision, we can use for other decisions. Let me show you an example of how we can turn laziness, or the rule that we follow the path of least resistance, into environmentally responsible behavior.

At American conferences, you often have to make a lunch selection prior to attending, usually between one or two meat dishes and a vegetarian dish. Most Americans are not very environmentally aware, for various reasons, and they tend to choose meat regardless of its greenhouse gas effects. Only 5 percent on average choose the vegetarian dish.

Awareness can help. At the annual Behavior, Energy, and Climate Change Conference, about eight hundred environmental scientists come together, and they know everything that Matthieu told us. They know that livestock generates 18 percent of American greenhouse gases. They know the harmful effects, and they're well intentioned to reduce them. With that level of awareness, the vegetarian lunch orders go up from a typical 5 percent to 17 percent, which is good—more than three times as high.

However, in 2009, the conference organizers made the vegetarian dish the default lunch offering. This option was prechecked on the registration form, so if you did not change it, you automatically got the vegetarian meal. Now the number of people eating vegetarian at that conference went to 80 percent!

This increase came from laziness, from inaction. This is in effect a passive decision on the part of the attendees, which was influenced by a proactive approach by the organizers. This is an example of how default options can be very powerful. They still allow for autonomy of choice—you could get that meat dish if you really wanted it—but produce a positive outcome from no choice.

Greater impact would come from having policymakers set positive defaults rather than attempt to legislate away harmful options. This tactic can be used in many contexts: building codes, food choices, and transportation choices. It has been used in the context of organ donations in many European countries where, by default, you are an organ donor unless you decide otherwise.

So, in summary, we can see that awareness is very important, but it is not enough and may be insufficient to stimulate effective action. Cognitive and emotional barriers also come into play.

Environmental problems are complex, interrelated, and pull on many different motivators and intentions. Just working with our automatic attention can be problematic, as we tend to focus too much on our ourselves and our immediate needs. We have to find ways to make longer-term goals active in our decisions. To cultivate sustained attention to longer-term goals, we need to frame things positively, and using defaults can be a powerful way to get results when low attention, inertia, or passivity are present.

It's also important to start locally, because local issues are usually a smaller slice of the bigger picture, and local people care about the problem, have more personal expertise and experience, and therefore have a higher chance of succeeding. Then small success can contribute to bigger successes.

I also want to repeat something I said earlier, which is that we scientists have to work harder at providing people not only with descriptions of the problems but also with effective solutions at the individual, social, and political levels.

Negative versus Positive Messages

JOHN DUNNE: I'm curious about the different contexts for decision making, and the fact that there are many factors that go into making a decision beyond rational examination and the analysis of costs and benefits. But I'm not sure I understand a decision that is purely emotional and not cognitive in any way. Could you tell us a little more about decisions that are motivated by negative emotion? For example, in Buddhist practice we talk about the contemplation of death and impermanence. This sometimes creates a state of concern or even fear that could be called a negative emotion but can also be used to motivate practice, especially in the beginning. Are you suggesting that when a decision is motivated by a negative emotion like fear, guilt, or regret, after you make the decision, you stop paying attention?

ELKE WEBER: That's what I was saying. Negative emotions, such as fear, are unpleasant, and therefore very motivating. It's a signal, a flag that goes up and says, "Look, something is wrong, something needs to be done; do something." We always have either a positive or a negative reaction to a situation that tells us this is safe or that is dangerous. And these emotional reactions were created in simpler times. They were created at a time when the danger was the tiger at the watering hole, and as long as you stayed away from the watering hole while the tiger was there, you would be okay. During those simpler times, simple actions removed the threat. In that sense, you could stop thinking about it; you took one action and you were done. Now our problems are not so simple anymore and require sustained attention. So that's one reason why negative emotion is less effective for long-term decision making.

The other reason is because the state itself is unpleasant, so we have a natural motivation to get away from it as quickly as possible. Instinctively, we know it's bad for our immune system to be in those negative states. It's adaptive to get away from negativity quickly. These emotions are good to capture attention, but then we have to somehow think about how to reframe the situation in a more positive way to maintain motivation and continued action.

JOHN DUNNE: Given the research showing that fear-based motivation leads to a simple action, resolves, and then is forgotten, it seems that a faculty such as mindfulness would cease to be active; the danger is over and you stop. I'm wondering if fear is a less effective motivator for all types of people, or just a percentage of the population. What about analytical people—are there cases where an analytical approach can overcome these different biases?

ELKE WEBER: That's a good question, and I think you're asking several questions in parallel. One of the questions has to do with individual differences, and we haven't talked about this very much in my talk or during this conference. We haven't talked about gender differences, for example, when we talk about environmental concern. We'll come back to that later.

But to your question about cognitive abilities, many cognitive abilities have to do with the way our brain is wired. We have some areas, the prefrontal cortex, for example, that are responsible for planned action and for cognitive-analytic processing. We have areas of self-control that help us override impulses or our natural focus on the here and now. The neural connectivity between those centers and other parts of the brain that process emotions differs as a result of genetics and prior training and experiences. The difference in how each person's brain is wired absolutely determines accessibility and use of different processing modes.

The studies that have looked at the effect of negative emotions have been done on different groups and populations: a hundred undergraduates at Harvard or eight hundred people in the general population in the United States via internet surveys. Unfortunately, we do not typically study people in developing countries. When we talk about "people," we're basically talking about Americans and Europeans. Until ten years ago, respondents were typically comprised of college undergraduates, but the scope has improved. Using internet studies, we can reach a broader range of socioeconomic backgrounds, ages, and education.

When we talk about the way our brain is wired, people all around the world have much in common, with the exceptions of age and possibly gender differences. But concerning the effects of culture, values, education, and physical and social context, we really have to look at a much broader sample of the global population. I would encourage everyone who can influence national or international science policy in different countries to lobby for funds for this type of research, because right now funding is not very available.

DIANA LIVERMAN: I would really like you to expand on the issue of differences between men and women in their response to the environment. Specifically, what do we know about whether women are more or less caring? Also, could you talk about how your research would apply to a specific attempt to change behavior? Suppose we want people to change their energy consumption in the United States, or middle-class India; how would you recommend we design a program, not necessarily a policy? My final comment is that you presented Garrett Hardin's "Tragedy of the Commons" without including the critique that Elinor Ostrom won the Nobel Prize for, in which she said that Garrett Hardin was actually wrong.

Key Determinants in Decision-Making Behavior

ELKE WEBER: I did say that this economic view of human nature was extremely limited, but I think it's worth noting that there is a lot of greed in this world, a lot of shortsightedness, and a lot of destruction of our public commons and our public resources. So we should not disregard that argument completely. At the same time, Elinor Ostrom was correct to downgrade the "tragedy" of the commons to a "drama," because the destruction of the commons is not a forgone conclusion, in part because not all of our decisions are made by calculation, and in part because we are not entirely selfish.

To the point of gender differences: there have been large US and international surveys over the last ten years or so that have found that the number-one determinant of environmental concern and even action is our ideology. How do we see the world? Are we more conservative and hierarchical, or are we more liberal and egalitarian?

The second most important determinant is education. In this case, the higher the education, the greater the level of the concern and action.

After these two key determinants, we get into other demographics, and that's where gender and other factors play a role. Income comes first; more wealth correlates with higher environmental awareness. This goes back to the point that concern for future generations and for the future of the environment is a luxury. If our immediate needs are taken care of, we can afford the luxury of being concerned about the future.

After wealth, gender comes in. Women are more concerned about the environment and they donate more to environmental organizations. The gender difference is significant, though not huge, and the impact of gender on decisions is reduced as we migrate back up through the other determinants.

DANIEL GOLEMAN: That's interesting, and as we know, women do the bulk of the shopping for families and are more informed and motivated around purchases. Bringing in some of Greg's points, environmentally informed women could create very powerful pressure for companies to clean up their supply chains.

HIS HOLINESS THE DALAI LAMA: Similarly, scientists who have studied gender differences, particularly with visual presentations of others in pain, have found that women have a stronger empathetic response. It seems that this would correlate with a greater understanding of the serious environmental situation. In fact, even for animals, this seems to be the case, as we witness the females nurturing the young while frequently the males are absent. And yet in the physical brains of males and females, there are not many differences, are there?

RICHARD DAVIDSON: A few differences, but not many.

HIS HOLINESS THE DALAI LAMA: So the potential is there for everyone. The potential for positive emotions is there for everyone. Again, so much depends on increasing awareness and education.

There are billions of human beings, and each person has unique qualities that cannot be taken for granted. We cannot say that any particular thing is the same for all human beings; even identical twins are significantly different people on emotional and intellectual levels. To say "this is the way it is with all people" seems to me to be unscientific. There's a Tibetan phrase from the scholastic tradition that cautions against picking up a grain of wheat and then arguing that all the grains should be exactly the same.

Educating and Inspiring the Younger Generations

GREGORY NORRIS: Speaking of education, and considering Jinpa's point about children influencing household awareness, are there studies that address this? How would you speak about the way in which research shows that children are a wonderful way to influence families, and why would that be the case?

ELKE WEBER: Now, I think that's a really good point. And, in this case, Jinpa's example is a good one. To consider how children can be a force for change, we must realize that many of our decisions are not deliberate. Many of the actions we take that impact the environment are habits, and quite a few are bad habits. We are old dogs and it's hard to teach us new tricks.

One way to think about influencing environmental change is to work generationally. As education instills better habits in young people, they will take actions that are better for the environment.

But it doesn't have to end there. Children can also become agents for change in the home, just as Jinpa was inspired to think more about the difference between trash and recycling. I've overheard many conversations in restaurants and public places where young people are the ones lecturing parents and grandparents about climate change or recycling. In some of my classes, the young men and women come to me and ask, "What can I tell my parents about environmental change? They don't think it's important, they don't believe it." They're familiar with the science, but what they really want to know is how to convince their elders that this is something they should act on.

HIS HOLINESS THE DALAI LAMA: I think one of the differences between younger and older people is flexibility and open-mindedness. Young people pay attention to new ideas whereas older people like to have more fixed ideas. Perhaps this has something to do with brain development as well. So our real hope is the younger generation. I am from the twentieth century, and our generation created a lot of problems, not only during the last century but lasting, ongoing problems. It may be late in the game for us to seriously influence older people, and we of the last century are getting ready to say goodbye. The youth of the twenty-first century are the planet's real humanity now. They have the ability and opportunity to bring change, to create a century of peace, dialogue, and compassion.

Even as global warming increases in intensity, they can work together in the spirit of brotherhood and sisterhood, share and find solutions. They are our real hope. Our work is to help them open their minds, to see and understand where we are and what is needed.

SALLIE MCFAGUE: Yes, those of us of the last century are certainly counting on the younger generation to help us. I have two granddaughters, and while, as Elke says, they are being trained in schools to be more concerned about these issues, one of the things that concerns me is their lack of what I would call "close encounters with the natural world." Television, the internet, and all indoor activities have made that connection very difficult. I was brought up in a one-room cabin, and I had a lot of close encounters with nature. I was able to run free in the woods, go looking for turtles, and things like that. A lot of today's children are deprived of that experience. Sitting in front of the TV, even if they are getting worthy instruction, can't take the place of the experience of having free time outdoors.

Kids aren't brought up that way now, and I wonder if that creates a deficit in developing profound empathy beyond intellectual awareness, through a feeling for the natural world that comes only with the experience of it.

HIS HOLINESS THE DALAI LAMA: Another challenge with today's youth, in addition to what you just pointed out, is the constant focus on external stimulation—for example, listening to music, watching sports, or going online. The reliance on external sensory stimulus has almost become a deliberate habit of seeking distraction, and that deprives them of going deeper into their own natural intelligence with focused attention. I think it would be interesting to do some research on this issue.

Motivating Youth versus Adults

ROSHI JOAN HALIFAX: This brings us back to Diana's question, which had to do with thinking about what kind of program would enhance young people's capacity to make decisions that are based more in discernment and moral responsibility.

ELKE WEBER: Diana's question was how to encourage everyone to be more energy efficient and to reduce the consumption of energy in the general population. Let's look at that for both children and adults.

Young children, in addition to having fresher minds, are also more idealistic, primarily because they have fewer material needs and obligations.

Their parents take care of their needs if they're fortunate, and so they have more space, and more attention for idealism and for the future. In the case of children, I would try to encourage them to make more conscious decisions that benefit the environment, and to think about how to trans-late their enthusiasm and intentions to others in their community and family. Children love to have an impact. One of the reasons we love video games is because there's always the promise of improvement. The next time around you might do better. It almost becomes an addiction to try to beat your last performance, and though that's bad at the extreme, the need to improve and cultivate mastery is very powerful. So for young children I would advocate a much more active, deliberate, and mindful approach.

When it comes to adults, we all have busy lives. We may worry about losing our jobs or our spouse, about making the mortgage payment. Con-serving energy becomes a much lower priority than our security needs. And there's the "drop in the bucket" syndrome—my action has such little impact on the big picture that it's not even worth worrying about. Given these barriers to making active decisions, I think, for adults, encouraging passive decisions is one of the more powerful tools. Setting defaults for everyone so that the nondecision is beneficial, such as the vegetarian meals or green suppliers of electricity to the grid. You can always choose cheaper, dirty energy, but if you don't bother with it, your passive choice has an impact.

Positive Messaging Is Best

CLARE PALMER: In line with the conversation about negative emotions, a few years ago two environmentalists named Michael Shellenberger and Ted Nordhaus published a paper called "The Death of Environmentalism." One of the things they argued was that environmentalism has always portrayed its message very negatively. They compared environmental-ism to the civil rights movement, pointing out that Martin Luther King didn't achieve anything with an "I have a nightmare" speech; rather, it was "I have a dream."

The argument suggested that environmentalists not frame the message as one of deprivation, not doing things, and restraint, but rather one about green jobs and the ways in which environmentalism could create a more flourishing economy. That kind of positive message would be more encouraging for people.

ELKE WEBER: That observation is very much in line with some of the points I've made this morning, and it's also in line with the idea of co-benefits that several of the speakers have articulated. These include health co-benefits, economic co-benefits, and even national security co-benefits. Our energy supplies are more secure when we generate energy from renewable sources, rather than importing them from the Middle East.

One thing to keep in mind is that you need to offer different positive messages for different groups. Some of us are concerned about too much consumption, the hedonic treadmill of doing more and working more so you can buy more. But in this state you are never satisfied, and you have to try harder. We all want to get off the hedonic treadmill, and that's a powerful motivation, and there's a lot of sociological and social science research that more consumption does not buy us happiness. That could be one message.

Other groups actually like the hedonic treadmill, but if they can save money by being more environmentally aware, by having a footprint that is smaller, because their workers are healthier and they can make more profits, that could be a good motivator for them.

Positive messages work best when they are specific, whereas the negative messages tend to be more general. We should all be worried about having to live in conditions of unbearable heat or about losing the world's glaciers. The negative messages tend to be more common and shared. The positive co-benefit impacts of action are more specific and localized, and therefore they are more complex. But in general I agree with that position.

HIS HOLINESS THE DALAI LAMA: With regard to the role of negative messages, if you do not also provide suggestions for solutions, then generally the negative approach is not effective. But if we underscore how these issues are due to our negligence and they are causing us and others suffering, perhaps that will get more attention. For example, if someone is ill but never goes to the doctor or takes medication, that is foolish. There seems to be a motivation to act in such a situation when we are faced with negative news. Similarly, the problems with the environment are our own creation, so wouldn't some negative message be appropriate to highlight what we have done and stimulate the initial inspiration to seek change?

Martin Luther King said he had a dream, but that was also couched in pointing out what was wrong with the treatment of others during the civil rights movement, how we were responsible, and the negative effects of our actions. It seems unrealistic to ignore the negative events.

JOHN DUNNE: Even in this discussion we have heard a lot of bad news, and you have said we need a method. Just hearing bad news without being provided solutions is one of the main problems. That's more like the nightmare without the dream. With the environmental movement, personally, I have often felt concerned that what needed to be done was, in a practical sense, beyond me. We also need practical guidance on what we can do.

Social and Religious Clout as Inspiration

DEKILA CHUNGYALPA: I became an environmentalist at a very young age. I was sent to the United States to study, and my friends and I created a recycling program that we were very proud of. We collected all the garbage, sorted it, and took it to the town center. When I went back home to Sikkim and proudly told my family about this, my grandmother was horrified. She said, "We didn't send you to the United States so you could become a street sweeper." I couldn't convince anybody at that time that the environment really mattered.

This is where I think the role of religion is so crucial. Over the years, His Holiness the Dalai Lama and His Holiness the Karmapa have really made the environment a focal point. A few years ago, I was home again and one of my aunts said she was very proud of what I did. I asked her why, and she said, "Because His Holiness the Dalai Lama thinks it's a very good idea that we protect the environment."

Even if people don't fully understand the problem, or haven't figured out the solution, there are other ways of motivating people to change their behavior. We don't have to convince every single person that this issue is the burning issue. Each person has a different set of concerns that he or she prioritizes. We, as environmentalists, demand that the environmental issue should be at the top. If somebody has a child that's seriously ill, that will be his or her primary concern. I think the real challenge for us is keeping people from shutting down around the environmental issue, which happens when information becomes overwhelming.

It seems to me that there are people like me who really enjoy getting information and come alive when we get a lot of science and facts. Then there's a group that shuts down and gets overwhelmed, primarily because they aren't being shown clearly how to make a decision. This is something we grapple with in the field every single day: Do I put the community's rights first, do I put the species' rights first, or do I put the forest's rights first? There have to be mechanisms to help us make decisions, and we need to design them.

Can Buddhist Debating Help Us Act?

JONATHAN PATZ: I fully agree that we've caused this problem, and therefore we can do something. It's not happening outside of us. I've been learning more about Buddhism and its incredibly intensive training, especially in debating. Since we're talking about a most difficult challenge of changing people's minds and behavior, I'm wondering if there are any best practices or approaches to changing people's minds and changing behavior from the Buddhist debating perspective?

HIS HOLINESS THE DALAI LAMA: In terms of the environmental issues, these are very new to us too. But yes, we do train in the art of debate, as it is very helpful to be able to understand the precise meaning of things, although sometimes this may not be the ultimate method, as debating training overemphasizes clarity and precision while reality is a lot messier than that. To approach more complex issues, you may have to use caveats such as "from this perspective."

On the other hand, debating can be a very powerful method in education, as it allows for precise conceptual distinctions, regardless of current reality, and can be very engaging for students.

There are essentially three levels of understanding: the first is hearing something, the second is acquiring information or knowledge, and the third is critical reflection. These are very important for going from hearsay to understanding, and even more so for being flexible about your opinion. When faced with new information, your prior convictions could be reevaluated or wrong.

Even the Buddha said, "Followers, scholars, and monks should not accept my teachings out of faith or devotion, but rather through thorough investigation and critical review." Now, that's a very scientific approach. There's always a distinction that needs to be made between the literal level, the definitive meaning, and provisional statements that require further interpretation.

I do feel that debating from the Nalanda tradition can make some contribution to the field of education. I have been making requests among the Tibetan scholars, those who have expertise in both modern scholarship and classical Buddhist scholarship, to develop teaching materials that would use the debating technique in contemporary subject matters. I recently saw a textbook by a young Amdo scholar on traditional Tibetan grammar that uses debating techniques to teach, and I'm hoping that we can approach more modern subjects with this method as well.

ROSHI JOAN HALIFAX: Thank you, Your Holiness and Elke. It's been an extremely rich session.

10 From Motivation to Action: A Buddhist View

PRESENTER: Thupten Jinpa, *Institute of Tibetan Classics*

ROSHI JOAN HALIFAX: Earlier, Elke explained the current psychological understanding of moving from motivation to action, and the challenges that we face in our decision making in the midst of this global dilemma. Thupten Jinpa will now explore this issue from the Buddhist perspective, to see what it means to move from a base of compassionate, or altruistic, aspiration to engagement, to actually engage in social and environmental transformation.

Jinpa will reference most of his insights from the Nalanda tradition; he was trained in the classical Tibetan monastic system. He is now a father, the main English-language translator for His Holiness the Dalai Lama, and also the translator of many Tibetan texts. He is an executive member of the Stanford Neurosciences Institute, a visiting scholar of the Center for Compassion and Altruism Research and Education, an adjunct professor at McGill University, and the Chairman of the Board of the Mind and Life Institute.

THUPTEN JINPA: Thank you. As Roshi Joan observed, this question of how we move from a set of beliefs and motivations to action and behavior change at the individual level is a question that has been approached by more than just contemporary Western psychology. This is a question that has also been considered quite seriously by most of the philosophical

202 ECOLOGY, ETHICS, AND INTERDEPENDENCE

traditions and contemplative traditions, and it has been a major focus of interest in the Buddhist tradition.

In the Buddhist tradition, the idea of spiritual liberation has been understood in terms of purification of the mind's toxic aspects and training the mind to perfect the beneficial qualities that are naturally present. This process has been conceptualized as a journey, a spiritual journey, and the term we use is "traveling the path." Part of traveling the path involves a strong belief in the possibility of change and transformation.

HIS HOLINESS THE DALAI LAMA: According to ancient Indian traditions, theistic and nontheistic, the concept is rooted in the law of causality. There are many levels of suffering, and suffering is due to wrong action. Wrong action stems from wrong motivation, and ultimately from ignorance. So in order to overcome suffering, we need only remove our ignorance. The ultimate source of suffering is ignorance, and the ultimate source of happiness is wisdom—they are both mental capacities. So the mind becomes very important, and the only way to overcome suffering is to train the mind.

Three Steps: View, Meditation, and Action

THUPTEN JINPA: I would like to begin with the larger conceptual framework, in which classical Buddhist tradition attempts to explain the mechanism of change and transformation. This is generally approached as a trio: view, meditation, and action.

View, or outlook, is the first stage. It includes understanding the nature of reality from a cognitive, or intelligence, perspective. From here, you can adopt an outlook, a way in which you see the world. Based upon this understanding, you develop certain attitudes toward others and the world, which, in turn, lead to aspirations and values. So this one area called *view* in fact refers to a whole set of processes.

HIS HOLINESS THE DALAI LAMA: The key factor here is the mind, and it is important to make a distinction between the sensorial mind and the mental, or thought, mind. Both ignorance and wisdom exist on the mental level, not on the sensorial level. Therefore, the concept of view does not apply at the level of the senses. However, in my discussions with modern scientists, there still do not seem to be clear, systematic distinctions between sensory versus nonsensory modalities, or conceptual and nonconceptual modalities.

When we talk about training the mind, it is not the same as sharpening the eyes with glasses or using hearing aids, or enhancing other physical senses. It's more complicated. We are talking about the mental level and thoughts.

THUPTEN JINPA: The second stage is referred to as meditation. When I use the term *meditation*, I'm using an English term to translate a Sanskrit and a Tibetan term. The Sanskrit term is *bhavana*, which means "to become," "to cultivate," and "to make it," whereas the Tibetan term, *gom*, means "cultivating familiarity" and "familiarization." The idea essentially refers to a process of habit formation. Through constantly learning a particular way of thinking, a way of seeing, and a way of experiencing, you acquire a habit. We could say it allows knowledge at the intellectual level to become internalized and integrated in two ways: on one side, through a wisdom component that includes intelligence, discernment, and insight, and on the other side, through a motivational component, including compassion and altruism. In other words, it includes elements of both value and affect in relation to the world.

This is Buddhism's response to the idea that to know good is to do good. Clearly, there are considerations here. Someone may know smoking is bad but continue to smoke. So the real question is, why is there often a gulf between knowledge and action?

The classical Buddhist, and perhaps Indian, traditions would argue that knowledge, on the intellectual level alone, is not enough. It needs to be internalized through some sort of cultivation. The Greeks explained this dilemma with the term *akrasia*, or weakness of will.

However, once you have formed a good habit through internalization and integration, you can move to the third stage: action. The kind of action we are talking about would arise naturally out of transformed states of mind.

This is why, when Clare talked about ethics, I raised the point that Buddhist ethics differ from Western ethics in that they aren't fundamentally rule-based, but rather more virtue-based. The focus is not so much on uncovering the right actions to take in each case, but more on the development of the individual's character. The right development of character will lead to natural, context-specific, ethical action.

So this is a very cursory road map derived from the Nalanda tradition. It is nonreligious, and it may help theorists and scientists look at the relationship between intellectual states of knowing and how those states can be translated into specific actions.

Spontaneous Right Action in Daily Life

THUPTEN JINPA: Of course it takes a long time to internalize and integrate knowledge, develop a value system, and spontaneously and naturally act from that place in the world. So the question becomes, how do we act on a day-to-day basis when confronted with various ethical challenges, be they environmental or other?

To address this, we'll draw from the writing of a great Nalanda teacher, Shantideva, who had tremendous influence on the Tibetan tradition. He wrote many texts, but two texts that are hugely influential are *A Guide to the Bodhisattva's Way of Life* and *Compendium of Training*.

As a quick clarification, Shantideva's influence was primarily in the area of bodhisattva activities, altruistic deeds, and actions. On the other hand, the Buddhist understanding of the nature of reality and the development of a worldview was mainly influenced by Nagarjuna and his immediate disciples.

These great Nalanda masters wrote extensively, and they wrote in prose, which lends itself to quite long texts, though they also wrote short verses that would summarize ideas, which lend themselves to easy memorizations.

In addressing learning in *Compendium of Training*, Shantideva says that refraining from engaging and indulging in fruitless activities that are essentially harmful is accomplished through constant mindfulness. And then he says that mindfulness comes from a deep dedication, and dedication arises from knowing the benefits of tranquility and striving for them.

There are causal connections being made between various mental factors, or processes. Shantideva is pointing out that, on a day-to-day basis, the key to living an ethical life is to bring into awareness your value system and your aspirations. This connects very beautifully to Elke's point that comes from contemporary psychological research: the important thing is to keep the intentions and goals active. This is exactly what Shantideva is pointing out here. We need to learn to have constant mindfulness in the face of everyday challenges. And this leads us to the next question: where does this kind of constant mindfulness come from?

Shantideva says it comes from a deep dedication to that particular pursuit. This is similar to Sallie's comments about deep awareness. Shantideva is talking about a form of profound motivation that is not just simple respect but a form of deep commitment and deep dedication. Then the question is, where does that kind of dedication come from? He says it comes from knowing the benefits of that particular pursuit, specifically the tranquility, peace, happiness, and joy that will arise from pursuing a particular course of action and striving for it.

Continuing, he identifies what he means by dedication. He says, "Now, as for dedication, this refers to turning your mind toward the concerned activities from deep within." It's a kind of character development, a value-system shift; not only do you turn your attention to it, but there is also a very strong and effective engagement with this particular pursuit. He describes this path as "an antidote against carelessness and negligence." Therefore, bringing mindfulness into awareness, one's values and aspirations become so important. But is deep dedication the only source of such constant mindfulness?

To answer this, I will cite from Shantideva's other text, where he acknowledges there are other ways of bringing mindfulness to the conscious level. He says, "Mindfulness comes easily through associating with one's spiritual mentor." This also implies that the kind of peer group with which you associate is very important, as are environmental influences. Of course he's primarily thinking about monastics, in which case associating with the right kind of people is very important. Those who are familiar with Tibetan Buddhist practice instructions know that there's strong emphasis placed on this. Another way to achieve mindfulness is "through the instruction of one's preceptor." The first directive has to do with being part of the right community, and this second one deals with specific instructions from one's teachers.

He also says fear is a powerful, motivating factor. This connects to our earlier discussions about the role of negative emotions as motivating factors.

The Positive Role of Negative Emotions

HIS HOLINESS THE DALAI LAMA: According to Buddhism, there are different varieties of fear. With certain fears, there is a real reason to be afraid, while with others, there is no real basis for the fear. The first kind of fear can be helpful by stimulating precaution, while the second usually causes unnecessary trouble.

As a negative emotion, fear can be helpful. Anger is similar. When anger is combined with compassion, a concern for others' well-being, it can bring out more essential, positive, and beneficial energy. On the other hand, when jealousy or hatred are combined with anger, that combination can bring out negative energy—it resides in a strong sense of "I" and "me," and can lead to bullying, harming, or exploiting others.

THUPTEN JINPA: When we are talking about mental processes, we are talking about a very complex phenomenon. Therefore we cannot pinpoint one mental disposition and say this is positive or this is negative. We have to take into account its function in a given context and understand the many other factors that are part of that process.

Similarly, in today's wider embrace of meditation, many people place a high value on thoughtlessness. Here, too, there are many different levels of thoughtlessness.

With any state of mind or emotion, we must consider the context and all the angles, otherwise we are at risk of going to the extreme and taking one grain of rice and saying all the grains must be exactly the same.

Shantideva acknowledges that fear can be an important motivating factor. He then indicates the ideal practitioners of mindfulness: they are "the fortunate who are dedicated." He refers to the people who have deep dedication as "fortunate ones," because in them mindfulness will arise quite easily.

Countering Laziness

THUPTEN JINPA: As Elke pointed out, human beings are very, very complex, with all sorts of competing values and mental processes operating at the same time. Additionally, there are many other conditions basic to our psychology, one of which is laziness. While Elke gave an interesting example of how one can turn that laziness into opportunity, laziness has been a major point of inquiry for the Buddhist psychologists, including Shantideva, and with this in mind, I thought it would be useful to share a classical Indian Buddhist take on how to deal with the problem of laziness.

This idea was most systematically developed in the writings of Asanga and his brother, Vasubandhu. They were both great fourth-century Indian Nalanda masters who came from the Peshawar region, which is modern-day Pakistan.

In classical Buddhist psychology, we unpack laziness into various components, or aspects.

One form of laziness is simple procrastination: "I'll do it tomorrow" is an attitude that we are all familiar with, probably a close friend to many of us. Another form of laziness, and an interesting one, is referred to as "habitual indulgence in contrary behavior." We don't normally see this characterized as laziness in contemporary psychology, but it is a form of laziness because it's a form of avoidance. A third but important form of laziness is being discouraged. This form of laziness is referred to as "self-deprecation"; in almost a self-insulting way, you lack confidence and have a kind of low esteem that makes you underestimate your actual capacity. This is seen as a form of laziness because it prevents us from taking action.

These great Buddhist masters offer several remedies, or antidotes, to counter laziness. One remedy is called *shraddha* in Sanskrit. This is a very complex term that is often translated as "faith," although that is probably the wrong translation in this case. It means something more like admiration, confidence, and trust. It has both cognitive as well as affective dimensions. One could say, "I have *shraddha* in my teacher," which is not purely cognitive, it's more a sense of entrustment: I entrust myself to the guidance of my teacher.

Three other remedies are aspiration (including the practice of cultivating strong aspiration), effort, and suppleness (a kind of fluency that comes from gaining expertise in contemplative practice). Suppleness includes a very strong component of joy as a counterforce to laziness. Here, it's worth noting that joy as a motivating factor is a very important concept that occurs throughout the writings of many great Indian Buddhist masters, including the great Nalanda masters. I think this is an idea that contemporary psychologists and behavioral scientists could consider carefully. Think of children learning an instrument or a sport. At first they may need encouragement, support, or discipline, but once they are competent enough to take pleasure in the activity, it's much easier for them to engage.

Joy can take different forms, including the pursuit of something very difficult, because of the value inherent in the goal. Athletes, for example, value winning, and this value can be so strong that they take joy in the pursuit of that goal, not just achieving the goal. This is an important insight from the classical Indian Buddhist and Tibetan traditions, which could have implications in the way we design curriculum for children, for example. Related to this, in Tibetan monastic debate, if you observe the monks debating, one interesting observation is that it is usually very joyful. They are laughing and it is very animated, although occasionally someone may lose his temper!

To summarize, from the Nalanda Indian and Buddhist traditions, we can see certain steps outlined. We begin with awareness, and as His Holiness always emphasizes, awareness needs to be deep. This kind of awareness comes from weighing the pros and cons and doing a cost-benefit analysis. Initially, cognition, intelligence, and discernment play a very important role; then, based on that awareness, you learn admiration and aspiration toward deeper awareness. From that develops a confidence and deep dedication, which in turn leads to more effort, joy, and enthusiasm. All of this activates a goal, and the pursuit of that goal, which can then lead to action.

Elke talked about how we use different mechanisms to move from motivation to action. Sometimes rules are more effective, and the Buddhist tradition would acknowledge that. Although the importance of discernment, insight, and intelligence is crucial to action, when it comes to dealing with life on a day-to-day basis, the ideal is to be able to respond immediately by bringing to mind whatever your values and aspirations are, which could be considered "rules" of action. I would argue that the role of intelligence, insight, and wisdom are important to cultivating and transmitting our values. This is especially true for teaching children.

The Role of Culture and Setting

THUPTEN JINPA: His Holiness gave the example of how Tibetan children instinctively avoid stepping on bugs. That's a culturally acquired value, and once you have internalized that value, then the behavior comes very naturally. When confronted with an actual ethical dilemma that involves competing values in a given situation, then the role of intelligence and wisdom become very critical. But in most of our lives, the ideal scenario would simply be to draw from our value system and aspirations, and act naturally in the best possible way for a given situation.

The great Buddhist masters of the Indian Nalanda tradition and the Tibetan masters also emphasize the importance of environment. For monastics, for example, a great emphasis is placed on avoiding situations in which you might be confronted with the possibility of breaking a vow. There's a beautiful line in one of Vasubandhu's texts where he says that those of us who haven't rid ourselves of our strong emotional afflictions, if we are confronted with a temptation, are likely to project qualities of attractiveness onto whatever is tempting us, and then we act in an afflicted manner. These kinds of insights suggest that both the individual work on the mind and the environment play important roles.

We talked about voluntary simplicity, or voluntary poverty. I've been living in the West for almost twenty years now, and people tend to look at simplicity in negative terms as lacking something or being deprived of something. But simplicity actually frees you. For example, if a family has two cars, then they also have the bills for two cars, the insurance for two cars, and need the garage space or parking for two cars. If there's only one car, then there would be times when there is a conflict, but you can take a taxi or public transportation. Maybe it's a little bit of an inconvenience, but economically it's cheaper and a more efficient way of dealing with the question of getting a second car. People tend to forget that simplicity actually can lead to a greater quality of life.

So, looking at the insights coming from contemporary psychology, the science of behavior, and also from Buddhist psychology, there are stages in the mental processes of going from knowing to action where people can take more proactive approaches to transforming their value system and aspirations. Each individual, each of us, can really make a difference.

ELKE WEBER: One thing that strikes me in what Jinpa outlined is a very nice integration of the different levels of analysis that Western psychology also emphasizes. On the one hand, we know things analytically after very carefully deconstructing a problem into its components and then reassembling it and deeply understanding it. But that's in our heads, and it's important to appreciate reality not only through analysis but also through more affect-based processes. I think what the Buddhist approach does very nicely—rather than saying they coexist and maybe they feed into each other—is spell out how they interact with each other, and how they go back and forth; awareness and cognitive processing actually can lead to an emotional experience that's positive and then can feed back into rational analysis.

Motivation and Deeper Awareness in Self and Others

GREGORY NORRIS: We heard from His Holiness this morning that there are three levels of understanding: hearing, critical reflection, and experience. This afternoon, we learned that there are these two levels of mind: the sensory level and then the deeper mental level. With this, I am realizing that I've been translating the term *awareness* much too shallowly. It's something about being full that leads to awareness. I'm asking myself, How, in the field that we work in, can this be applied? I'm feeling a challenge to our field. We tend to just convey information at the surface level: "this is a green product" or "this is 22 kilograms," but we're missing the other levels. So I'm asking myself how we can cultivate practices that deepen the awareness of both the environmental impacts of our actions and the benefits that we might achieve.

HIS HOLINESS THE DALAI LAMA: I think in most cases, you first learn from your teachers and books; that is the first level of awareness, or understanding. Then you undertake research, and through your own research and experimentation you uncover trends, patterns, or truths. With this, you develop conviction, the second level. And after time, this experiential process becomes internalized and automatic, and that's the third level. In strict Buddhist terms, the third level of understanding is also defined in terms of concentrative power, but generally speaking, one can apply this to the question of being and becoming habituated in action.

To address your question further, which was about how to communicate with others beyond the first level of understanding, you need to set up some kind of challenge that engages others in those deeper levels. For example, students studying the environment would be given a particular situation or issue by the teacher, but then asked to analyze that issue, raise questions, and look for contradictions, and perhaps they would be encouraged to do so through some kind of award system. That's a way to bring enthusiasm to the inquiry and engagement at deeper levels of understanding.

Even in a monastic debate, it's not always the case that the person dedicated to debating is being motivated by higher ideals, such as seeking liberation; rather, they may be, in fact, trying to put someone on the spot. And when someone succeeds in doing this, people say, "Oh, he was brilliant, he put that guy in his place," and then people get a deep sense of satisfaction. And that outcome may serve as the motivation for the debater. So you need to find a way to encourage and bring enthusiasm to your students to engage in more critical and analytical considerations of the "surface understandings." And then give them praise when they do so.

It's a function of the teacher's skill. Even in monasteries, you see different styles of teaching. Some teachers and scholars just go through the texts word by word, but the more skilled instructors say, "You can read the texts on your own," and then they pick out some of the more difficult points from the texts and engage the students in analysis and debate.

Now, in the debating tradition, the custom is to always cite the authorities and important thinkers of the past, and not go beyond these boundaries. However, on certain subjects, such as Middle Way philosophy or epistemology, I think we should move away from this custom and pursue a more open line of critical inquiry.

Overcoming Depression and Exhaustion through Commitment and Joy

DEKILA CHUNGYALPA: I appreciate the reference to joy and enthusiasm, because I think most environmental activists are actually optimists pretending to be pessimists. At the same time, I read an article recently that said environmental activists are facing a particular kind of depression because they're screaming as loud as they can about the environmental problems we're facing and it feels like nobody's listening. So there is a real issue of depression and exhaustion that's taking place among environmental activists. My question to His Holiness and to Jinpa is, when that happens, how do we, from a Buddhist perspective, change this feeling of exhaustion and depression?

HIS HOLINESS THE DALAI LAMA: Shantideva makes the point that before you commit yourself to a particular line of work or take on a challenge, it is important to evaluate that pursuit, to see whether you are capable or not. And once you are committed, then you should not have second thoughts about it. But you should not just rush and grab on to something that you are not able to handle.

Another practice for when we are in the thick of it, in the middle of a pursuit such as environmental activism, and we feel overwhelmed or alone because nobody is listening, is to step back and take a wider perspective on the issue. Often we get so focused on the issue that we lose sight of the context, and simply shifting the contextual view on the issue can provide a change in perspective and perhaps some relief to the overwhelm.

One important practice is continuously making an effort to cultivate joy. Even in my own life, if I look at progress over short periods of time, there isn't always something to be joyful about. But if I look over a decade or two decades, then there is tremendous room for joy. This is true with the environmental movement, too. There are many areas where environmentalists have had tremendous success. In most schools in developed countries children are being taught about and engaging in projects on the environment. Environmental awareness and concern is reaching into wider cultural values. These are important achievements.

Carrying the Message to Skeptics

DIANA LIVERMAN: I'm wondering if there's anything I can draw from this perspective to help in conversations with people who are very skeptical about climate change, especially those who are actually taking actions like funding politicians who don't believe in climate change. On the occasions where I have the opportunity to talk to these people, is there anything I can learn about how to approach somebody who would look at the graph of rising temperatures and almost be in denial about it? Are there any lessons I can learn about converting skeptics?

HIS HOLINESS THE DALAI LAMA: There is a classical Indian text by Aryadeva, a senior student of Nagarjuna. In his text, called *Four Hundred Stanzas on the Middle Way*, he talks about the skillful ways and means of teachers when communicating certain ideas. One important point is to take into account the sensibilities and mental disposition of the listener or the student.

In my own experience, when I talk with someone who may have different views or be in disagreement, first I consider that on the human level we have no differences. We both want to be happy and have close connections in life. If we start from a place that emphasizes differences, such as nationality, faith, or race, we will encounter an inevitable barrier. To remove that barrier, we need to start with a common human goal: living a happy life. In my opinion, to achieve that we have to have this commonality in our own view, which often enables a shift in the other person, allowing more openness, connection, or closeness. If we lead with the differences, we risk encouraging defensiveness, which is usually followed by offense or attack, and there's no way to connect.

Information Overload: Internet versus Deep Awareness

SALLIE MCFAGUE: I'm wondering how to address bringing superficial knowledge to deep awareness. Today, we have so much information on the internet; it is very easy to find out information about everything. People think that that the information is going to give them quick solutions, like a magic bullet. What I hear is that we need deep knowledge. One can see how with monks who live lives of deep meditation, this could occur. I have been studying the lives of the saints for many years and have learned about the same gradual journey of spiritual development in their lives. But for most people, how do we answer the question "What should I do?" when what they really mean is "What is the quick solution for this?" What would the Buddhist answer be for moving from superficial knowledge, such as information from the internet, to deep knowledge?

HIS HOLINESS THE DALAI LAMA: This is a serious question and challenge for those of us who live in the information age, with multiple emails daily and Google creating a superhighway of information. The general attitude—not only in the West, but also in the East, and excluding authoritarian societies—is that more information is better. But we know that more information is not necessarily better as we become paralyzed by information overload. To address how to deal with this, I would again refer to the great Nalanda masters and ask the fundamental question, what kind of value system do we want?

Once we are clear in this regard, then we can set priorities and aspirations based on that value system for both immediate and long-term considerations. From this place, when confronted with a deluge of information, we will have quick discernment and the ability to sort what's relevant and what's not.

Cultivating Deeper Attention

JOHN DUNNE: You have a term to describe one function of mindfulness as that which blocks carelessness, but I think that the Tibetan term you have in mind can also convey a sense of being overcome or even defeated by distraction. Is that right?

THUPTEN JINPA: Yes.

JOHN DUNNE: Usually mindfulness is described as that which prevents distraction, stopping the mind from wandering off. What's interesting about that term is the implication. When you say that mindfulness prevents us from being overcome, you are saying that there's a hook in the distracter, so to speak; there is something actively pulling the mind away. Something is becoming salient, and one is losing track of the main goal. In other words, instead of keeping the eye on the prize, one is now distracted by something else. I think what this term is implying is that the role of this kind of mindfulness is to prevent that kind of scatterbrained effect. To some extent, I think that is a function of your value system, but it's also a function of a certain kind of training, a capacity for concentration, a capacity to maintain a calm mind, especially in difficult situations. Maybe this means that a little bit of basic meditation, maybe a secular style of mindfulness meditation or something along those lines, might actually be part of the solution. I think there is a great tendency for our modern lives to create this effect of being overcome or defeated by distraction. Our attention is pulled away by things that seem to be important, when actually they're not; they're just superficial. So, in some ways, part of the Buddhist answer here is really about the development of certain kinds of cognitive capacities for concentration, a stable form of concentration.

SALLIE MCFAGUE: Simone Weil, a French philosopher, said that even a child working on a math problem would increase his or her attention. It doesn't have to be prayer; just seriously trying to solve a math problem can be a lesson in in-depth awareness and attention. It's so rare that we really pay attention to something outside ourselves. I agree, the internet has helped students access numerous connections to different kinds of information, but they don't go deeply into the center. How to help educational systems and people develop radical attention in an age where the computer is fast becoming the main way people read and learn is an important question.

Addressing Addiction

JONATHAN PATZ: To add to our discussion, you may have heard the saying "Chance favors a prepared mind." Unless we're really prepared and paying attention, we won't learn and we won't make discoveries. With regard to awareness, and first becoming mindful and then aware and then taking action, I'm curious about addictive behavior. With smoking, even with awareness, people can't just decide to quit, because they're addicted. Many of our behaviors are addictions. People argue that we are addicted to oil and that many of the things in our lives are connected to oil addiction, because they use or are made from oil. So how do you deal with these extra challenges of addictive behavior?

HIS HOLINESS THE DALAI LAMA: One obvious thing would be to weigh the pros and cons of a particular behavior. When we speak about weighing the pros and the cons, again we are coming back to the point about awareness, the role of awareness.

We also see societal differences. In some parts of the world, cigarette smoking is prohibited in public spaces. There are signs and people modify their behavior accordingly. In other countries there isn't the same awareness and explicit caution, and in those areas we see more people smoking.

So there are two ways in which we need to deal with addiction. One is the individual's self-motivation, and at the same time there could be more societal measures taken.

Where Change Happens: Individual versus Society

ELKE WEBER: Both my presentation and Jinpa's dealt primarily with individual action. I'm wondering what prescription, or what diagnosis, your framework gives for collective action; how do we coordinate actions between individuals?

HIS HOLINESS THE DALAI LAMA: If you look at psychology, whether it is contemporary Western psychology or classical Buddhist psychology, generally it speaks from the perspective of an individual. That is the nature of psychology. When we try to take into account the societal impact, social psychology becomes a much more complicated business. One important consideration in both Western and Buddhist psychology that relates to

218 ECOLOGY, ETHICS, AND INTERDEPENDENCE

society is the important role that the surrounding environment plays in our behavior.

THUPTEN JINPA: If you look at many of the instructions in the Buddhist texts, there are constant reminders of this effect, although it was never systematically developed as a subfield of psychology. And in the end, whether we talk about society or community, ultimately the units are individuals. It is a collection of individuals that compose society, that compose community. At the emergent level there may be certain properties that the collective displays that the individual may not display, but the fact is communities and societies are collections of individuals. Therefore, the Buddhist approach overall has been to emphasize the individual. If the individuals within the collective change, the collective will naturally change as well.

When it comes to environmental issues, which are the topic of concern here, it's much more complicated. Part of the challenge comes from the fact that what needs to be done is not that clear, and the recommendations have huge immediate implications for our current lifestyle and behavior.

More than twenty years ago, I had the honor of accompanying His Holiness to Germany soon after the collapse of the Berlin Wall. There was a lot of discussion about a new world order, and His Holiness was part of a small group of thinkers that spent about two days discussing this idea of a new world order. I remember very vividly His Holiness making this very important point: "At some point," he said, "the affluent Western societies, as well as Japan and others, need to take seriously the whole premise of modern economy and their belief in perpetual growth as a measurement of economic success. Sooner or later, people living in the affluent societies will have to learn to lower their standard of life in terms of consumption." I remember being very struck, because that was one of the first times I had ever been to the West. And this theme of consumerism continues today. We are so used to thinking that this is the way to live, and the governments are so used to assessing their success, or failure, by using only growth as a measurement. So the question is, how do we change that? To do so, there needs to be a movement, both on the individual level and on the societal level.

HIS HOLINESS THE DALAI LAMA: If I may add one thing, in addition to material value, there is also inner or spiritual value. Material value is limited; spiritual value is limitless. And while daily we hear people talking about these two values, I'm not convinced that people fully understand inner value, even just the ability to rest and relax on a mental level. In modern society, material value is more prized as a path to contentment, but it is limited. The truer path to contentment is found in spiritual value, which is not concerned with material and physical things, and is limitless. But, again, I think this misunderstanding stems from a lack of awareness.

ROSHI JOAN HALIFAX: The question I just want to bring forward has to do with the lack of contentment of probably everybody in this entire room with regard to what's happening to our earth and to human beings on our earth, and all of the living systems. I think that lack of contentment is really essential. It has to do with addressing the truth of suffering, the first noble truth. Is there a mandate within Buddhism to engage directly in social and environmental transformation, to actually become proactive, to deal with psychosocial and political issues directly, or are we taking another approach?

HIS HOLINESS THE DALAI LAMA: When the great Nalanda masters were alive, the society of India was very different from today. We probably need to invite them to come back and ask for their advice. But if they had written in our age, they would have definitely talked about social issues. For instance, the *Jewel Garland*, which was written by Nagarjuna as a letter to a king, has very explicit sections dealing with the king's social responsibilities to his subjects. Such texts are seen as a genre of text, referred to as *nitishastra*, which means a treatise on governance.

ROSHI JOAN HALIFAX: That's really important for us to hear, because the prevailing view of a Buddhist practitioner is that the practitioner is somewhat individualistic and somewhat passive. I think that having an engaged perspective is something that we need to rearticulate, or perhaps is a new articulation of Buddhism, but looking for sources in traditional texts is helpful.

JOHN DUNNE: There are also a number of sutras that consider this issue. And there is a way in which I think a Buddhist version of social policies and social activism and responsibility could be created. I think that's probably emerging in the Buddhist world, a vision of social responsibility, now that Buddhism is becoming part of the modern world.

THUPTEN JINPA: Thailand is quite well developed, and that is a place where the monastic members have attempted to write treatises dealing with contemporary issues and social issues.

JOHN DUNNE: And in Sri Lanka as well, there's what's known as Sarvodaya, the Uplift Movement, which has been very active in this way. And of course Thich Nhat Hanh, who is Vietnamese, is an important figure in this regard. It's interesting that in the modern Buddhist world, some of this movement has begun.

HIS HOLINESS THE DALAI LAMA: While we are exploring the possibilities in Buddhism, I want to reiterate that no one religion, no matter how popular, will ever be universal. So when we are discussing issues that concern the whole world, seeking a solution from Buddhism alone is not right. There are many different religious traditions, and out of genuine respect for them, I don't think we should create the impression that Buddhism has all the answers. It's important to emphasize that contributions from our tradition deal primarily with working with the mind and dealing with destructive emotions, and that Buddhist practice has certain goals and objectives without which it's not Buddhism. Take for example someone engaged in shamatha meditation, or some other form of concentration meditation. If the practice is not motivated by the aspiration to seek liberation, you cannot call that a Buddhist meditation.

So, in characterizing our conversation, it's not so much Buddhism and science but Buddhist science and philosophy and Western science.

JOHN DUNNE: When we think of the philosophical idea of interdependence, it seems to be an important view in how we approach science. It took Western science quite a long time to come to the point of view where interdependence is the nature of reality. I'm wondering whether that's because there wasn't a philosophical tradition in Europe that strongly upheld the notion of interdependence, whereas if there were great physicists in the Buddhist world, perhaps the notion of an interdependent reality would have come up earlier. I am curious about the role of philosophy and ideas in interdependence. Do these play an important role in changing the way we do science?

HIS HOLINESS THE DALAI LAMA: When engaging in discussions with scientists, the concept of origination by means of dependence comes up continuously. On the other hand, not all Buddhists subscribe to this concept.

There could be areas where the Buddhist understanding of dependent origination could make a contribution. For example, in quantum physics, at some point, the very notion of reality breaks down, which could lead to a nihilistic position that nothing really exists. In these types of situations, the Middle Way philosophies and characterizations of reality in terms of radical dependence could be helpful contributions.

11 Presence and Action Are Needed

PRESENTER: His Holiness the Seventeenth Karmapa

JOHN DUNNE: It is now my pleasure to introduce His Holiness the Karmapa, a highly respected teacher within Tibetan Buddhism and the leader of the Karma Kagyu lineage. The many practitioners and monasteries in the Karma Kagyu lineage—and in other lineages as well—look to his Holiness the Karmapa not only for spiritual guidance but also for practical advice and guidelines for the effective and ethical management of monasteries, retreat centers, and other such institutions. In this context, His Holiness has placed great emphasis on the importance of environmental awareness as an aspect of spiritual practice, and he has also initiated concrete environmental policies in Kagyu monasteries and other institutions. Monastic institutions have traditionally been guided by the ancient code known as the Vinaya, and now it's as though His Holiness the Karmapa has offered us a green Vinaya—a set of precepts for helping the earth. As I now ask His Holiness to speak on the topic of this meeting, I hope that he will be willing to share with us something about his approach to caring for the environment, including the types of policies that he has implemented and also the underlying rationale within his tradition that provides the motivation for environmental awareness and action.

A New Perception

HIS HOLINESS THE KARMAPA: Actually, a lot of the points that I wanted to discuss have already been covered, including scientific, spiritual, and philosophical considerations.

223

My own effort on environmental issues is really quite small. I appreciate John's nice words, but I am not as engaged compared to many others.

I can't recall a specific catalyst that first engaged me with environmental work, but one thing that I do remember, which was an important factor, was a conference on the environment that I participated in. At that conference it became very clear that we interact with all aspects of the environment every day, such as water and trees. I realized that we are part of an interdependent system, even though we often naively think of these things as being somehow external to ourselves. In other words, it became very clear how the presence of things like water and trees is deeply intertwined with the well-being and survival of the human species on the planet. That left a very strong impression on me and also in the minds of many monastic colleagues who attended the conference.

Prior to that, in our naive attitude toward the environment, we saw trees and water as only part of the landscape, without a sense that they are alive or that they have a unique significance. After the conference, when I looked at trees, there was a qualitatively different perspective that included an awareness of the importance of the interconnectedness between human well-being, human beings, the trees, the water, and the natural world altogether. That also leads to a sense of connection, a sense of, one could even say, affection toward these natural things.

In my case, I was fortunate to have been born and raised in a rather isolated, nomadic region where day-to-day living brought one very close to nature. There was a lot of wild, open space and lots of greenery. There were beautiful, snowy mountains and an abundance of wildlife. Because of this, I had, from an early age, an aesthetic appreciation of the natural beauty of the environment. And because of this appreciation and my personal experience, I have a sense of affection, a kind of valuing of the environment and nature.

Therefore, when the question of environmental conservation and protection came up, it seemed very logical to me because of my upbringing. Later, when I came to India and was engaged in talking about the environment, I was fortunate enough to be able to tap into these memories from my youth and recall the natural beauty of those experiences.

Many people in our modern society live in cities and huge metropolitan areas, so they do not have the kind of fortunate experience I had, the opportunity to really have an experiential appreciation of nature. Perhaps for them it may be more difficult to have that kind of emotional connection with the beauty and importance of nature.

For All Sentient Beings

HIS HOLINESS THE KARMAPA: One thing I strive toward is to find a way of making sure that environmental protection does not remain a mere philosophical concept. Rather, I want to find a way to enable people to connect emotionally with the idea of environmental protection—that is something that I feel is very important.

Because of my conviction, I started an ecomonastic initiative in 2009, where monasteries and nunneries were able to become trained in environmental science and solutions, and learned how to manage environmental projects in their own sites and communities. After the first two years of such training programs, the monasteries that were involved came together and requested that they be known as an ecomonastic association under me: this is now known as Rangjung Khoryug Sungkyob Tsokpa. At first, I wasn't sure what I would be able to accomplish; I doubted my ability and whether or not anything could be achieved through this initiative. But later I realized that this is an extremely worthy pursuit because in the Buddhist tradition, particularly in Mahayana Buddhism, the highest ideal—one could even say dream or aspiration—is to help as many sentient beings as possible.

When we think about it, the environment is the basis for the survival and well-being of all sentient beings. It is clear that by protecting the environment, we are serving the needs and welfare of all the sentient beings that depend upon the environment in which they live.

Furthermore, I would argue that protecting the environment is perhaps one of the best opportunities that we have as Buddhist practitioners to bring the ideal of serving sentient beings' needs into practice. Therefore, it is a pursuit and a goal in which Buddhist practitioners need to engage with great joy and recognition of the opportunity this offers us. This is something very valuable that we need to embrace.

For example, in Buddhist texts, such as in Shantideva's *Guide to the Bodhisattva's Way of Life*, if we look at the aspirations that Shantideva expresses for a bodhisattva, we see him intending, "May I be able to serve sentient beings even as resources for their everyday use," such as water, trees, and even as space. Of course, in reality, we cannot become these things that sentient beings need, but we can protect the natural environment, which the sentient beings directly depend on to live. So by taking care of the natural environment, in a sense, we are also trying to fulfill these aspirations of the bodhisattvas.

The Barriers of Fixed Ideas

HIS HOLINESS THE KARMAPA: Unfortunately, as we have been discussing in this meeting, trying to impress upon an audience the specific and urgent aspects of environmental issues is not an easy matter. For example, I attended a conference where Dekila was a presenter and the topic of biodiversity came up. As part of that discussion, the importance of protecting tigers was introduced. Some people responded by saying, "We don't need to protect tigers. Actually, they are harmful; they eat all the deer and livestock." I understand that Dekila had a lot of difficulty arguing for the importance of protecting animals that are predators, like tigers.

At a later conference, we were again discussing the importance of wildlife protection, and I took the opportunity to readdress the point about protecting or not protecting tigers. I told the assembly that if we did not protect tigers we would not have tigers, and then how would one understand the *Jataka Tales*, the stories of the Buddha's previous lives? In one of those stories, the Buddha sacrifices his life to feed a tigress. How would you explain that if there were no tigers?

That was one point I raised, which I followed with the scientific point about the importance of all species, even predators, in maintaining the balance in the food chain. If we get rid of one particular species, even though it may be a predator, that action will impact the entire food chain, which will have a greater impact on the environment. In fact, if you think about it, human beings are more dangerous than tigers, because tigers only eat what they need, but we kill everything whether we need it or not. Earlier, Matthieu talked about how millions of animals are killed, especially in the breeding and farming processes, to provide meat for humans to consume. So if you use the argument that predators are harmful or evil and therefore shouldn't be allowed to live, we would have to conclude that it is actually human beings that shouldn't be around—not tigers.

Dispelling Ignorance

HIS HOLINESS THE KARMAPA: From a Buddhist perspective, the root of environmental degradation is really our own ignorance, as well as self-centeredness, selfishness, and other similar attitudes and traits. For example, our juvenile attitude when we think about "me," "I," and "mine" perceives "I" and "me" as somehow being completely autonomous and independent. But the reality is, if we look at everything that we interact with—our clothes, or food that we eat, even the air that we breathe—we are completely dependent upon factors outside us, other than us. And it is through this dependence that our survival is ensured. Once we recognize this fact, we should value those things outside of ourselves because we understand that they are crucial for our own survival and welfare. Further, we should see that their survival and welfare is deeply intertwined with our reality, actions, and behaviors. Until this interdependent relationship is understood on a fundamental level, it is very difficult for one to make a shift in thinking.

People may listen to such rationale and say, "Yes, yes," but if there is not fundamental change in the way they see the world, they will continue in the perceptions and actions they have now.

We can take Buddhist concepts such as emptiness and no-self, which can be explored in sophisticated philosophical analysis, and use them simply in our everyday lives to cultivate the understanding of interdependence, that everything is part of our existence. If we are able to do this, to relate Buddhist teachings such as no-self and emptiness in this manner, then there is a real chance that people can be awakened from the slumber of ignorance, that their eyes can be opened to see the world in a new way.

The Prison of "I" and "Mine"

HIS HOLINESS THE KARMAPA: I often say that many of us who are caught in this self-centered way of thinking are, in a sense, living in the prison of "I" and "mine." When you're living in a prison, then there are boundaries and limits imposed upon your ability to interact with the world. You may be able to interact with a few of your close relatives and family members, but beyond that, the outside world is closed for you. Although the outside world is there, because there's no connection to your day-to-day life, you are not relating to it.

Similarly, if we live in this prison of "I" and "mine," then, although in reality we are all interconnected, we live a life as if we were separate, where our interactions with the rest of the world are very, very limited.

For example, with this way of thinking, someone living in India who hears about the production of a particular hazardous chemical in a US factory will probably not make any effort to connect it to their own well-being because it is so far away. "It's in the United States," they'll say. "I'm here; there's no connection." If we reverse this example, people living in the United States may not care about the climate-change impacts that we are suffering so drastically from here in the Himalayas.

A Fundamental Change

HIS HOLINESS THE KARMAPA: If we move out of the prison of "I" and "mine," we can begin to relate to the world from a wider point of view. His Holiness the Dalai Lama often talks about the importance of seeing the bigger picture and that the reality of the modern world is that interconnectedness is increasing. So, in order to change our behavior, we are first going to have to make a very fundamental change in the way in which we see the world.

This fundamental change in the way in which we see the world is so crucial that it could be compared to the analogy of a tree. When we think of economic growth today, it is as though we are looking at the beautiful foliage of a tree—the modern world is so attracted by and caught up in admiration of its shiny leaves and branches that we neglect what is most important: the health of the roots underground. Similarly, all we care about is what we get from nature; we don't notice that nature is being completely emptied of its resources.

When I watch the news on TV, what is immediately evident is that our world leaders are, for the most part, obsessed by two topics: economics and politics. Beyond that, few people seem to be really paying attention to the fundamental questions of human survival and well-being, or to the environment as the basis for our survival and well-being. And once we've lost that fundamental perspective, even if we succeed at the economy and politics, we will still be lost and without a basis for survival. We will continue to admire the leaves and chose to ignore the rotting roots of the tree, and it might be too late by the time we wake up.

So that is essentially what I have to say, and I wound up saying a lot.

Many of the speakers have come here from great distances specifically to discuss this topic, and this conference has been organized partly at my request. So in sharing I would also like to say thank you, and that I am happy to have had this opportunity to learn from you. Also, over the past few days, all of the speakers have offered their insights and enthusiasm, and for my part, I would like to make an effort to ensure that these proceedings get more widely shared in the Tibetan community, particularly the monastic community. Personally, this has been a wonderful, educational experience. I learned a lot, and I also felt very, very touched and moved. The speakers spoke not only with expertise and knowledge but also with passion; it is obvious that each one of you is very committed to this in your day-to-day life. All of this made me feel very moved and touched, and also encouraged. I would like to look to you, when it comes to environmental issues, as models and examples to try to follow. Thank you.

SALLIE MCFAGUE: First, I want to thank you deeply for the journey that you have shared with us, and especially to point to your important experiences as a child. We're back to the trees, again—trees that moved you to be able to see another natural being, not as an object, but as a subject. Martin Buber, a Western philosopher, has said the difference between the prison of "I" and "mine," which I thought was a wonderful expression of yours, and the ability to say "I" and "thou," or "I" and "you," is to see the whole world as subject to subject rather than subject to object. I think your journey from development as a child is a wonderful illustration of how one moves from these early experiences to become an environmental activist, as you have become, and able to move the community in this direction. I think the way you have expressed and embodied the raising of consciousness from the imprisonment of the self to the gesture of seeing another as a "thou," as a subject, is beautiful, and I want to thank you, deeply, for sharing that story with us.

ELKE WEBER: Your Holiness, you're clearly a very important role model in your own right. We talked a lot about vegetarianism at this conference, and I know you are vegetarian, and you asked your followers to follow your example. Can you say a little bit about that?

HIS HOLINESS THE KARMAPA: When I was in Tibet and living in Tsurphu Monastery, I was actually known for loving meat. In Tsurphu, there is a uniquely prepared dried jerky that is famous all over Tibet. It is quite popular; it could be used as bribery for the officials in Lhasa. So when I was in Tibet, I was especially fond of this jerky and used to eat great amounts of it. But after coming to India I found that, first of all, the kinds of meat that Tibetans love—like yak, sheep, and lamb—are very rare here. You have to buy goat meat, which is a bit smelly, and not as delicious. So that's part of what influenced me!

But putting jokes aside, I first noticed this issue while watching documentaries about hunting on the Discovery Channel. What became very clear to me was that the people who were hunting animals really had no consideration that what was being hunted was as a living being. They treated them purely as objects, and that had a huge impact on me. I felt that, even though in this life I was fortunate enough not to be involved in hunting, there was no guarantee that in my successive lives I would not end up being born as someone who is going to hunt and kill animals. That led to my aspiration that in my successive lives I be reborn as a form of life that would not have lost the regard for other living beings. That was an important moment for me. That's what led to me giving up eating meat.

Initially I didn't really think about sharing this experience and decision with others, or trying to encourage others to follow the same example, but over time, the inspiration to do so developed.

Perhaps the seminal moment was at an important gathering, a prayer festival in Bodhgaya known as Kagyu Monlam, which is a very large gathering of monastics. At that time, I spoke about the importance of vegetarianism, although I did not say that everybody should just stop eating meat, which is how it is usually reported. I gave several options if people wanted to make some commitment toward this choice. For example, it is part of the Tibetan cultural custom to avoid eating meat on important days of observance: during the new moon or full moon, or on the eighth or the fifteenth day of the month, and so on. So I offered choices for people to either follow the traditional way, which is to not eat meat on those important days of observance, or to choose to eat meat at only one of three meals a day, or maybe only once a month. One of the options was also to immediately give up meat and become a vegetarian.

What was surprising was that while I thought the majority of the people would choose the traditional way, which is not eating meat on important days of observance, at that gathering about 70 percent of the participants chose the option of immediately becoming vegetarian. That was quite interesting, and I'm not entirely sure how that happened.

Later I found out that this kind of shift was occurring inside Tibet as well. Once, a lady from Lhasa came to see me and said, "Because of what you have talked about, vegetarianism and the negative consequences of excessive meat eating, the cost of meat has gone down in Lhasa."

I don't know if this is actually true, but all I said was, "If you could commit to this new choice as a kind of prayer for the long life of His Holiness the Dalai Lama and as a prayer for my longevity as well, I would be grateful."

So that's one way of presenting this kind of option: offering it so that . it has direct relevance to the aspirations and practices of the people of the community. That has generally been my approach.

Furthermore, I often tell people that it is not enough to quote sutras and scriptural citations on this or that, particularly when it comes to adoption of lifestyle. Instead, I tell people, "You should find for yourself the reason that is compelling for you, rather than trying to find a reason elsewhere."

This generally seems to be a much more effective approach. But, of course, on a global level, often people are not awakened by the need for behavioral change. It seems that unless the whole ocean turns red, or the whole Himalayan mountain range turns red with blood, people will probably not respect these issues in a large-scale manner. But this is essentially my own approach, and that's what I wanted to share with you.

JONATHAN PATZ: You mentioned being entrapped in the "I" and "mine." It's the same with countries' national sovereignty, and countries saying, "That's mine, and this is mine." You've also talked about and written about the Himalayas as the Third Pole upon which the entire region depends. This is not so much of a question, rather perhaps a strategy of how to think this way, and how to encourage more collaboration across countries that are dependent on a single resource: the Himalayan mountains.

HIS HOLINESS THE KARMAPA: Jonathan, as you mentioned, the Himalayan range is important for the global environment, and particularly the Tibetan Plateau. I, of course, personally consider this critically important. But the unfortunate thing is that often when people talk about Tibet, the conversation tends to be dominated by politics. It's almost as if saying the word *Tibet* implies politics.

Of course, the issue of Tibet has a lot to do with politics. In fact, it's an issue of the protection of basic human rights, the protection of culture and religion, the protection of people, and the right of people to survive. But another thing I feel strongly about is people also looking at Tibet from the environmental point of view. The advantage of doing this would be, in addition to the humanitarian issues, the opportunity to talk about environmental protection in the area. This has relevance not only to the people on the Tibetan Plateau but also to millions of people in the greater region whose lives are related to the welfare of the plateau.

For example, Tibet is the source for many of the major rivers in Asia.

MATTHIEU RICARD: It's estimated that 47 percent of all the agricultural food production in China, India, and the greater region depends on the rivers of Tibet.

HIS HOLINESS THE KARMAPA: India, China, and many neighboring countries and their people are connected to and impacted by the environmental situation of Tibet. The Tibetan Plateau plays an important role in the weather patterns in the region. I feel that if we can somehow bring awareness to the critical consideration of the Tibetan Plateau from the environmental point of view, of its role in the weather, this would be very important. At this point, this environmental perspective of Tibet isn't very prominent. But this is something that scientists could make public through their research and studies.

DIANA LIVERMAN: Your Holiness, I was asked a question yesterday by one of the monastics about the long-term history of the Tibetan Plateau. I thought this might be an opportunity to answer that question because of your own interest in the environment.

I discovered a fascinating paper by Lonnie Thompson ("Tropical Glacier and Ice Core Evidence of Climate Change on Annual to Millennial Time

Scales"). He has been taking the ice cores that we talked about in Tibet and in particular on the Guliya ice cap on the Tibetan Plateau. He was able to extract an ice core that was 130,000 years old, a piece of Tibetan environmental history. Inside, he was able to see in the layers of this ice core the differences in precipitation, temperature, and dust levels over the years, showing when the earth was dry or wet.

Based on his research, you can see the ice ages that occurred on the Tibetan Plateau, as well as the temperature change that happened ten thousand years ago. It also has been used, together with the tree ring evidence, to reconstruct the history of the great droughts on the Tibetan Plateau.

By observing long-term environmental history through methods used by Dr. Thompson and others, we see that whenever the Tibetan Plateau is warmer, it's wetter, and when it's cooler, it's drier. This would suggest that warming might lead to more rainfall, unless the monsoon is disrupted, because most of the precipitation is from the monsoon. Finally, I would like to say that there are dozens of papers being published on the environmental and climate history of the Tibetan Plateau, mainly by Chinese scientists.

THUPTEN JINPA: One question, Diana: Is there any way, through this ice-core analysis, of finding out about human habitation?

DIANA LIVERMAN: That's unrelated, although there is some interesting evidence, and actually a theory that I didn't discuss earlier. Some people believe that the rise in temperature ten thousand years ago was not the catalyst for the development of agriculture, but rather that the development of agriculture caused the rise in temperature.

The reason for this theory is that ten thousand years ago is when the great rice paddies of Asia were built, and wet rice production produces methane, which causes warming. There's a scientist named William Ruddiman who has suggested that the increase in temperature, including in Tibet, was actually caused by the expansion of rice production. This theory flips the traditional causal relation.

However, to address your question further, we can detect human habitation by measuring the pollen content in ancient lakes. Different types of pollen are indicative of specific grasses related to the domestication of animals, which helps us estimate human habitation.

12 Environmental Activism: Strategies and Ethics for Today's World

PRESENTER: Dekila Chungyalpa, *World Wildlife Fund*

ROSHI JOAN HALIFAX: We've discussed science, ethics, decision making, and motivation, and now we're into an exploration of action. What does it mean to actually engage in work to transform the conditions on this planet? Dekila Chungyalpa addresses the skillful means of activism, and how activists apply ethics, science, and direct knowledge of ecoregions—and work both from the bottom up and from the top down. She uses her work at the World Wildlife Fund, specifically her work in the Mekong region, as an example of such activism. Born in Sikkim, and a person of the twenty-first century, Dekila has described herself as a problem solver. She did five years of conservation work in the Himalayas, designing community-based projects for issues such as forest encroachment, poaching, and human-wildlife conflict. From there she moved to the Mekong region to work on climate-change strategies and policy changes for sustainable hydropower. She has recently launched a new program at the World Wildlife Fund (WWF) to work with religions on preserving the biodiversity, habitat, and ecosystem services that we all need for survival.

What Is Activism?

DEKILA CHUNGYALPA: To begin, I'd like to say that I'm presenting the work of hundreds of environmental activists in the Mekong region and around the world.

Next, allow me to give you an overview of what I have to share: The first part is activism, and why it's relevant to our world. The second part is the challenges we face and the strategies we have developed to meet those challenges. The case study that I will raise concerns the Mekong River; it exemplifies the skillful means of activism we've developed as an environmental community.

So what is activism? Activism refers to an intentional act done to create positive change in our society. Successful activism occurs when the positive change that is created becomes a social norm, something that we take for granted. Some examples are laws against child labor, the protection of wildlife reserves, and laws against casteism in India. The famous Indian activist B. R. Ambedkar was himself born in what is now called a Dalit caste; that is, he was born into a caste on one of the lowest rungs of the social ladder in India. Yet he was also one of the main authors of the Indian Constitution, and he used activism in a very skillful way to create laws requiring the inclusion of individuals of tribes and castes that were traditionally discriminated against. This is a great example of how activism is relevant in our world.

Generally speaking, there are three kinds of activism. First, grassroots or community activism is usually performed by people outside of the power structure. Second, market or private sector transformation happens when the activists are working within a system. And third, government lobbying and policy change are ways for developing alternatives to governance systems. WWF, the organization I will be talking about today, is often criticized for working with large corporations, but in reality it uses all three types of activism in almost every instance.

Overcoming Obstacles to Change

DEKILA CHUNGYALPA: As activists working for change, we face many obstacles in our efforts. Elke mentioned several of these earlier. Apathy, or what we sometimes call "fatalism," is a very common one—even when people know about the environmental problem, they don't care enough to do something about it. Inadequate or overwhelming amounts of information are another obstacle. What we've seen over and over again is that providing not enough information and too much information have the same result. People become frozen, they become immobile; they don't want to make a decision. Disinformation, where somebody's actively spreading the wrong type of information, is another obstacle. This is in line with what Elke mentioned earlier about the "tragedy of the commons," where everybody thinks the problem is somebody else's. The lack of alternative solutions also thwarts progress. Finally, costs outweighing benefits is a major obstacle. There are certain tactics that the environmental community uses all over the world to engage the public and to address these obstacles.

One example I would like to use is that of tigers. There are less than 3,200 tigers left in the wild today. One small bowl of tiger soup can cost five hundred dollars in local markets around Asia. The threat is incredibly high for tigers. When we talk about species extinction, and the fact that the population of tigers has declined by 30 percent over the past few decades, people usually shut down. They don't want to hear the bad news.

So instead of focusing on the bad news, what WWF and partners did is create a very compelling, positive vision. They declared 2010 as the Year of the Tiger and held a very large tiger summit in Russia, inviting the heads of state of the twelve tiger-inhabited countries. These leaders came together and made a commitment that by 2022 they would double the number of tigers. The NGOs who were involved in this process used the skillfulness of having a positive vision, speaking to all levels of power, and personalizing the issue to get people to care about tigers.

However, one thing we know is that working purely on species conservation is not enough. If we don't engage the communities, and if the local communities don't benefit from this work, then we won't have lasting success. In the last ten to fifteen years, there has been an evolution inside the environmental community. We've realized that the means we used in the past to awaken the collective consciousness to reach our goal, such as signing a petition or attending a meeting, are actually also the ends.

An example of a community-based approach is the management of the Koshi River basin in Nepal. There, the various collaborating agencies seek to represent every aspect of the eco-community—including people, species, different kinds of industry, and the private-sector businesses. This type of whole-basin management means that every person who impacts that ecosystem or is impacted by it has the right to be involved and should be engaged in decisions affecting them. This is a new way of doing conservation.

Turning now to the examples of river basins emanating from the Tibetan Plateau itself, the impacted community is very large: it includes vast areas stretching from Kashmir in the west, and into northern India, Bangladesh, Myanmar, Thailand, Laos, Cambodia, Vietnam, and large regions within China. This enormous environmental connectivity is a result of the fact that seven major rivers descend from the Tibetan plateau: the Indus, Ganges, Brahmaputra, Irrawaddy, Salween, Mekong, and Yangtze. For this reason, the Tibetan Plateau is of great environmental significance, and various environmental NGOs such as the WWF are very concerned with this region. We heard earlier that climate change is a big threat for these rivers, but another enormous threat is large-scale hydropower, an issue of particular importance for our case study, the Mekong River.

The Mekong River Basin

DEKILA CHUNGYALPA: The Mekong flows nearly 5,000 kilometers from the Tibetan Plateau, through Yunan, Burma, Laos, Cambodia, Thailand, and Vietnam to the South China Sea. As a source of water and protein it impacts more than 300 million people. The river produces an estimated 2.6 million tons of fish every year. It is home to 25 percent of all inland fisheries, meaning it produces 25 percent of the world's farmed fish, and 2 percent of all the fisheries, marine and other, in the world. So this is an incredibly important river.

The Mekong is the lifeline of this entire region. More than 70 million people get their protein from the fish in the river. It provides transportation, food, life, and livelihood. The Mekong River is the second most

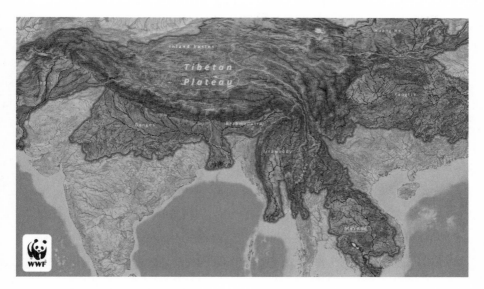

Figure 19. The river basins of the Tibetan Plateau, from left to right: the Indus, Ganges, Brahmaputra, Irrawaddy, Salween, Mekong, and Yangtze.

Figure 20. This is a satellite map that shows where the Mekong River flows into the South China Sea. There are nine mouths in the delta where it enters the South China Sea.

biodiverse river in the world, with more than 1,300 species of fish. Nobody has figured out why the Mekong has so many giant fish. It has the same geomorphology as the other rivers next to it, the Salween and Irrawaddy, but this is the only river that has more than ten giant freshwater fish species. The Mekong giant catfish, which grows to 9 feet in length, is unique to this river, as is the giant stingray. The Mekong is also home to the threatened Irrawaddy dolphin.

The Threat of Hydropower

DEKILA CHUNGYALPA: The largest threat facing the Mekong at this time is the possibility of large-scale hydropower on the main stem. The Greater Mekong region is fast-growing in terms of population and economy, and there is definitely a need for new sources of energy to support this growth. Hydropower has the potential to provide a clean source of energy. But this brings up a point that Jonathan made: we must always have a holistic vision. While climate change could mean that hydropower may be a good source of energy compared to coal, in the case of the Mekong it would have a devastating result.

The Mekong is already one of the most heavily dammed rivers in the world, with dozens of existing hydropower dams. And amazingly, more than one hundred new dams are under consideration. At the same time, there are more than 150 migratory species of fish in the river that go all the way upriver to spawn and come back downriver as adults. Any one of these dams would be a major obstacle for fish migration connected to reproduction, and several species could go extinct. That is one major impact.

Another impact is that, as more dams are built, the natural water flow becomes altered—the seasonal water patterns would thus be changed by additional dams. Depending on the magnitude of the change, this could affect irrigation and farming. Sediment that contributes to the richness of the delta and provides soil that grows food for an entire region could be blocked. And the delta is one of the three most vulnerable deltas to climate change in the world. Because of a rise in sea level, the coastline is also being eaten away by the sea. If sediment was blocked, and the sea rises, at least 17 million people would be affected or displaced.

HIS HOLINESS THE DALAI LAMA: I recently read an article that said when a river is dammed, the water remains more still, which leads to a rise in temperature and increased vaporization of the river. So you have temperature impact and loss of river water.

DEKILA CHUNGYALPA: That is accurate. In the case of the Mekong, because there is so much water, that impact isn't immediately obvious, but is nonetheless happening.

WWF has been working on sustainable hydropower in the Mekong region for the last decade. It has carried out several environmental-impact assessments and worked hard to educate and influence decision makers. I would say that for the first five years we made absolutely no progress. We hoped that providing the scientific evidence would be enough, but not surprisingly, it wasn't.

Environmental Partnership with Corporations and Leaders

DEKILA CHUNGYALPA: This is when WWF developed the second part of its strategy: institutional analysis. For each level, from local to global, starting with species, habitat, and communities, and then moving to national, regional, and global, we identified which institutions were the best levers to bring about policy change, benefit the community, or benefit the species we were trying to protect. We built a broad partnership base. We work very closely with communities to protect species, to make sure their fisheries are sustainable, to provide livelihoods. We worked as a technical partner to the Mekong River Commission, which is an intergovernmental body that oversees the Mekong River. We worked with organizations and banks, such as the Asian Development Bank, as well as Coca-Cola, which is invested in protecting fresh water in the region.

A big part of our strategy is picking the right ambassador. Currently, the supreme patriarch of Theravada Buddhism in Cambodia is our ambassador for the Irrawaddy dolphin. About 98 percent of Cambodia is Buddhist, so we find that when he talks about the importance of preserving the river, almost everybody listens.

One of the reasons why WWF works with the corporate sector is because this region has incredible economic growth possibilities. There are plenty of corporations investing in countries like Vietnam and influencing how business and, therefore, everyday life is carried out. When we're able to explain that climate change is going to directly threaten their investment, we find that they are very responsive to us. They want to preserve the place that they're investing in.

Another reason why WWF works with the corporate sector is to mitigate the threat of indecision due to lack of clarity. One of the things that we've invested in with partners is developing the tools needed to make decisions. We've mapped out the main stem of the river, as well as the tributaries, in terms of fisheries. This way, it's easy to see if you were to put a dam on the Mekong main stem, what the impacts would be for fisheries. Similarly, if you dammed a tributary, you see what the impact would be. This way, decision makers can assess how their communities will be affected by different decisions.

Another very important strategy that WWF has led is to develop a tool based on the idea of "integrated river basin management," which I mentioned earlier. The approach here is to look at the entire river basin. This helps designers see where to put the dam, how to design the dam, and then how operationalize the dam.

WWF has also reached out to the different dam investors. We held a summit for financial institutions, more than seventy of them, that were planning to invest in the Mekong dams. We explained our analysis in language that they understood, making the arguments that the type of dams they invested in and the locations they were placed could increase or decrease their own long-term financial returns. So we have used financial arguments with the financial investors to explain how much it matters if the Mekong is dammed.

The final thing that WWF has done is to identify and reach out to the global community in influential countries that are committed to the well-being of this region. One such example is the United States. We were able to get the US Senate very involved, to promote and financially invest in a dialogue on this idea of integrated river basin management with all the governments of the lower Mekong countries. The result was that some of the premiers of the countries involved—Vietnam, Laos, Cambodia, and Thailand—began expressing their concerns, and finally three of them came out with a statement saying that they would not dam the Mekong's main stem. Further, they called for a moratorium on dams on the main stem. They actually put the needs of their communities, biodiversity, and their own long-term interests first, versus a short-term economic gain.

We see a great deal of good that has come out of this process. It is unprecedented that governments are actually putting the notion of sustainable economic development before immediate short-term gains. Local communities are very engaged and empowered on river basin management. And there is now a precedent for a very strong, cross-sector partnership that engages the private sector, public sector, the NGO community, and local communities. Such a strategy works to protect the future of people and species.

I would like to end with the lessons that we've learned from applying strategies for skillful activism. The most important thing is that there needs to be a positive vision. We've learned that the hard way. As Elke discussed in her presentation, with a negative vision, people get engaged for a very short period of time but lose interest in the longer term. When the vision is positive, and we keep the goal in the future, people respond to it more consistently. Also, the vision needs to feel personal. Every individual who can make a decision that leads to either the protection or destruction of the environment has to feel a personal connection. Activists need to engage all stakeholders; we shouldn't leave anybody out, because we don't know who might be the right lever at the right time. And finally, dialogue and negotiation are critically important. We must continue to seek dialogue and negotiation all the time everywhere.

Damming the Deltas

JONATHAN PATZ: To follow up on your comment about blocking sediment that builds up the Mekong delta, even in the United States we've seen repercussions from dams and levies on the Mississippi River. Hurricane Katrina wiped out the city of New Orleans and more than a thousand people died—in our wealthy country. That was because we have held back sediments, and so the natural protection of that coastal city disappeared. Satellite images show that in the Mississippi delta, the protective vegetation and barrier islands are gone, which made New Orleans more vulnerable to the hurricane.

DEKILA CHUNGYALPA: We've seen the same thing in other parts of the world. One example is a protected area called Tram Chim National Park in southern Vietnam. When WWF first took over managing the park, it had been completely concretized. The park managers had put cement barricades everywhere in this protected area because they were trying to protect the land from flooding. But the park is actually a wetland that merges with the sea, where water should be flowing back and forth naturally. As part of the management, we took away all of the barricades, and when we did, the biodiversity actually improved. The fish were able to move in and out of different habitats, and the rising sea was no longer as big of a threat because the wetlands were self-regulating, unlike before. Removing barricades in almost any ecosystem seems to be beneficial for climate-change adaptation.

To Protect Individual Beings or Species?

CLARE PALMER: Your example sounds a bit like a case of protecting the river in order for people to continue eating fish. I was wondering whether there was any discussion about that among the team? If so, what were the different positions people took, and were there long-term ideas, such as people should eat less fish? Was that part of the discussion within the WWF and with the local communities?

DEKILA CHUNGYALPA: It's a very complicated issue. It brings an ethical dilemma to almost any decision activists make about natural resource management. Do we prioritize the communities' needs, do we prioritize individual wildlife species, do we prioritize the ecosystem? It's always a challenge for us to figure out if we're making the right decision because it is not an objective one and really depends on the personal paradigm. In the case of the Mekong fisheries, the team had differing views. Some members felt that, since the communities actually fish the endangered Mekong giant catfish, we should institute no-fishing zones, and other members felt that 70 million people need their daily protein so communities have the right to fish. Every dilemma has a compromise, and our compromise was that in the areas where the fish spawn, called "deep pools," where most of the biodiversity is, there are no-fishing zones. We work with the community to say, "If you actually protect these areas, you are more likely to have fish in the future." Communities continue to fish in the areas that are open, and NGOs don't try to restrict or manage that.

CLARE PALMER: It seems like the reasons you were protecting fish were based on protecting species of fish that were becoming endangered, rather than protecting individual fish or preventing the suffering of individual fish, for instance. I'm wondering about the reasons for protecting species rather than being concerned about individuals, given this Buddhist context.

DEKILA CHUNGYALPA: Most wildlife ecologists and conservationists have to be unemotional about this topic, because protecting biodiversity often means that we select species that best represent the largest amount of biodiversity or an entire ecosystem. That means that we don't really get to be emotional, for example, about deer, when we pick tigers as the representation for an ecosystem or all of biodiversity. It doesn't mean that we don't get emotional, but that we can't let that affect the decision. It's the same with this issue. We picked the Mekong giant catfish as the umbrella species, the species that, if it were to disappear, would most alter the food chain, and alternately, if it were to be protected would result in the protection of the entire ecosystem. I think almost all wildlife ecologists I know would choose to protect the ecosystem rather than the individual, although I am not saying it's always the right thing to do. But this is also why environmental teams need to represent all points of view—we cannot assume that one point of view is inherently more important than another, although everyone might think their own is.

CLARE PALMER: I think that's particularly interesting, because it seems like you are saying, "We're protecting the species in order to protect the ecosystems, and we're protecting the ecosystems in order to protect all the individuals in the ecosystems, so we're sacrificing some individuals, as food, in order to ultimately protect the whole system." I'm not quite sure how this all fits together.

DEKILA CHUNGYALPA: Biodiversity isn't just about one species, it's about all the species, as well as the habitats and ecological processes in the region. Whether we're talking about a tiger or a Mekong giant catfish, those are individual species that get a lot of attention, because they represent biodiversity, so we invest a lot in protecting them. And in some ways, they are sacrificed, because they are so prized by communities or people. So they are both a sacrifice and a rallying cry.

Ethical Dilemmas in Environmental Action

JOHN DUNNE: We've spoken about the problems, and we are also speaking about the good news. Certainly activism is part of the good news. One question that does come to mind is this question of difficult choices. There are times when, as we've seen in the context of the Mekong, one makes a choice knowing that there will be some suffering in order to achieve some other goal. Another example of this would be making the choice to kill mosquitoes—not just the one that's biting me, but a whole population of mosquitoes—because they bring such danger from malaria. What are our guidelines for these choices? How do we sort out the difference between creating suffering and creating benefits? Is it about trying to create maximum benefit, even if some suffering must occur?

HIS HOLINESS THE DALAI LAMA: We touched on this already through Shantideva's text. When we are confronted with a particular situation where we have a clear choice, then of course we need to make the right choice. But if the choice is only to sacrifice the well-being of one for the benefit of another, then we have to weigh the pros and cons. What are the negative implications or consequences of a particular course of action versus another? We also have to take into account the greater view and consider the greater benefit for the greatest number of beings. These kind of considerations need to be brought in, and it may differ from case to case.

Clare brought up the ethical consideration of compassionate concern for individual beings that have the capacity to suffer and experience pain, versus protection of the species. With each of these positions, there are different motivations and considerations at play. In the first scenario, we would seek to protect the individual beings because they have feelings of pain and pleasure, and that could be held equally for each and every individual being. Another motivation would be to protect the things we love. With trees and flowers, we favor the ones that are beautiful, rare, and make us feel good—not because they have feelings of pain and pleasure, but because of their value to us. So protecting species versus caring for individual sentient beings because of their capacity to feel pain and pleasure are two different considerations.

If we think about fish and tigers in captivity, sometimes we capture live fish and feed them to other fish that we have in captivity. Likewise, I have seen documentaries of live chickens being fed to tigers. Yet from a moral consideration for sentient beings, they all have the same rights. The best thing would be for the tigers to become vegetarian!

DEKILA CHUNGYALPA: That brings up a very interesting ethical dilemma: if we try to make tigers vegetarian, we're interfering with the natural order of things.

HIS HOLINESS THE DALAI LAMA: In that case, I think Buddha's teachings and Buddhist practice is actually against our nature. Consider anger and attachment. These are part of our nature, yet we deliberately try to reduce these. So serious Buddhist practice is against our true expressed nature. But ignorance enables us to continue with these behaviors regardless of negative outcomes. Because we are happier and benefit more without these natural tendencies, we deliberately and intentionally go against our own nature.

JOHN DUNNE: I want to be sure I understand. When we face a difficult choice where individuals will be harmed, we choose the path or the action that will lead to the maximum benefit for the longest period of time, for the most beings, based on what we know?

HIS HOLINESS THE DALAI LAMA: Maybe we can find a solution with the mosquito. Perhaps in places where there are a lot of mosquitoes we can provide them with water and food or blood and the humans can wear nets!

MATTHIEU RICARD: That may be difficult, because mosquitoes will spread out of control. But to the point, much of what we are talking about sounds like the style of ethics called utilitarianism in the West.

The problem with the utilitarian view is that it's about maximizing pleasure. From that view, if you have a hundred slaves making a thousand people happy, that's fine. It's missing the ideas of well-being and avoiding suffering. We need a compassionate and wisdom-based utilitarianism.

JONATHAN PATZ: I want to expand on your earlier example of taking one grain in the field and saying "this grain represents all grains." One mosquito is not the same as another mosquito. In fact, there are 422 mosquito species in the genus *Anopheles*, and of those 422 species, only approximately 60 species carry malaria. But there are some species of mosquitoes that are extremely dangerous, that cause suffering all over the world, and that kill approximately one million children every year. I read recently that there are currently five hundred cases of mosquito-borne dengue fever in Delhi. We have not succeeded in eliminating them; it's only when we accidentally destroy an ecosystem that we eliminate species. And yet they cause tremendous suffering. In the difficult-choice scenario, we may want to get rid of them.

HIS HOLINESS THE DALAI LAMA: The term "human rights" seems to imply that we have special rights to use other living sentient beings for our own purposes and gain. Really, we all have the same right for survival and to not be intentionally disturbed or threatened.

In the Vinaya, Buddha said that certain types of meat should not be eaten. In particular, any animal that was specially killed for you should not be eaten. On the other hand, I recall a conversation with one monk from Sri Lanka about thirty or forty years ago, in which we talked about this. He said he was neither vegetarian nor nonvegetarian because he did not have a private kitchen, only a begging bowl. In this case, he couldn't be preferential about his food; whatever he received he was obliged to accept, vegetarian or nonvegetarian. This is one case in the Vinaya that Buddha did not prohibit.

Look at India; there are more than 400 million vegetarians. One time I was at a prayer gathering with millions of Hindu pilgrims who were all vegetarian. I think if Tibetans gathered in such numbers, the butchers would get rich. I often share this with Tibetans—millions of Hindu people can gather, and not a single life is taken. The American lifestyle also needs to put more effort toward vegetarianism, as does Western Europe.

Dis-Activated: When Discouragement and Depression Arise

ROSHI JOAN HALIFAX: Steering our inquiry back toward activism, I would like to begin with a question that I feel many activists are asking themselves: What do we feel are skillful means for activists who are dealing with issues relating to making choices that create suffering for an individual, or for large groups of individuals, but might be the best decision in the long term? How do activists deal skillfully with a decision-making process where there's a moral dilemma, where suffering is going to be created in the short or long term for a number of beings? Many activists suffer as a result of this and become discouraged.

JOHN DUNNE: Is there a method, when one feels disappointed or upset in the context of having to make a difficult choice, that one can use to counteract that feeling?

HIS HOLINESS THE DALAI LAMA: As we discussed earlier, in these situations, of course people can respond with despondency and discouragement, but on the other hand, there is always the possibility of responding with greater enthusiasm and commitment.

DEKILA CHUNGYALPA: Almost every activist I know is actually an optimist at heart, because to become an activist you really have to believe that the society will be better off. I think there is a natural ebullience, an enthusiasm that comes from inside. We're convinced, no matter what the odds are, that we will win. And when the reality crash happens, it happens very hard, but everybody goes through that.

I became an activist at fifteen, so I have some years of experience now. If we have a long-term goal, and we see that we're advancing toward it, even if it is one tiny step at a time, it makes a big difference. If it is a short-term goal, and we're just doing it to stop something, or we're angry and we're protesting from anger, then it never goes anywhere. So finding that joy that Jinpa talked about has been my solution.

HIS HOLINESS THE DALAI LAMA: When we face difficulties, or obstacles, one important factor is that your own stand must be truthful, honest, and genuine—an altruistic attitude. With the strength of altruism, there's no reason to feel discouraged. But if we are hypocritical, saying one thing and doing another, our inner being weakens and we may not have the strength to face challenges.

In my own life, at sixteen I lost my freedom; at twenty-four I lost my country. For sixty years I've faced a lot of problems, but the ultimate source of my strength is based on moral principles, so there is no reason to feel discouraged. It's important to ensure you have the right kind of motivation and sincerity in your pursuits.

Look at people like Mahatma Gandhi, Martin Luther King, or Nelson Mandela. Initially, they faced many challenges. Mahatma Gandhi's struggle for freedom through nonviolence was laughed at and dismissed at first. Now nonviolence is a practice in some countries. These are clear examples of the power of truth, sincerity, and honesty. These are the key motives, because we are not working only in our own self-interest but in the interest of life.

Sometimes you see people start something important and work hard, and if it doesn't materialize right away, they lose interest. But these bigger, important goals are almost impossible to materialize in one lifetime. We're talking about humanity, and over time humanity can change. But someone must start. Our generation must start these important changes, even if the results don't materialize in our lifetimes. That's okay! Even the Buddha did not see the broader results of his teachings materialize in his lifetime, but the benefits are still here today. So it's our responsibility to begin to shape the world for the better, even though at present it is only a dream. Yet we must make the effort through education and through awareness; we must inspire the younger generation.

Sometimes the cause seems hopeless. Everyone says they want peace and freedom, and yet millions remain silent in their circumstances. But we stand with the wisdom of Buddha or Nagarjuna as sources of courage, inner strength, and determination. In fact, if there were no challenges or obstacles in human life, then there would be no need for great teachers like the Buddha or Jesus Christ. Both said that the extreme self-centered attitude is the source of our problems. Whether rooted in the philosophical view of causality or in a theistic reverence to God, both espoused reducing self-centeredness and increasing altruism. The main goal is more or less the same.

How Can Science Help More?

DIANA LIVERMAN: I am very moved by this discussion. I wanted to ask a question about the link between science and activism. Dekila, you could be a scientist, but you've chosen to become an activist. I'd be trying to recruit you as a student if I didn't think the work you are doing is so important. I am wondering if, in your work, you feel that you get enough support from scientists? Are there areas where scientists could better help the activist community? I'm really interested in the role of science in supporting the work that you do.

DEKILA CHUNGYALPA: Because the organization I work for, WWF, is so science-based, we don't have that much of a divide. About half of our staff are conservation scientists. We're very interested in understanding and applying the latest scientific research. I think where the divide usually happens in our larger community is in the processes of engaging local people or policymakers. For example, on the issue of climate change, I sometimes witness scientists—not all of them—sit back with the attitude that mainstream advocacy is the job of activists. In reality it's everybody's job. We should all be finding ways to make this information available and real. Science is the original problem solver, but it's not always the case that we get a positive response when we ask scientists, "Help us come up with new ideas; help us come up with new alternatives." That is where science could actually make the biggest contribution. The scientists here are a rarity because all of you are so interested in solutions. At other times, I have come up against the obstacle of a scientist being very interested in the theoretical piece and not so much in the solution.

THUPTEN JINPA: I have a question about your mention of "good" dams. It seems that public opinion from the environmental point of view is that all dams are bad.

DEKILA CHUNGYALPA: There are different types of dams. Generally speaking, large dams are very dangerous in terms of the impact, but there are many smaller dams that are called "run of the river," which means that the river actually goes through the dam, and a major diversion isn't created. The dam allows the water to go through unimpeded, including the fish and the sediment. There are also lots of technological innovations that improve the water flow and habitat.

THUPTEN JINPA: In terms of energy production, are these dams less efficient?

DEKILA CHUNGYALPA: Yes, but in the long term, they're actually better because they're sustainable. If you're from the Himalayas, most of you know that there are plenty of hydropower dams that are functioning at very low efficiency, which is always the argument for building new dams.

In the past, we haven't tried to make dams sustainable in the long term; we just try to get as much energy in the short term. There are technological innovations, such as the "fish ladder," which is used in North America. This allows salmon, which go upriver when they're ready to spawn, to cross the dam. This works in North America because there are very few fish species that travel upriver to spawn. In the Mekong, which is a tropical ecosystem, there are 150 migratory species, so that wouldn't work. But this is where science can help us come up with other innovative ideas.

Finding Common Ground in Unlikely Partnerships

ELKE WEBER: When you do activism, you always have the alternative of engaging a group on their own terms, in their own language and within their own value system, or you can try to change the value system. For example, you can talk to people at Coca-Cola or at the World Bank, and put an economic value on the environment, and get them to include that value in their calculations. Or you could argue that economic calculations of costs and benefits shouldn't be the only determinate of decisions, and that there are other rights-based considerations that should play a role. How do you deal with that tradeoff?

DEKILA CHUNGYALPA: Institutionally, we don't. When WWF works with a corporation, it's a partnership on equal terms. The idea is that the corporation invests in conservation, so there is a financial transaction, and they benefit from conservation. We also talk to them about their footprint.

Using the example of Coca-Cola, they have made many commitments to source sustainable sugar, citrus fruit, and water. They have become water-efficient in almost all their factories. They have a goal around this issue and WWF helps monitor it. This is an ideal partnership with a corporation, but it took ten years to cultivate and may not be replicable in the same way.

What I notice is my evolution as an activist. When I was younger I was always yelling, "Everybody should change!" What I realized through experience and hard lessons is that, by *not* yelling, activists are able to create partnerships that may be much more beneficial in the long term. Coca-Cola was initially just a philanthropic donor. They gave some money to WWF for the preservation of three river basins worldwide. Gradually, it evolved to a conversation, where they began expressing their concerns about water. Over time, this conversation turned into one around protecting entire river basins, and that's when they made a major commitment, saying, "We are going to change and we want you to help monitor the change." The ripple effect created includes aluminum producers that sell to Coca-Cola expressing to WWF, "We would like to invest in making our own supply chain efficient." The ripple effect has been enormous, and part of the reason is that we took the values discussion off the table. It doesn't mean that as activist that I didn't want this to happen all along, but by creating this conversation without polarization, it's been more beneficial.

HIS HOLINESS THE DALAI LAMA: By emphasizing the common benefit?

DEKILA CHUNGYALPA: Exactly.

The Role of Women in Environmental Activism

CLARE PALMER: I was wondering if you could tell us something about the role of women in the activism projects you've been engaged in? Do women participate more, less, or equally? Do they have different roles to men? Are there any patterns you can pick out, or does it vary from place to place? And do you find that there are issues where women feel oppressed by men in some of the campaigns?

DEKILA CHUNGYALPA: That is a fantastic question. In the field, I'm often the minority. It's not rare that I'll come to a room and find I'm the only female. I think there are two components to your question: one is what actually happens in the communities where we work, and the other is about the conservation community. What we know is that when we work in the field, most of the resource managers are women. If you think about who goes out from the community to gather fuel wood or carry water, who is in the fields on a daily basis, most of that labor is performed by women. And such women seem to understand the connection with nature almost instantly. There isn't a separation that exists, because they are dealing with it in their daily lives. We also find that when we discuss health issues—such as fuel wood being bad for your health because inhaling the smoke creates respiratory disease and your children suffer—and make recommendations to switch to bio-gas, women instantly understand. I think they naturally have the ability to have a more holistic perspective. In that sense, I think women have a very strong, positive reaction to environmental protection.

The interesting thing is that as you start climbing up the decision-making ladder, there are fewer and fewer women. On a personal level, I have found that I have to make a shift from making these holistic sorts of arguments to making arguments based on finances and facts. You have to make a decision to do this because the people you're interacting with, whether gender-influenced or not, are decision makers and are held accountable for these concerns. Decision makers are not being held accountable for a holistic vision and making everybody happy, although they should be. They're held accountable for GDP and income generation. I find I'm forced to make those arguments in order to create relationship and commonality.

Within the conservation community there are many women. I would love to see more women scientists coming up in the conservation field, and more women project managers. Certainly, there are quite a few who are incredible and whom I really look up to. Wangari Maathai, a Nobel Peace Prize winner, is probably the biggest inspiration for women conservationists. She fought a lot of inequity within her own culture and created the Green Belt Movement in Kenya that not only improved the environment but also empowered her community. I can't think of a better inspiration.

Engage the Leaders for Sustainability

JONATHAN PATZ: I have a general question about engaging the communities. You said that when you're trying to protect the ecosystem and the river basin, unless you get the communities engaged and taking ownership, a sustainable solution is not possible. I've been involved in all sorts of assessments and community engagements, and the greatest challenge is to maintain the engagement. With limited resources and time, what is the best way to engage a community and have a solution be sustainable?

DEKILA CHUNGYALPA: I think I speak for almost all environmental NGOs I know that are doing field conservation work when I say that the best thing to do is to invest in the leaders of local communities. Every place I've been sent to design a project, one of the first things I do is pick out who I think the future leaders are going to be. They should be emotionally invested already, have a personal connection to the issue, and feel that courage that His Holiness was referring to, the energetic motivation to take it on. That's where most of our energy goes. As an NGO, even when we have been in places for decades, we're really still short-termers, and it's the community leaders who will carry the work in the years ahead.

I've begun working with religious leaders in the last couple of years. This was partly an understanding that emerged for me after ten years of working on community-based conservation. It was also advised by His Holiness; the fact is that religious leaders are the spiritual backbone of a society. If they buy into a project and take it on, they will propagate something that becomes locally owned. So the effort doesn't become something that's coming from the outside world or from an external point of view, but rather from within the community. I think that's really important.

Changes in the Himalayan Region

JOHN DUNNE: I wonder if you could share some concrete experiences you've had with conservation and environmental issues in the Himalayan region? I've heard a little bit about some of the activity in monasteries. I saw a wonderful picture of a group of monks from Nepal wearing their robes and a special vest. They had brooms and garbage cans, and they had just gone out in the neighborhood and cleaned up garbage. Previously, such activity was almost unthinkable due to the reverence and devotion for Buddhist monks in the Himalayas—they shouldn't be associated with garbage! Could you share some concrete activities that are happening in the monasteries and elsewhere in the Himalayan region?

DEKILA CHUNGYALPA: The work that you're referring to is by Rangjung Khoryug Sungkyob Tsokpa, the organization headed by His Holiness the Karmapa. There are forty-five monasteries and nunneries that are doing environmental projects of all kinds. The association put on several training conferences where I worked with a team of trainers to explain things such as the carbon cycle, and we worked together with each monastery to select goals and design projects. Some monasteries are clustered close together, as in Boudha, Nepal, and decided to work as a team. They wear the apron you were describing as a uniform and go out and clean Boudha. They told me that they were so tired of seeing Boudha very dirty. Some of the monastics are very senior geshes and khenpos, and this created a lot of consternation in the community, because of course the community members are used to visiting them and offering *khatas* rather than watching them literally getting their hands dirty.

This group of monastics represents twelve monasteries and nunneries in the area. Initially, the community tried to stop them. People were coming out and saying, "Please don't do this." My understanding is that the monks from Thrangu Monastery were adamant that they were going to do regular cleanups, and so some community members started joining in. Now they clean every second Saturday of the month. A few months later, a community member came forward and said that she had gathered donations from all the community members to pay a *jamdar*, a cleaner, so the monks don't have to do it anymore. So this is just one example of how collective action can have an impact, and how much of a difference the monasteries and nunneries can make.

ROSHI JOAN HALIFAX: What happened when the Karmapa addressed the issue of vegetarianism in Bodhgaya?

DEKILA CHUNGYALPA: His Holiness offered it as an option to people. He said, "You could, if you want to, give up meat for short periods or give up meat entirely," and almost everybody raised their hands to give it up entirely. I think many thousands of people became vegetarian, including myself, without overthinking it. It was a very instinctive reaction. But the other thing he did, which from an environmental perspective was incredible, happened during prayers for the long life of His Holiness the Dalai Lama. He said, "If you actually want to invest in this, you really want to think about increasing the longevity of His Holiness the Dalai Lama, then you should plant a tree." And he said, "If you protect this tree, then you're actually doing an act that benefits so many people that it infinitely multiplies the well-being prayer that you're making." The monasteries and nunneries can get competitive, so all of a sudden we had one monastery saying, "We'll plant one thousand," then the other monastery saying, "We'll plant two thousand." My understanding is that all the way into

Tibet there is a lot of planting happening because of this request that His Holiness the Karmapa made for the longevity of His Holiness the Dalai Lama. I think that was very special.

The Intersection between Activism and Religion

SALLIE MCFAGUE: His Holiness had talked about the common ground among the religions as not being about beliefs in God but about human flourishing and well-being. I'm wondering about the connections between the religious organizations and the NGOs that work with you on the ground level. Do you find that there are special places of connection between you and the religious groups, or special places of conflict or differences, and are there any connections that have generated the most success? What is it like working with the religious organizations, and has it been a good thing, and in what way?

DEKILA CHUNGYALPA: Many NGOs work with the local faith community. If there is a faith leader in a project area, usually that faith leader is involved in some way or another. WWF created a sister organization called the Alliance of Religions and Conservation, based in the UK, many years ago. It has been very successful at getting religions globally to hold themselves accountable for environmental sustainability and to make declarations that they live up to. One thing that was planned for 2012 is a declaration of a green hajj—all the religious leaders in Mecca and Medina are making a commitment to turn the pilgrimage green. Maybe that will provide an inspiration for Buddhist communities to do something similar in Bodhgaya. I think the fact that more than 80 percent of the world identifies with a religious faith gives religion an incredible power that we should not ignore.

Maybe not all religious people are necessarily good, but the potential for positive influence is inescapable. In the United States, there was a study by the Pew Research Center that found more than nine out of ten Americans say they believe in God or a higher spirit. If you break that down further in terms of where they live, or how they vote, that also makes a big difference.

HIS HOLINESS THE DALAI LAMA: When I look at areas in the Middle East and hear both sides crying "Allah" while they kill each other, it doesn't make sense. The same thing in Ireland: Catholics and Protestants hating each other while both believe in Jesus Christ. Even among the Buddhists we have, at times, quarreled and even killed each other. These are not serious practitioners and followers of their respective faiths, so I am skeptical of the 80 percent figure.

What often happens is that instead of using their religious faith and resources to transform their own personality and character, they impose their personality on the religion and change it. It's very sad. Otherwise, there's no reason to kill each other in the name of religion. It's very tricky when people manipulate religion.

From this view, antireligious people are more honest. They don't believe and may even have a negative view of religion, and they are quick to say so publicly. At least that is clear and honest.

DEKILA CHUNGYALPA: I have a slightly different point of view. One of the big challenges in the United States surrounding climate change is this great divide between science and religion. People who identify themselves as religious have been quite antiscience. Especially people who identify themselves as conservative Christians in the United States don't believe in the science of climate change because they do not accept some of the scientific facts and findings.

HIS HOLINESS THE DALAI LAMA: If I may add something. There are narrow-minded Christians who have a singular point of view. I have heard some say, "The Dalai Lama is coming frequently to America, so he may lead many Americans to hell." It's understandable, because according to their belief there's only one truth, one religion, and the other religions are invalid. But this is due to lack of knowledge and not realistic. Ignorance is the problem.

DEKILA CHUNGYALPA: I think the scientific and religious communities have a lot of common ground, no matter how uninterested the religions are in science. For us, the challenge is finding the common ground. One thing I've discovered is that I have many scientist friends who don't understand why we should work with religions. I don't find as much of an objection in the religious community as I do in the scientific community. So the challenge is to find a bridge between these different communities that don't always agree with each other. With the religious community, of course, I can talk about the sanctity of life. Every religion does have that in common, even though they might go to war over God. With the scientific community, I find that if we talk long enough about why each one of us became an environmentalist or got interested in this issue of the ultimate truth, almost everybody I know has had a moment when they were in nature, in a forest, or in a great body of water and they felt they were one with the universe. I think that just those two understandings from each group can be enough to build this bridge, enough to unite us, because we do have a common cause, which is to save life on Earth.

HIS HOLINESS THE DALAI LAMA: Shantideva has a line that says, "Given the diversity of people in the world, if even the Buddha is not able to please all of them, then how can I even pretend that I could do that?" The point is that you need to reach out to those who are receptive instead of trying to make everybody come to your side.

I think we can really learn from India's example. For a thousand years there have been different religions—Buddhists, Jains, Hindus, Zoroastrians, and Muslims—that live happily without risk of danger or persecution. Because of the diversity of religions, as well as nonbelievers, everyone is granted respect. In today's world, we really need that attitude.

13 Solutions for a Sustainable World
Group Discussion

JOHN DUNNE: One of the main issues that we now face is that we are responsible for some very profound changes to our planet in this time we call the Anthropocene age. The good news is this: since we've made the mess, maybe we can clean it up. We're not only looking at the problems but also the possibilities and solutions. There seems to be a tremendous human capacity to correct these problems. We have not only a footprint but also a handprint. The ways in which our economic consumer activities impact the entire planet create an opportunity to do something positive. And despite the great complexity of the ethical difficulties, we can find common ground and keep those common ethics in mind as we go forward. That "wild space" that Sallie introduced is something that we can tap into to see the world differently, to gain a new perspective. All of these are incredible possibilities. They offer hope for the future.

We've considered how we can foster positive environments for decisions rather than being overwhelmed by the negative. We've looked at the Buddhist approach, which involves commitment, dedication, and mindfulness. And we've explored successful activism. We can certainly see that there are problems, and now we'd like to focus on what we might be able to do, what concrete steps can we take as we move forward.

Practical Environmental Solutions

DIANA LIVERMAN: There are some very simple things that we can all do to stop the march toward planetary boundaries, and they don't necessarily require ethical considerations or deep mindfulness. Some of these include taking a shorter shower or installing a low-flow showerhead. With a low-flow head, and going from a ten-minute shower to a five-minute shower, you reduce average water usage from 20 gallons to 5 gallons per shower. Turning the air conditioning thermostat up 2 degrees probably won't be noticeable, but it saves energy. Only using one fan to cool off or wearing extra layers instead of turning up the heat when it's cold all help reduce global warming. Another big one would be to fly less and use videoconferencing for work meetings and gatherings instead.

DANIEL GOLEMAN: I think the individual is very important when we're talking about multilevel change. I was very moved by a book Pico Iyer wrote about His Holiness (*The Open Road: The Global Journey of the Fourteenth Dalai Lama*; Vintage Books, 2008). It's a wonderful book, and on the last page he recounts that after a meeting, when they're leaving the room, they closed the door and His Holiness stopped, went back, and turned the light off. That really impacted me. I started to do that, and I think to the extent each one of us becomes more mindful about the little ways in which we can do better, the cumulative effect will make a huge difference.

JONATHAN PATZ: On a personal level, we could engage more with urban planners and city policies. This kind of engagement by others has resulted in many changes, including green roofs—growing vegetation and/or produce on rooftops. Green roofs cool the climate in the summertime and prevent flooding from excessive rainfall and runoff.

DIANA LIVERMAN: A town, a community, a university, a hospital, or any organization can take advantage of the methodology Greg presented to do more sustainable sourcing, including power, paper, building materials, and anything else they use. This could send a sustainable ripple effect through the supply chain.

Making Big Decisions Count

GREGORY NORRIS: Earlier, Jonathan proposed that we are addicted to oil, and I would refine that by saying our infrastructure is addicted to oil. Studies of different populations found that people who deeply care about the environment may make small decisions on a daily basis, but in the big picture, there wasn't a tremendous difference in impact between those who care more and everyone else.

In addition to the smaller activities, we also need to consider that there are a few moments in our lives where we make decisions that have a major impact because of their long-term nature. These include where you live, what kind of car you buy—a ten- to fifteen-year commitment to energy use—the energy efficiency of your house, and so forth.

The message is not to ignore the daily practice, because that makes a difference and raises awareness. But we must also bring that awareness to the key moments in life when we make larger infrastructure decisions, personally and at the community level. For example, Washington, DC, implemented a building code saying that all new construction and renovation must be compliant with US Green Building Council standards. Once you make that kind of community decision, it mandates a positive habit.

ELKE WEBER: There's a lot of inertia in our own habitual behavior, and even more inertia in institutions. I think we are responsible for changing our institutions. That means going to planning meetings, engaging in dialogue and even mundane activities, but in the long run, these efforts and the changes they generate can make a huge difference.

To the extent that we reduce our own footprint, we can put pressure on institutions and organizations in our lives to help them become more "mindful." A collective of people to which a given institution is responsible can influence the institution in positive ways.

DIANA LIVERMAN: There is an organization, ICLEI – Local Governments for Sustainability, that has a program called "Cities for Climate Protection," where cities share information about successful strategies. A similar program for corporations, the "Carbon Disclosure Project," includes an annual report that shares the activities and changes businesses have made to reduce their environmental impact.

JONATHAN PATZ: I have been thinking about the attempts at the international and national levels to engage in environmental sustainability through treaties and policies, and there's been a lot of frustration. I would like to endorse what Bill Clinton and Michael Bloomberg have done. The Clinton Foundation has a climate change initiative where they seek to effect change in cities at the local level.

When Bogota took out a lane of the expressway and converted it to public transportation, they modeled a change that other cities are now adopting. I think getting engaged at the local level will allow each of us to support interventions that are the best fit and will have the greatest impact in our communities.

JOHN DUNNE: Dan Goleman wrote a book called *Ecological Intelligence* (Broadway Books, 2010) that covers some of the bad news and also a lot of good news and success stories. It discusses approaches one can take in order to really make a difference. Another thought is the power of grassroots initiatives, as Dekila's work shows.

Transparency as a Model for Change

ROSHI JOAN HALIFAX: We should practice transparency—personal transparency and public transparency, as well as corporate and governmental transparency. In a way, this meeting has been a model of that. I appreciated the fact that His Holiness said, "I'm not entirely a vegetarian." Taking personal audits and being open is an important step to putting pressure on communities, corporations, and our government to disclose exactly this kind of information.

DANIEL GOLEMAN: I have a data point on that. About twenty-five years ago, the US government required factories and production sites to report their emissions. All they had to do was report how much goes into the air, how much goes into the water, and how much goes into the soil. Even with that simple transparency requirement, emissions have been reduced by 75 percent since then.

Planetary House Rules

SALLIE MCFAGUE: I want to expand a little on the planetary house rules that guide us to treat our planet like our home, not like a hotel. Everybody who lives in the "house" follows the rules. The first rule is "Take only your share." On the individual level, we know that most of us are taking too much. The call for restraint and limitation is very important. What does this mean at the public level? That is more complicated, but as a quick illustration, during World War II, we had rationing. One of the things people felt good about was all being on the same ration plan. Perhaps today we could seek legislation for a similar plan of limiting or rationing use of resources.

The second rule is "Clean up after yourself." Individually, many of us are already recycling. At the public level that could mean a shift from punishing companies after they've destroyed the environment—as with the Exxon Valdez—to factoring in the cost of nature on the front end and adjusting prices and protections accordingly.

The third rule is "Keep the house in good repair for others." On a local level it's important to educate children well. We focus so much on the importance of the next generation, and many environmentalists have said that deep down we're generational people. Whether we have children of our own or not, we all want the next generation to flourish. Many schoolteachers act as mentors, as if their students were their own children, educating them as deeply and effectively as possible. At the public level, we also need to consider the future generations. I'm from Canada, and the First Nations there talk about seven generations into the future. That is, the decisions we make are not just for now; we have to consider how our decisions today will impact future generations.

These are sound rules we could apply on a planetary level. It may be difficult, but not impossible.

An Imbalance of Global Responsibility

THUPTEN JINPA: The lifestyle we lead, particularly in developed countries, is so consumption-based that in some ways there isn't a lot of room left for individual choices to make a huge impact. This ties into the ethical question of asking developing countries to make more of a contribution to environmental protection while they are trying to up-level lifestyle and communities, versus the developed countries that have decimated resources to get where they are at today. For every society, environmental protection will demand sacrifices in the pace and strength of economic development. And with that, we need to consider and balance the economic impacts, not just First World countries' GDP, but also the impact on laborers, workers, and people's livelihood across the globe.

CLARE PALMER: There are several positions on this. One says that it's the developed countries that caused and produce greenhouse gas, and so they should carry special responsibility for fixing the problem. Further, it would be particularly unfair to force nations that didn't cause the problem to cut emissions to correct the imbalance we've created. Related, there's the argument that developed countries have greater wealth and therefore greater capacity to address environmental issues, while developing countries are putting all of their efforts and resources into improving their economy and quality of life.

These are some of the historical arguments and distributive arguments about climate justice. Diana may be able to say more about the actual policies from international climate negotiations that govern transfer of resources from developed to less developed countries.

DIANA LIVERMAN: In the absence of an international agreement, some steps are still being taken to address this issue. The Copenhagen Accord set a goal to raise 100 billion dollars per year through 2020 to help developing countries cut carbon emissions and has other provisions to mitigate deforestation. Also, organizations such as Oxfam and others play a role in supporting environmental action and relieving suffering, as with the Pakistan floods in 2011. We can help these initiatives by supporting and contributing to such organizations.

Help the Environment, Save Money, Change the World

JOHN DUNNE: Greg, did you tell us that one of the main issues that we can manage is heating our homes?

GREGORY NORRIS: How your home is heated is somewhat important. What's more important is the size of your home, because heating and cooling energy use is proportional to home size. Other big levers we have are how much you earn, where you live, your distance from work, shopping, and other activities. Another big one is air travel. Typically, city dwellers are more efficient because they drive less and use public transport. But because they fly more, their emissions balance out with their rural peers.

A few more points: the three areas of spending that have the biggest impact on climate change are food, home energy, and transportation. And when you start to change habits—fly less, take shorter showers, turn back the thermostat, ride your bike—you are going to be saving money. Now, you have to be careful where you spend that money you saved. If you fly to Tahiti for vacation, you'll negate your other efforts. You could give it to a nonprofit, or put it into a fund and retire early. Then you can tell your friends they're missing out, because you are retiring early as an incentive to get others to take pro-environmental actions!

And if you're on this path, then we need to rephrase "retirement" to something like "graduate early from the workforce into a fuller life of voluntary action."

However, we also have to address what happens to the people in the margins of our economies when those of us with luxury lower our consumption. We need to deeply engage with economists to figure out how lowering our consumption will also help, and not hurt, other economies.

DIANA LIVERMAN: Is your point that when we consume less, many people lose their jobs?

GREGORY NORRIS: My point is that if we consume less, the economy may shrink, and the flow of money drops a bit. In our own countries, early graduation from the workforce, stepping out of a job into activities that are more fulfilling, leaves that job open for people who are coming into the economy. Also, some of the money we are spending promotes economic development in other countries, developed and developing, so we have to address those outcomes, too.

JOHN DUNNE: In some ways we are looking for the emergence of a new paradigm.

ROSHI JOAN HALIFAX: A new economic paradigm; not a paradigm of growth, a paradigm of generosity.

MATTHIEU RICARD: The ethical dilemma has been presented in the extreme, that if the wealthy nations curb consumerism, the developing nations will remain in abject poverty. I think a middle approach could be more effective. We could work to bring people out of poverty and provide decent healthcare, wages, and education, and then at some point the wealthy nations could work toward voluntary simplicities. We would also have to temper aspirations so that the developing nations wanting to copy the developed nations—two cars and all the amenities—don't overshoot the goal.

THUPTEN JINPA: Even with this plan, I think messaging is very import-ant. For people in Third World countries, who are often focused on sur-vival and their own economic development, the environmental message can sound moralizing. We need to create a compelling case that includes everyone's participation, especially those of us in the developed world.

Investing, not Preaching

DEKILA CHUNGYALPA: I want to build on what Greg said, that it's actually the infrastructure that needs this energy; the habit exists with the infra-structure. If investors would invest in clean energy for the Third World, where new infrastructure is being developed, that would bring hope for innovation and change.

But even on a simpler level, there was a story about a young Malaysian man who filled Coca-Cola bottles and put them on the roof as a way of accessing solar energy. That was so innovative and it was so simple. And he didn't let any social or economic barriers get in the way.

So if we can shift from preaching to investing, that's part of the real solution. I'm personally skeptical about aid to Third World countries because we're making them dependent on foreign aid and creating another habitual tendency.

The question is, what is realistic? It is a little unrealistic to think that we will solve all the problems quickly. It may take a lifetime, or more. But what is the incentive that will make us evolve? It cannot be preaching and it cannot be aid. Perhaps we can harness the motivation found in competition, that now resides in consumerism, and refocus that on a sustainable future.

JONATHAN PATZ: The focus doesn't have to be asking everyone, especially developing nations, to consume less. That's not practical. And the solution isn't a matter of either/or, but of changing and evolving. We have devel-oped and grown our economy based on oil and coal. Now we know better. We know it's dirty and harmful. And there is new technology, low-carbon transfer technology, that we can use to help developing nations create more sustainable energy standards than we did decades ago.

We build our developed countries and economies on more and more. Unfortunately, developing countries are following our bad habits in the worst way possible, and I think it's important that we bring the message of new possibility as they grow.

SALLIE MCFAGUE: In the interim, while we're in transition, we need to work with the system we have and do our best. All of these suggestions are very valid, and, at the same time, we need to be constructing a new vision of how we live at a deep level. This is happening in the education of our children. They are being introduced to the new worldview of inter-dependence and interrelationship.

We need basic changes to our current economic model. Currently, we are imprisoned in the consumer model, and that's the meanest kind of capitalism. There are other economic systems and models. We should work toward legislating elements of our vision for change, such as fair distribution and sustainability, into our current model in the meantime.

DANIEL GOLEMAN: While we're changing the system, I'd like to suggest that we change the materials we use to build our world. We've been using the same materials—brick, glass, cement, and others—for a long time, and some of these are very costly in terms of energy usage and pollution. We need innovation in the materials we're using as well as continuous upgrades to our infrastructure to shift its dependency away from coal, oil, and other limited resources. This could also be an enormous entrepre-neurial opportunity, creating jobs and providing sustainable technology to developing countries.

JOHN DUNNE: This points to something His Holiness says repeatedly: science can be a huge innovator and motivator. The more we look at our consumer culture and the environmentally unfriendly way we live, we see that our actions aren't even scientifically sound because we are heading toward a critical point of diminished resources and a compromised planet.

DANIEL GOLEMAN: That's why the transparency that Roshi Joan talked about is important. It makes everything we have or do visible in terms of environmental impact. Today, we own and do things with little if any knowledge of their true environmental cost. Once we have transparency, we can make better choices and better buying and spending choices, which will be drivers for environmentally friendly innovation.

ELKE WEBER: In addition to the systemic solutions and innovations we have been discussing, I would like to add to the list the empowerment of women, and the influence of that on population growth.

JOHN DUNNE: That's a good point. As you mentioned earlier, there's a direct correlation between women's education and population. It's also interesting, as Dekila shared, that women are more naturally connected and empathetic to environmental issues.

REDD and Carbon Credits

JOHN DUNNE: To return to the systems we currently have, one of them is REDD. What is that and how does it work?

DEKILA CHUNGYALPA: It stands for Reducing Emissions from Deforestation and Forest Degradation. REDD is basically the idea that most of the carbon is stored in forests, and because of the high rate of deforestation, there's a lot of carbon going into the atmosphere and contributing to global warming and climate change. The idea is that there could be a global financial mechanism that primarily encourages people not to deforest, while also promoting reforestation. First World countries and several Third World countries, as well as many governments, would put money into this mechanism, and whenever a government made a commitment to protect a forest, it would have access to some of this funding. Basically, it's a financial-incentive mechanism.

It's been renamed to REDD-Plus, because it now includes biodiversity and indigenous rights. Conserving trees by creating a plantation is much different from conserving a forest and all of its biodiversity. Also, many indigenous people live in and rely on the forest. So projects that protect biodiversity and/or indigenous rights qualify for the "Plus" factors of the program.

What REDD is trying to do is get all the governments around the globe to agree on this system of conservation and protection.

JONATHAN PATZ: Foresters tell me that there's a big distinction between intact trees, especially in primary growth forests, and planting new trees. My understanding from the forestry sector is that more carbon is stored in original forests. Research shows that if you were to cut down an existing forest and grow biofuels in place, it would take more than a thousand years to recoup the carbon you lost. On the other hand, if you plant trees on land that's already degraded, you achieve sequestration, and more carbon-retention value added.

DIANA LIVERMAN: Just to make sure people aren't confused, REDD is not primarily about planting new forests; it's mostly about protecting the old forests.

There are two ways in which finance and developing countries can intersect around climate change. One is to pay for environmental services, where wealthy countries send money to developing countries that maintain the forests that are the carbon sinks and the source of oxygen for the whole planet. The other is market-driven, where a country can invest in forest protection and reduced emissions by getting solar cookers or efficient woodstoves for women and families, and get credit for that. It's the idea of carbon offsetting, and while it's controversial, it can be done is a way that is sustainable.

The controversy is in the choice. Say you have $20,000 to invest in sustainability. Do you put it toward yourself and install solar panels on your house or give it to a nongovernmental organization that's providing people in developing countries with efficient woodstoves? You might actually create a greater reduction in emissions with the latter. Part of the debate is that some call it carbon offsetting, while others see it as paying for our carbon sins and indulgences.

DEKILA CHUNGYALPA: Expedia has a voluntary option that you can choose when booking a flight to offset carbon. It calculates how much your flight will use and what your contribution will restore. But I don't think many people are aware of this tool. And that brings us back to the big challenge: raising awareness. There are many voluntary mechanisms already in existence. If we could get an entire economic sector focused on sustainability, that could help.

ELKE WEBER: We talked about the possibility of vegetarian meals as the default meal on airlines, but I think carbon offset should be automatically priced into an airline ticket. At least it could be a default with the option to decline.

DIANA LIVERMAN: Through my affiliation with the University of Oxford, we made strong efforts to persuade British Airways to do exactly that, but they didn't want to shift from voluntary opting in to voluntary opting out. There are companies that have made this change, however. If you buy a Land Rover in Europe, part of the price goes to offset the first 35,000 miles of driving and the impact of manufacturing. They have made this an opt-out choice, and close to 95 percent of people who buy are keeping the option. I think having these options and offsets is a legitimate way for people to see and be involved with offsetting carbon emissions.

JOHN DUNNE: While we're on the topic of carbon offsets, is that a short-term mechanism toward transition or a long-term solution?

DIANA LIVERMAN: It's short-term, and to fully explain it would be very technical, but basically we need a global cap on emissions. And once you reach a global cap on emissions, offsets really don't work. So the offsets are a short-term way to generate reductions in emissions as we work toward a global cap on carbon emissions.

THUPTEN JINPA: Out of curiosity, do these various offset programs donate to NGOs or have their own branches of community action?

DIANA LIVERMAN: Sometimes companies—say an airline that charges thirty dollars to offset the carbon on a flight—will give money to an NGO, and sometimes it will go back into their company or into projects they've developed in other countries.

I've just supervised twenty different graduate dissertations that have evaluated offset projects in various countries. They included solar energy projects in rural Guatemala, efficient woodstove projects in Madagascar, wind farms in China, and small-scale hydro projects. These are projects that wouldn't have happened without your money. They are legitimate offset projects where they would have otherwise used a generator and fossil fuels. Using the offset money, they have access to solar energy, or wind, or another solution. We call this an "additional carbon reduction," since it wouldn't have happened without the offset funding.

JOHN DUNNE: So one possibility would be to take some action—say, reducing meat consumption—save the money otherwise spent, and donate it to offsets when one travels, for example. Would that be reasonable?

DIANA LIVERMAN: I think that you should only use carbon offsets after you've done everything possible to reduce your own emissions. In fact, our research shows that individuals and companies that offset are often the ones that have done the most to reduce their emissions. It's really a quantitative calculation. You say, "Okay, I've reduced my carbon footprint from 15 tons a year to 4 tons a year, but it should only be 2 tons, so I'll offset those other 2 tons."

Changing Our Lifestyle: Embracing Wild Space

JOHN DUNNE: The concept of a lifestyle change can be quite difficult, unless it's forced upon us, and even then it can still be difficult. I'm wondering if there are ways in which people can experience a taste of their wild space, of living in a very simplified environment, even temporarily, even just a weekend?

SALLIE MCFAGUE: That's a very good question. The notion of a person in lack of wild space is based upon the conventional Western male, who is fit and trim, educated, probably white, hasn't really known any kind of deprivations or discrimination; he simply is the hegemonic human being. Anybody who does not fit that description in any sense probably already has a little bit of wild space. But a lot of middle-class folks do fit that pattern. And in that case, you would have to create some wild space.

For example, when people travel to developing countries and experience for the first time what it's like not to have a good bathroom or food that they like, it is a disorienting movement outside the box. That is where you can begin to think differently. Any pattern you can develop or experience that allows you to imagine another way of living helps cultivate wild space.

Your wild space is some of the most precious space that you have. Never underestimate its possibilities; it is what allows us to dream, and to dream differently. One of the great things about being human is that we help construct the reality in which we live. We live within our world, but we have constructed that world, and it can be a different world. When I grew up it was a man's world; today, that's changing.

DANIEL GOLEMAN: There's a wonderful wild-space opportunity run by Bernie Glassman of Zen Peacemakers. It is a *sesshin*, a Japanese Zen retreat, which is held on the streets of a city while you live as a homeless person. You become invisible. That's pretty wild.

ROSHI JOAN HALIFAX: I think this work that Bernie is doing is so important, because it means we're stepping out of our frame of reference, where we feel safe and familiar, and we have the opportunity to look out of the eyes of the so-called other. Suddenly our behaviors, which have contributed to adverse homelessness, become very apparent to us, as does our treatment of people who live in the margins of the world. This is critical.

This is one of the functions of pilgrimage in Buddhism. We leave our monasteries and we have a chance to go to holy places, but to get to those holy places, such as Mount Kailash, a tremendous amount is asked of you physically and psychically. These are places of tremendous power, and having visited some of these places as a pilgrim I have to say that one of the things that I've hoped for is more respect for these spaces. Having been to and circumambulated Mount Kailash seven times, it's devastating to see the increase of trash there since 1987. My hope is that there would be a call among Tibetans, and among Chinese, who have respect for wild space, so that we would take care of these holy natural places, where the narratives of our culture are also held.

I also live in a valley that's surrounded by three million acres of national forest, where we're completely off the grid. That's where I go to restore myself, so that when I come back to the monastery, or to conferences like this, I have had the experience of being restored and revivified by being in the natural world. I think it's important that people have refuges, take time to step away from the so-called civilized world—"the backward step," Zen Master Dogen called it—and move into the wild space that Sallie has been talking about.

THUPTEN JINPA: Since we're on the topic of fundamental shifts in the way we envision our life, and questioning assumptions underlying our consumerist model of life and society, one of the things we need to take into account is that environmental protection demands that we accept some degree of inconvenience. Most lifestyle choices that we make in a consumerist model have to do with convenience and efficiency. We tend to define efficiency in terms of speed. In our culture, speed and convenience seem to be important values.

JOHN DUNNE: There is certainly a kind of intensity in the speed of modern life in the West. One could ask, "If I didn't have that convenience and therefore life had to slow down, might that actually be more enjoyable?" Might it be more enjoyable to relax in the train station and read a book versus rushing home in a car in traffic? We have this image sometimes that the life of voluntary poverty or simplicity requires us to be dressed in bark with barely enough to eat. One of my favorite images of a person with a very simple life is Matthieu Ricard, who has written a book about happiness. Matthieu is living a very, very simple lifestyle, and he seems to be really quite happy.

SALLIE MCFAGUE: Another example of changing worldview is the transition to what is now the accepted status of women in the West. In most of the world, the regard toward women is still abysmal. But during my lifetime—I am now seventy-eight—there has been a paradigm shift in the West in the view toward women. The hegemonic human being is no longer just a male but also, at least in the West, female as well. The status of women in any culture is a deep indication of the health and well-being of the entire culture.

Simplicity and Empathy

JOHN DUNNE: I'm going to ask my colleague Venerable Lobsang Tenzin, the founder and director of the Emory-Tibet Partnership and the Emory-Tibet Science Initiative, to make a comment from the monastic perspective.

GESHE LOBSANG TENZIN NEGI: Thank you. This has been a great learning experience for me, with such great minds. Buddhism has a motto: "fewer needs, fewer deeds"—and that's exactly what Geshe Jinpa-la was saying. The accelerating speed with which we are moving is based on how much want we have, and therefore our greater needs. I think this ties to greed. Frans de Waal, the biologist, has written a book called *The Age of Empathy* (Three Rivers Press, 2009), and it starts with the idea that "Greed is out, empathy is in." We are at a place where we are see-ing the consequences of the unchecked greed and individualism our society has prized, where it is okay to maximize your profit within a set of rules. The problem is that it doesn't matter who gets hurt in the process.

The need for empathy is becoming much clearer now. As Sallie was say-ing, the fundamental worldview that we currently hold has a tremendous impact on how we act. We need to address the question that Sallie asked: how do we cultivate deep awareness? That happens through meditation. Meditation doesn't have to mean sitting cross-legged on a cushion in a Buddhist setting. It simply is a process of deepening or fine-tuning our perspective. I think the opportunity for deeper awareness is growing, thanks to His Holiness the Dalai Lama and many of the people here in this room. Adam Engle had the courage to support His Holiness's vision and, with Francisco Varela, to create Mind and Life. I think that due to efforts like this, we are at a point where there is a truly great opportunity to draw from the modern science that is shedding more and more light into this fundamental nature of our living being.

What is it that drives our survival; what is it that is most crucial for our survival? Is it greed, or is it empathy? With these new insights we are seeing that empathy, not greed, is the key to our society and our survival.

Through these meetings, where exchanges take place between the con-templative traditions and scientists, we model a mechanism by which we can deepen insight and shed light on new perspectives.

To build on new perspectives, we have to engage in a transformative process, and in the Buddhist world, we think of this in terms of, first, the training in right view, that is, seeing things as they truly are. This leads to right motivation. How then do we deepen right motivation? Through right concentration, or right mindfulness. Those have impact on our actions; they bring right action, right livelihood, and right speech. This is the kind of transformative process that we find in Buddhism, but it is broadly applicable.

In these meetings, we are just scratching the surface, but I think there is a great potential present. Just being here in the presence of such great scientists and contemplatives, and hearing all the presentations, gives me a deep sense of appreciation and awe for the impact of His Holiness the Dalai Lama's vision.

With regard to the Emory-Tibet Science Initiative, it's a project to create a comprehensive and sustainable modern science education for monks and nuns. Many of the monastics present at this meeting have studied science through this program. In the beginning we struggled. People thought we were corrupting monastics with science. We struggled to demonstrate the real purpose behind it. My colleague Geshe Lhakdor played a critical role in this movement, in some ways revolutionizing monastic education. What has become clear is that His Holiness's vision here is not just to bring modern science to monks and nuns to offer them scientific facts, but rather it is a way to facilitate a deep dialogue and exchange between scientists and contemplatives. Contemplatives are the holders of the deep wealth of understanding mind and emotions, the processes of cultivating deep awareness, and the resulting spontaneous right action and behavior. I think that is what the Emory-Tibet Science Initiative is really about: expanding knowledge and also contributing a method for humanity to face some real problems. These problems cannot be addressed simply by having more wealth, or more materialistic gain, but through combining knowledge with the inner science of the mind.

Carry the Message; Live a Good Life

JOHN DUNNE: Your Holiness, we've had a great conversation. We would like to hear some of your final reflections to close our meeting.

HIS HOLINESS THE DALAI LAMA: First, it's very encouraging to see our dialogues strengthening year after year. It's also great to witness people participating not just at the academic level but also with a genuine sense of care and concern. When we go our own ways, if each of us reaches out to ten people, and they to ten, and so on, we can continue to build the awareness needed to help our world. I will do this; I will stay committed each day to the well-being of sentient beings, until my death. In the morning when I wake, I remember the Buddha and set my intention and commitment on making some contribution to creating a better, happier world. In our own ways, each of us has that same opportunity. I may have a fancy name, "the Dalai Lama," but I am just one human being. Each of you can have a great impact. And then, when your last day comes, you will feel happy that you have lived a good life and made an important contribution. That will be more fulfilling than worrying about where your money is going to go when you die. But before that day comes, I am looking forward to our next meeting.

14 Appreciation and Thanks
Group Discussion

JOHN DUNNE: Your Holiness, we really appreciate your time this week. The Mind and Life Institute is very grateful, and we, too, look forward to the next meeting. Diego Hangartner, the chief operating officer of the Mind and Life Institute, will now offer some thanks to people who've produced this meeting.

DIEGO HANGARTNER: Many, many people were involved. Foremost thanks to His Holiness the Dalai Lama. You have been an unwavering force of determination in our efforts. We're very grateful. Also our thanks go to His Holiness the Gyalwang Karmapa, who is involved in the preservation of the environment. A big thank you to all of our speakers, who have come from very far, and to the moderators, who have dedicated not only this week of their time but also time to meet, discuss, and shape this program.

It has been wonderful to work with the planning committee—Dan, John, and Jonathan—to create and implement this program. None of this would have been possible without the incredible support of the Hershey Family Foundation. Since 1987, the Hershey Family Foundation has been supporting these meetings. Thank you very, very much. They also support other initiatives of the Mind and Life Institute, such as the Varela Awards, and other events related to the advancement of this emerging field of contemplative science. We also wish to thank all of our other donors who have been contributing over the years to the flourishing of this new area of dialogue and inquiry. The Office of His Holiness the Dalai Lama has been very supportive—particularly Chime-la and Tenzin Taklha have been very dedicated.

We would like to thank our translators, Druk Tsering, from Dehra-dun, and Tenzin Tsepak, who have been translating all the proceedings here into Tibetan. We also send appreciation to the team managing the webcast that has enabled more than ten thousand people to watch these proceedings. Special thanks to our camerapeople: Don, Choejor, Lehpa, Chime, Dzogchen, and Pasang.

I would like to extend my thanks to the Mind and Life board and Program and Research Council. Our ongoing work with this incredible group of people is guiding the vision for the organization. I would also like to thank the Mind and Life staff, those who are here, and those who are in other places but played a role in making this meeting a success. And I would like to thank Middle Path Travels for helping us with travel and logistics, making sure everyone got here okay. Finally, I would like to thank Adam, who has been instrumental in this vision and in bringing us together, and Betty, who has been an unwavering support for me.

JOHN DUNNE: Thank you, Diego. I'd like to ask Richie Davidson, a senior and long-term member of the Mind and Life Institute board of directors, to say a few words.

RICHARD DAVIDSON: I want to say to Your Holiness that your time and involvement with us over the years has been deeply inspiring. One of the things I often tell people is that the scientists who come to Dharamsala to be in your presence leave different than when they first came. They are deeply affected by being in your presence. We do the best we can to bring the best people in the world to Dharamsala; these are the thought leaders in different areas of science. After being here, they are changed in very beneficial ways. So on behalf of the board of directors, I'd like to extend a deep bow of gratitude for all the time that you give to us.

This is a special moment in Mind and Life history. We are going through a transition, and this is the last meeting in Dharamsala at which Adam

Engle, our chair of the Mind and Life Institute, is present in his role as chairman. Adam is the cofounder of Mind and Life, a real visionary and strategist, and he has engineered this organization in ways that I don't think any of us dreamed about when we first became involved. Through his tireless work, his commitment to the cause, and his incredible ability to listen to scholars, he has enabled Mind and Life to rise to a certain position where the rigor, honesty, and ethical sense that we bring to our mission has been recognized worldwide. The penetration of this collective dialogue and new kind of epistemology that brings together contemplative traditions and modern science could never have occurred without his extraordinary work. It is my great honor to be Adam's close friend and colleague, and I'd like to ask him to say a few words.

ADAM ENGLE: Your Holiness, we've been through a lot since 1983 when I first heard the rumor that you were interested in science and came up with the crazy idea of organizing a science meeting with you. Reflecting on what we've done together with Mind and Life, we've been through two developmental phases. Phase one began in 1987, when we started the dialogues. For a dozen years, we pioneered how to develop rigorous dialogue between Buddhism and science and the scholarly world. In 2000, we enhanced that dramatically when you requested that the scientists and the scholars actually investigate contemplative practices to see how they affect brain behavior. You asked that any beneficial findings be taught in a secular environment. That shift has been dramatic in the world. If we think back to the way the world was in 2000 and the way it is today, there was little reputable research on contemplative practices in those days. Through these dialogues, the establishment of the Summer Research Institute, the Varela Awards, and contemplative studies fellowships, and the Mind and Life International Symposium on Contemplative Research, we have cultivated thousands of people and hundreds of scientists and scholars in the world who are doing this work in dozens of centers and laboratories.

There are faculty now that are receiving tenure in contemplative studies and contemplative science, and I suspect eventually there might even be faculty departments on contemplative science and studies. More important, there's been a huge change in public awareness on the effects of contemplative practice, what I call "mental and emotional fitness training for health and well-being."

My personal aspiration for Mind and Life has been that through our work and the work that stems from us, a global awareness of the value of purposeful mental and emotional fitness training will grow. The fact is, it can be done, and there are age-appropriate and culturally appropriate tools available so that everyone in the world has the opportunity to practice in whatever way or context is most effective for them—in education, healthcare, and leadership in the workplace.

When we sat for the first time in 1986, one of the things that I asked you was, "What's in it for you, what are your desires here?" And one of the things you said at that time was that you wanted education to go into the monasteries. I just want to acknowledge how the Emory-Tibet Partnership and Science for Monks have actually done that. There are many people who have contributed to these programs over the years, and many have been acknowledged. I especially want to acknowledge your brother, Ngari Rinpoche (Tenzin Choegyal), who was the original go-between for us, and who has been a champion of Mind and Life for decades.

From a personal point of view, I want to thank you from the bottom of my heart, and on behalf of my family as well, for being my teacher and my friend. Your kindness, generosity, and blessings have transformed my life. I am incredibly grateful to be able to use my few skills in service of your vision, in service of the Dharma, and in service of humanity.

I recall that in 2002, shortly after Francisco died, we had started our first public meeting at Harvard, and then you got sick, and we had to cancel it. Mind and Life was virtually bankrupt. I came here, put a picture of Francisco on the table, and said, "Your Holiness, Francisco's gone. Is this something that you want to continue to do?" You looked at me very clearly and said, "The work that we're doing here together is much too important to depend on any one life, whether it be Francisco, whether it be Robert Livingston"—who had recently passed—"whether it be me, or whether it be you." You said, "I want you to build this, so that it outlives us." I am grateful today to be able to look at you, and say, "Mission accomplished."

JOHN DUNNE: Thank you very much, Adam. We really appreciate it. The Mind and Life Institute is very grateful for all of your work and contributions. We wouldn't be here without you and Your Holiness.

HIS HOLINESS THE DALAI LAMA: Once more, we have this gathering. Last year, in Delhi, after my interview with CNN, I mentioned that I was looking forward to complete retirement. I was asked, "Oh, what will happen to this kind of meeting if you retire?" To this I say, don't worry. As far as political responsibilities are concerned, I decided to retire. Not only to retire myself but also to retire a four-centuries-old tradition by which the institution of the Dalai Lama is both head of state and spirituality. That responsibility, I happily, voluntarily, and proudly ended. But my other commitment is the promotion of human value, and this kind of meeting is part of that commitment. Our meeting proves to you that my retirement has no effect on this commitment.

I must also say that for so many years, a number of people—including Adam Engle, Daniel Goleman, and so many others—have really worked hard, right from the beginning. I want to thank you. Some participants, like Francisco Varela, are no longer with us, but we carry their wish and their spirit continuously—as we do with Buddha Shakyamuni, who came here 2,600 years ago. His spirit continues like other great masters. For those people who have real vision but are no longer physically with us, it is our responsibility to carry on their spirit and their vision. I very much appreciate these visionaries and those who carry on their work.

Afterword

Daniel Goleman, *Mind and Life Institute*

As we reflect on the impacts of our meeting, the connections between ethics, the environment, and interdependence that we made are being echoed by a louder chorus. One of the strongest voices added to this chorus is that of Pope Francis, who in his 2015 encyclical framed the climate crisis as a social justice issue, calling the fight against global warming a moral imperative and "one of the principal challenges facing humanity."

Of course in voicing this concern he joined the Dalai Lama—among other spiritual leaders—in seeking to motivate people worldwide to rise to this challenge. And each of us, it seems, was touched by our meeting—and by the keen participation of the Dalai Lama—and spurred on in our given corner of this great challenge.

Dekila Chungyalpa

In her presentation at our meeting Dekila Chungyalpa mentioned in passing that she was starting a new initiative at the World Wildlife Fund (WWF). This is Sacred Earth: Faiths for Conservation. The program trains religious leaders in the basics of environmental understanding as well as in organizing tools for implementing an environmental project relevant to their own mission. So, for example, the Catholic Church in Kenya focused on an environmental education track for its hundreds of schools, teaching students these same basics.

After fourteen years at WWF, Dekila left the staff to become a senior fellow there. And she won a prestigious environmental honor: the Yale School of Forestry and Environmental Studies' Dorothy S. McCluskey Visiting Fellowship in Conservation for 2014. While at Yale University she designed a program where Yale and Princeton, among other universities, offer funding for their graduates to receive a year's training to learn methods for organizing environmental projects in cooperation with local religious leaders. She continues to direct this program as head of Sacred Earth.

Thupten Jinpa

Our meeting gave Thupten Jinpa the opportunity to step out of his role as His Holiness's chief English-language interpreter and draw on his classical Buddhist philosophical training to make explicit a theory of action that had only been implicit in Buddhist thinking—and present that theory to us. He later fleshed out that theory of action in his 2015 book, *A Fearless Heart: How the Courage to Be Compassionate Can Transform Our Lives* (Penguin Publishing Group, 2015), integrating that model with new findings from cognitive neuroscience, including the neuroscience of habit formation and change.

In doing so, Jinpa explained how systematic mental cultivation can create new positive habits. One key distinction here is between "motivation" and "intention." In his book *Thinking Fast and Slow* (Farrar, Strauss and Giroux, 2011), Daniel Kahneman gives an analysis of two mental systems, one conscious and one unconscious: intentions are our conscious choice, while motivation remains unconscious, though powerful, and not easy to see or change. In Jinpa's model, by contrast, we use conscious intention-setting to change motivation. And a compassionate motivation—genuine concern for others—offers the best basis for this theory of action, as well as our personal ideals.

Diana Liverman

For Diana Liverman the impacts of her meeting with the Dalai Lama took many forms—for one, she has continued to have a keen interest in his leadership on climate change. She has supplied data to another meeting participant, Matthieu Ricard, sending him material on the climate crisis for his books. She has helped the Tibetan government-in-exile's environmental team get accredited to attend international climate negotiations, including the Rio+20 summit, by adding them to a university delegation.

Her work has been recognized with honors like the Presidential Achievement Award of the American Association of Geographers and a Guggenheim Fellowship. Her environmental activism continues apace, with cochairing the planning group for a better "Future Earth" that was launched at the Rio Earth Summit, and she was an author of a US National Climate Assessment report. Her scholarly work also continues at an impressive rate, with writing more than a dozen coauthored journal articles and book chapters since our meeting, many reflecting themes like environmental justice and her research on the local impacts of global patterns, and others speaking to the urgent need for stronger policy to slow the degradation of our planet's environment.

On a more personal note, Diana has started a meditation practice, joining a loose group at the University of Arizona working on mindfulness. And she commissioned the preparation of a slice of an ancient tree showing in its rings differences in climate over the centuries—a gift presented to the Dalai Lama by her fellow University of Arizona professor (and Mind and Life fellow) Al Kaszniak.

Sallie McFague

For Sallie McFague our meeting came at a time in her life when, as she says now, "I needed new juice to keep working on matters of climate change and worldviews." She reported feeling thankful for the stimulation she received that week.

What she calls the fortunate timing of our meeting reinforced her own notions of a compassion-based restraint and the concept of kenosis: the "self-emptying" of one's will that allows more receptivity to a divine will, a key organizing principle in her own thinking. The Buddhist insights, she found, were different enough from the Christian ones that they widened her views considerably.

Many of the themes and concepts we reflected on together are echoed in her 2013 book, *Blessed Are the Consumers: Climate Change and the Practice of Restraint* (Routledge), a collection of essays that spans forty years of her writing. Sallie continues to teach an advanced seminar at the Vancouver School of Theology on climate change and postmodern views of transcendence and immanence, continuing a line of thought articulated in her 1993 book *The Body of God: An Ecological Theology* (Fortress Press), which used that physical metaphor for caring for our planet.

Gregory Norris

As he told the Dalai Lama, Gregory Norris had been teaching life-cycle assessment at the Harvard School of Public Health for years, and each year when his students finished his assignment of calculating their personal carbon footprint, they were shocked and dispirited. That led Norris to the insight that flipping the calculation around to a *handprint*, where you get the footprint as a starting point and then just measure all the ways you can reduce it, would be far more motivating.

At our meeting this idea received a key endorsement from cognitive scientist Elke Weber. She had been puzzled by the fact that when people received information about global warming and their role in it they tended to become less motivated, rather than more, to do anything about it. When she heard Norris explain the handprint concept she immediately recognized that this approach was far more artful, marshaling positive emotions and motivation rather than negativity and denial.

Gregory Norris's presentation on handprints at our meeting was one of the first times he had shared the idea with an audience beyond the specialized world of industrial ecology and public health. Weber's endorsement, and the general receptivity of the group, gave him greater enthusiasm for promoting the concept. He worked on clarifying the description of handprints and how to calculate them and put up a website about the concept. This led to two donations to help him further advance the idea, a crucial boost at the time.

At about the same time, I (Daniel Goleman) wrote about the handprint idea in *Time* magazine for their "10 Ideas That Are Changing Your Life" issue. When it ran in March 2012, Norris found a wider audience for his concept and that the idea was being given more credibility and visibility. That boost helped create an initiative at the Harvard School of Public Health, called SHINE (Sustainability and Health Initiative for NetPositive Enterprise), in which five companies are now road-testing handprints in their own operations. "My main projects at Harvard these days," Norris told me, "are on making handprints more and more real by working with companies on advancing the methodology."

In recognition of the need to "reinvent everything" in the material world not only to have zero impact but to actually replenish nature, Norris also works with the International Living Future Institute on "living products." Their goal, according to their website, is to "re-imagine their design and construction" so they "function as elegantly and efficiently as anything found in the natural world."

Clare Palmer

For Clare Palmer, the ethicist, the impacts of our meeting were immediate, as shown, for instance, in her giving several talks to student groups about the Dharamsala meeting on her return to Texas A&M University. She now routinely discusses the Dalai Lama's views in her classes on environmental ethics, especially when considering the value of the lives of beings, including animals. The meeting spurred Clare's interest in environmental psychology and what moves people to change their actions (or not)—reflections that stemmed from Jinpa's and Elke's presentations.

The very format of our meeting made Clare see the value of interdisciplinary thinking and action, a track that has led her to try to break down barriers between disciplines, especially regarding the environment. She has been bringing the ethicist's perspective to other fields, particularly genomics. As co-principal investigator on a grant from the National Science Foundation, she has been designing an online course that explores social and ethical questions raised by genetically modified crops and animals, as well as the ethical issues surrounding genomics in general.

Another influence of the interdisciplinary perspective is in Clare's writing, where she has more actively reached out to coauthors in disciplines such as biology, environmental science, and genetics for books, chapters, and journal articles. The topics include some rather provocative issues like the ethics of pets (or, as framed at a Yale conference, "Is Keeping Pets Immoral?") and what kinds of life we should make special efforts to protect.

Jonathan Patz

When we contacted Jonathan Patz to learn how our meeting had impacted his thinking and work, he was in Ethiopia for five months, part of a sabbatical year from his post at the University of Wisconsin. This research opportunity continues his immersion in the disproportionately negative health impacts of the global climate crisis on the world's poor. Meeting with the Dalai Lama, he has found, has made him more mindful of the ethical issues raised by these disparities.

The moment that has continued to resonate for Jonathan was when the Dalai Lama asked him a simple, yet penetrating, question: "Now that you Americans know that burning fossil fuels harms people around the world, why do you continue to do it? Your country is not showing much compassion, is it?" He has repeated that question to his audiences in countless public lectures and explored it in more detail in his research and writing.

That writing includes a new book he has coedited with Barry Levy, *Climate Change and Public Health* (Oxford University Press, 2015). In the book fifteen experts argue the case that climate change will worsen health problems like deaths due to soaring temperatures and diseases like asthma and allergies, as well as malnutrition, mental disorders, and even violence.

He highlighted the ethical dimension in an article coauthored with Levy, "Climate Change, Human Rights, and Social Justice"(*Annals of Global Health*, 2015). And he brought the ethics of the climate issue to the attention of the medical world in an article in the *Journal of the American Medical Association* (*JAMA*) that was timed to appear during the September 2014 UN Climate Summit in New York City: "Climate Change: Challenges and Opportunities for Global Health" (*JAMA*, 2014). That article spurred a *JAMA* editorial encouraging physicians to consider climate change a public health issue akin to good hygiene and sanitation.

A 2007 research article coauthored by Patz on the ethical dilemma of climate change pointed out that while the richest people on the planet cause the largest portion of global warming and related impacts, the poorest suffer the worst results, particularly in damage to health ("Climate Change and Global Health").That theme continues to organize much of his ongoing thinking, such as an article with Tony L. Goldberg, "The Need for a Global Health Ethic" (*Lancet*, 2015). That article caught the public imagination, going viral. A key cartogram map from that piece showing the disproportionate impacts from climate change on rich and poor countries continues to get prominent display at places like the World Health Organization. And Patz's work has been honored both locally and internationally: he has been awarded an endowed chair at the University of Wisconsin and given an award for his work from the world's largest public health organizations.

Matthieu Ricard

In the years following our meeting Matthieu Ricard returned to his academic roots to write a scholarly argument for compassion, *Altruism: The Power of Compassion to Change Yourself and the World* (Little, Brown, 2015). Several chapters reflect his presentation at our meeting on the plight of farm animals and the humanitarian case for vegetarianism.

This argument became the focus of a subsequent book, *A Plea for Animals* (Shambhala, 2017). First published in France, the book created a stir in that country, with Matthieu meeting with members of the French Senate. A month after that meeting the French civil code was changed, altering the status of animals from "mobile furniture" to "sentient being" (Matthieu found it amazing this had not been done before). And a new law has been proposed creating a vegetarian option in all school cafeterias; as of this writing Matthieu has been involved in the parliamentary debates on the law, but there has not yet been a vote.

As for his own humanitarian projects through the charity he founded, Karuna-Shechen, the organization now treats 120,000 patients a year in India, Nepal, and Tibet, and there are 25,000 children studying in the schools the group has built in that region. After the 2015 Himalayan earthquake, the group came to the aid of 210,000 people in 560 villages, supplying two to four weeks of food for each person and medical assistance. The organization has been preparing for the next two or three years of rebuilding after the earthquake damage, including rehabilitating damaged schools, food security, solar electricity, and organic agriculture. They also fight trafficking in children and women among desperately poor families.

Elke Weber

For Elke Weber the meeting's immediate impact was to strengthen her belief in a set of interlinked principles, all research-based—and all strongly reinforced by her meeting with the Dalai Lama.

The first of these, decisions about the environment—like human impacts on planetary boundaries for survival—need to be aligned with "moral, ethical, or religious rules of conduct," instead of cost-benefit thinking that favors just oneself or one's own group. Stewardship of the earth and its resources is more important, for example, than profit and more effective in motivating action that will safeguard our planet for future generations.

The second draws on her own behavioral decision research (as was true of her presentation at the meeting), and was underlined by other presentations like that of Gregory Norris on "handprints": the importance of positive messaging.

Such messaging encourages the third point: that each of us needs to feel we can act to change things for the better—that we have agency, the sense of being able to act, and efficacy, the feeling that what we do makes a difference, and the responsibility to act to protect the earth. Our choices can matter.

Along with this affirmation of her earlier assumptions, Professor Weber has been engaged in a number of initiatives that demonstrate her own agency and efficacy in helping protect the earth. She has undertaken, pro bono, a project to help the US Navy with a culture-change initiative to reduce energy waste through better efficiency. Part of her contribution has been to "lower the cognitive effort"—that is, make it easier to know what to do—needed for Navy personnel to make these changes. This includes, for example, better labeling of thermostats in Navy barracks and efforts to make energy-efficient products the default options during procurement decisions.

Her writing projects follow the same lines. She has been lead author of a chapter for the United Nations' Intergovernmental Panel on Climate Change (IPCC) in their Fifth Assessment Report: "Integrated Risk and Uncertainty Assessment of Climate Change Response Policies" in *Climate Change 2014: Mitigation of Climate Change* (Cambridge University Press, 2014). In the chapter she reviews what cognitive science has learned about how people make decisions to integrate principles from motivation, goal-setting, and decision-making research as it could bear positively on environmental decisions.

His Holiness the Seventeenth Karmapa

As for His Holiness the Seventeenth Karmapa, the meeting offered several kinds of data that he has used in his public talks when he addresses environmental issues. Diana Liverman's presentation was particularly eye-opening, especially the data on "carrying capacity" and the overshooting of the upper boundaries for the safe operation of the planetary life-support systems. His Holiness not only has used these concepts in his talks but has also shown Professor Liverman's slides on the topic as part of his presentations. He continues to speak strongly about climate change, both to his own followers and in public talks around the world.

The sessions also have helped His Holiness in making a case for vegetarianism. A vegetarian himself, he urges others to become such. While he makes the traditional argument based on compassion, he also gives the case for vegetarianism as a way to slow climate change and other breaches of planetary boundaries for life support. He has sometimes shown a short video that Matthieu Ricard had hoped to show at our meeting but did not: a documentary about the cruelty of how livestock are treated in industrial farming.

The Karmapa has an increasing appeal among young people worldwide and often speaks to college students. At Princeton and Yale on a recent visit he addressed students there—a group of whom have become participants in Dekila's projects, training them to become environmental activists. And the Karmapa continues to be deeply involved in Rangjung Khoryug Sungkyob Tsokpa, his network of Tibetan Buddhist monasteries and nunneries that implement guidelines for sustainable life and work for monastics and laypeople—ranging from solar energy projects and reforestation to basic education in the environment.

His Holiness the Fourteenth Dalai Lama

Finally, the Dalai Lama has himself repeated in his own global public talks many of the scientific facts and messages from the meeting. To be sure, he may have learned many of these points earlier in his far-ranging meetings with public officials, scholars, and scientists. But this meeting resonated with his perspective, giving him more "ammunition," as he once called the information he acquires in his many encounters with scientists.

In my book *A Force for Good: The Dalai Lama's Vision for Our World*, written for release with his eightieth birthday on July 6, 2015, the chapter on his vision for protecting the environment repeats many of the key points from this meeting (Bantam Books, 2015). While the sight of violence, he notes, makes us recoil, the damage wrought by what we are doing to the environment takes place "more stealthily." What we need, he adds, is compassion at every level—and that includes for our planet.

As the Dalai Lama says, "The earth is our home, and our home is on fire."

Bibliography

Atran, Scott. *Cognitive Foundations of Natural History: Towards an Anthropology of Science*. New York: Cambridge University Press, 1996.

Dennehy, Kevin. "Sacred Earth: McCluskey Fellow Merges Religion and Conservation." Yale School of Forestry and Environmental Studies, May 6, 2014. http://environ ment.yale.edu/news/article/dekila-chungyalp-mccluskey-fellow-merges-religion-and-conservation.

De Waal, Frans. *The Age of Empathy: Nature's Lessons for a Kinder Society*. New York: Three Rivers Press, 2009.

Gamborg, Christian, Clare Palmer, and Peter Sandoe. "Ethics of Wildlife Management and Conservation: What Should We Try to Protect?" *Nature Education Knowledge* 3, no. 10 (2012): 8.

Goldberg, Tony L., and Jonathan A. Patz. "The Need for a Global Health Ethic." *Lancet*, July 15, 2015. https://doi.org/10.1016/S0140-6736(15)60757-7.

Goleman, Daniel. *Ecological Intelligence: The Hidden Impacts of What We Buy*. New York: Broadway Books, 2010.

Goleman, Daniel. *A Force for Good: The Dalai Lama's Vision for Our World*. New York: Bantam Books, 2015.

Iyer, Pico. *The Open Road: The Global Journey of the Fourteenth Dalai Lama*. New York: Vintage Books, 2008.

Jinpa, Thupten. *A Fearless Heart: How the Courage to Be Compassionate Can Transform Our Lives*. New York: Penguin Publishing Group, 2015.

Kahneman, Daniel. *Thinking Fast and Slow*. New York: Farrar, Strauss and Giroux, 2011.

Kunreuther, Howard, et al. "Integrated Risk and Uncertainty Assessment of Climate Change Response Policies." In *Climate Change 2014: Mitigation of Climate Change. Contribution of Working Group III to the Fifth Assessment Report of the Intergovernmental Panel on Climate Change* [O. R. Edenhofer et al.], 151–203. New York: Cambridge University Press, 2014.

Leiserowitz, Anthony, Edward W. Maibach, Connie Roser-Renouf, Geoff Feinberg, and Peter Howe. *Climate Change in the American Mind: Americans' Global Warming*

Beliefs and Attitudes in April 2013. New Haven, CT: Yale Project on Climate Change Communication, 2013. http://dx.doi.org/10.2139/ssrn.2298705.

Levy, Barry, and Jonathan Patz. "Climate Change, Human Rights, and Social Justice." *Annals of Global Health* 81, no. 3 (2015): 310–22.

Levy, Barry, and Jonathan Patz, coeditors. *Climate Change and Public Health*. New York: Oxford University Press, 2015.

McFague, Sallie. *Blessed Are the Consumers: Climate Change and the Practice of Restraint*. Minneapolis: Fortress Press, 2013.

McFague, Sallie. *The Body of God: An Ecological Theology*. Minneapolis: Fortress Press, 1993.

Patz, Jonathan, et al. "Climate Change: Challenges and Opportunities for Global Health." *JAMA* 312, no. 15 (2014): 1565–80.

Patz, Jonathan, Holly K. Gibbs, Jonathan A. Foley, et al. "Climate Change and Global Health: Quantifying a Growing Ethical Crisis." *EcoHealth* 4, no. 397 (2007). https://doi.org/10.1007/s10393-007-0141-1.

Ricard, Matthieu. *Altruism: The Power of Compassion to Change Yourself and the World*. New York: Little, Brown, 2015.

Ricard, Matthieu. *A Plea for the Animals*. Boulder, CO: Shambhala, 2016.

Rockström, Johan, et al. "Climate Change: The Necessary, the Possible and the Desirable: Earth League Climate Statement on the Implications for Climate Policy from the 5th IPCC Assessment." *Earth's Future* 2, no. 12 (2014): 606–11. https://doi.org/10.1002/2014EF000280.

Shantideva. *A Guide to the Bodhisattva's Way of Life*. Ithaca, NY: Snow Lion Publications, 1997.

Thompson, L. G., E. Mosley-Thompson, M. E. Davis, P.-N. Lin, K. Henderson, and T. A. Mashiotta (2003). "Tropical Glacier and Ice Core Evidence of Climate Change on Annual to Millennial Time Scales." In *Climate Variability and Change in High Elevation Regions: Past, Present & Future*, edited by Diaz H.F., 137–155. Dordrecht: Springer. https://doi.org/10.1007/978-94-015-1252-7_8.

Weber, Elke. "Climate Change Demands Behavioral Change: What Are the Challenges?" *Social Research: An International Quarterly* 82 (2015): 561–81.

Wilder, Margaret, Diana M. Liverman, Laurel Bellante, and Tracey Osborne. "Southwest Climate Gap: Poverty and Environmental Justice in the U.S. Southwest." *Local Environment* 21, no. 11 (2016): 1332–53.

Zaval, Lisa, Ezra M. Markowitz, and Elke U. Weber. "How Will I Be Remembered? Conserving the Environment for Legacy's Sake." *Psychological Science* 26, no. 2 (2015): 231–36.

Image Credits

Figure 1 is courtesy of International Geosphere-Biosphere Programme.

Figure 2 is courtesy of International Geosphere-Biosphere Programme.

Figure 3 is courtesy of International Geosphere-Biosphere Programme.

Figure 4 is reprinted by permission from Macmillan Publishers Ltd: Nature, 1995.

Figure 5 is courtesy of NASA Earth Observatory / Robert Simmon.

Figure 6 is courtesy of International Geosphere-Biosphere Programme.

Figure 7 is courtesy of International Geosphere-Biosphere Programme.

Figure 8 is courtesy of www.terraprints.com.

Figure 9 is courtesy of Stockholm Resilience Centre, Stockholm University: http://www.stockholmresilience.org/research/planetary-boundaries.html.

Figure 10 is courtesy of Stockholm Resilience Centre, Stockholm University: http://www.stockholmresilience.org/research/planetary-boundaries.html.

Figure 11 is courtesy of Nelson Institute Center for Sustainability and the Global Environment, University of Wisconsin–Madison.

Figure 12 is republished with permission of American Association for the Advancement of Science, from David. S. Battisti and Rosamond L. Naylor, "Historical Warnings of Future Food Insecurity with Unprecedented Seasonal Heat," *Science* 323, no. 5911 (Jan. 9, 2009); permission conveyed through Copyright Clearance Center, Inc.

Figure 13 is courtesy of Jonathan Patz.

Figure 14 is reprinted from UNEP/GRID Geneva; University of Dacca; JRO Munich; The World Bank; The World Resources Institute, Washington DC.

Figure 15 is courtesy of Jonathan Patz.

Figure 16 is courtesy of Gregory Norris.

Figure 17 is courtesy of Gregory Norris.

Figure 18 is courtesy of Clare Palmer.

Figure 19: This HydroSHEDS map was developed by the Conservation Science Program of World Wildlife Fund (WWF). Please visit their website at http://www.worldwildlife.org/hydrosheds for general information.

Figure 20 is courtesy of Jacques Descloitres, MODIS Rapid Response Team, NASA/GSFC.

Index

Page references to figures are in *italic*.

A

activism. *See also* education; motivation, motivators; science

  barriers and limits, 2–3, 5, 37, 83–84, 179–82, 212–13, 216, 238–39

  Buddhist approaches, 174–75, 199, 205–9, 219–20

  co-benefits from, 197, 213

  connecting emotionally with, 225

  concrete approaches/solutions, 2–3, 38, 43, 63–64, 184, 197–98, 266–67

  cross-sector partnerships, 243–45, 248

  decision-making about, 248–49, 252

  defining success, 238

  environmentally conscious businesses, 97–98

  and feeling powerless, 181

  the importance and need for, 39–40, 299

  individual vs. collective initiatives, 79–80, 183, 217–18, 238, 271–72

  intentions and goals, 155, 182–83, 238, 292

  involving children, 193–94

  laziness, failure to act, 155, 179, 207–8

  lifestyle changes, 150–51, 153, 266–68, 271–72, 279–81

  and negative motivations, 186, 188–90

  and optimism, 107–8, 252

  and passive decisions, examples, 187–88

  and political considerations, 33–34, 43, 102, 109, 189, 213, 229, 233

  proactive, 219–20

  public-goods dilemma, 178–79

  role of women, 257

  service to sentient beings, 225–26

  small actions, importance of, 266

  sustaining for the long-term, 245, 253

aerosols, planetary boundary limits, 28

Africa, greenhouse gas emissions, 53–54

The Age of Empathy (de Waal), 281

agriculture. *See also* deforestation; meat consumption

  "buy local" campaigns, 99–100

  genetically modified crops, 296

  grain production, 131–32

  during Holocene period, 15

  industrial farming, 130–33

  land conversion, 28, 46

  monoculture vs. biodiverse, 66

  and rising global temperatures, 234–35

climate change
  anticipated rise in temperatures, 32,
    55
  and carbon dioxide, 28, 30–31
  as environmental problem, 43–44
  as ethical dilemma, 297
  as global, 75–76
  heat waves and hot spots, 39, 56, 72
  mechanisms associated with, 38–39
  modeling, 68–72
  perceptions of, 37–38
  regulation to address, 104–5
  and the responsibility of developed
    countries, 270–71
climate science. *See* science
coastal environments, human impacts
  on, 21, 24
Coca-Cola, involvement in Mekong
  River basin protection, 244, 256
cognition. *See also* awareness; education
  barriers to action, 37, 179–81, 213, 216
  motivators associated with, 185–86,
    190
*Cognitive Foundations of Natural History:
  Towards an Anthropology of Science*
  (Atran), 161
Cold Mountain poems (Hanshan), 175
collective action, 79, 116, 123, 183. *See
  also* activism; interconnection/
  interdependence
  and Buddhist emphasis on the indi-
    vidual, 218
  and education, 171
  and long-term perspectives, 7
  and seeing the larger context, 217–18
communication. *See also* motivation,
  motivators
  and co-benefits concept, 197

importance for motivating action,
  40–41, 299
positive vs. negative messages, 40–41,
  167, 185–86, 189–91, 195–97, 206,
  299
relevancy, 36–37
resistance to, 35, 40
and sustaining long-term commitments, 245
community organizing. *See* grassroots
  activism
compassion
  anger and fear with, 167, 184, 206
  and concern for others' well-being,
    103, 163, 165
  the Dalai Lama's call for, 301
  extension to all living things, 5, 135,
    158
  and a holistic perspective, 54, 165
  and levels of caring, 162
  as motivation for action, 5, 292, 294
  Ricard's explorations of, 297–98
  and separating the act from the actor,
    173–74
  as source of happiness, 104
  sustaining, 170
  tonglen practice for, 173
Compendium of Training (Shantideva),
  204–5
consumerism, consumption. *See also*
  poverty, voluntary; sustainability
  addictive, 216–17
  appeal of, 47, 49
  and belief in material progress,
    141–42
  "buy local" campaigns, and the com-
    modification of animals, 133
  Dalai Lama's questioning of, 218

as explanation of reality, 9

as fundamentally interdependent, 2, 18–19, 161, 227

and health, 58–60

human impacts, 19

human-centered vs. nonhuman centered concerns, 112–14, *113*

ice-core analysis, 233–34

industrial ecology, 82

intact ecosystem, defined, 66

the monetary value of healthy ecosystems, 84–85

moral significance, 114

and the planetary boundary concept, 27, *27*

pollen content analysis, 235

valuing, 116–17

ecomonastic initiative, 225

economics. *See also* consumerism, consumption; cost-benefit analysis

and concern for others' well-being, 103

costs associated with climate change, 77, 138

as focus of world leaders, 229

and the profit motive, 81

ecophilia, 161

ecosystem services, 60, 112, 237

ecosystems. *See* ecology, ecosystems

"Ecosystems and Human Well-Being," 60

education. *See* awareness; science

and cognitive barriers to action, 179

and communicating inner values, 164

engaging students, 41, 211–12

and ethical responsibility, 9, 55

incorporating Buddhist practices, 175

and information overload, 214–15

and joy in learning, 208

lack of respect for in the United States, 181–82

and mindfulness, 203, 205

and motivating activism, 41, 168–69, 171–72, 192

moving to action from, 202–4

and the three levels of understanding, 200

and the value of Buddhist debate, 199–200

effort, as remedy for laziness, 208

ego

at core of environmental difficulties, 103

egoic separation as a lie, 144

as root cause of environmental damage, 227–29

The Eight Verses on Training the Mind, 165

electricity, cost-benefit analysis, 99

electronics, supply chain relationships, 89–90, *89*

elephants, self-sacrifice in, 168

Emory University

Emory-Tiber Science Initiative, 282

Secular Ethics program, 164

empathy

as natural, in children, 162, 195

value of, for sustainable living, 282

energy reduction programs, 90–91

engaged Buddhism, 174–75

Engle, Adam, 282, 287

environmental action. *See* activism

environmental degradation. *See also* consumerism, consumption; science

accelerating, 13–14, 16–21, *17*, *21*

climate change, 75–76

and corporations, 105–6

and ecosystem management, 27
limits for, 28
listing of, 27, 27
and multiple, simultaneous stresses,
43–44
and nitrogen pollution, 29
overstepping, impacts, 26–27
and phosphorous pollution, 29
tracking and monitoring, 29–30, 31
planetary house rules, 149, 269–70
plastic bags, environmental footprint
of, 90
polar ice melt, impacts of, 1–2
pollution controls
economic costs and benefits, 61–63
interdependent positive effects,
90–91
poor, the
dependence on nature, 168
and desire for Western lifestyles, 46
dietary needs, 131
health impacts of climate change, 54,
296
unintended impacts of reduced consumption, 272
population growth
during the Holocene period, 15
and medical advances, 15–16
as root cause of environmental damage, 139
since 1950, 16, 17
slowing of, 77–78
Portland, Oregon, promotion of sustainability in, 47
poverty, voluntary, 145–47. *See also*
sustainability
predator species, ecosystem role, 226–27
Priyadarshi, Tenzin, 121, 123
procrastination, 207

profit motive. *See also* consumerism,
consumption; corporations
in consumer economies, 96–97
reevaluating relationship to climate
change, 81
public health. *See* health effects
public transportation initiatives, 48
public-goods dilemma, 179

Q
quality of life calculations, 49–50

R
Rangjung Khoryug Sungkyob Tsokpa
breadth of environmental projects,
300
cleanup work done by, 259
organizing of, 225
tree planting by, 260–61
recycling, 83
regulation, environmental impacts,
104–5
relative nature of all things, 121
religion
and distrust of science, education,
181–82
failure to cultivate compassion, 170
fostering ecological balance, 138
and the lie of egoic separation, 144
and the message of restraint, 140
potential for helping solve environmental problems, 45, 138, 244
religious leaders as motivators,
198–99, 259–60
and selfless love, 158
and spirituality without religious
faith, 142
teaching ethics, 10, 162

responsibility. *See also* activism;
    education
  consumer, 106
  corporate, 95, 98, 269
  of developed countries, for addressing
    climate change, 270–71
  and educating others, 41, 111
  and ethical behavior, 9–10, 55, 228–29
  and mindfulness, 163
  social, 98–99, 103–4, 144–45, 162, 214,
    219
  and taking action, 126, 270–71
  and understanding of interconnected-
    ness, 143
restraint/sacrifice, 140–41, 149–50
Ricard, Matthieu
  on altruism, 123, 164
  background and accomplishments,
    297–98
  on Bhutan, 46–47
  on fear of suffering, 123
  and links between simplicity and
    happiness, 281
  Liverman's data exchange with, 293
  Mars candy company, 101
  meat eating, environmental and ethi-
    cal impacts, 130–35
  mind print concept, 101
  on promoting longer-term views of
    satisfaction, 47–48
  on the removal of suffering as univer-
    sal right, 129
  on types of fear, 36–37, 206
  on utilitarian ethics, 250
  on vegetarian diets, 4–5
Rio Earth Summit, "Future Earth"
  initiative, 293
Rockstrom, Johan, 27–28
rule-based ethics, 125, 204, 209

Russia, production of greenhouse gases
  in, 53–54

S

science. *See also* education
  and awareness vs. action, 33, 35, 172,
    254
  and climate change skeptics, 34–35,
    181–82, 213–14, 262–63
  demonstration of the impacts of
    greed, 143
  ethical responses to, 9, 35, 109
  and evaluating effectiveness of solu-
    tions, 105
  individual responses to, 199
  and industrial ecology, 82
  and modeling climate change, 68–72
  scientists as gurus, 36, 107
  sharing with activists and organizers,
    33, 41, 111
  and the value of measurement, 184
sea level rise, impacts, 57, 58
Secular Ethics program, Emory University, 164
self-awareness. *See also* altruism; awareness; love, selfless; the wild space
  and altruism, 163–64
  and the ecological self, 175
  for handling addictions and bad
    behaviors, 217
  and maintaining a holistic perspec-
    tive, 165
  and readiness to take action, 209, 213
  and self-interest, 35, 107, 123, 232
  and spiritual impetus for changing
    lifestyles, 143
self-emptying. *See* kenosis (restraint,
  self-emptying); no-self, emptiness;
  the wild space

About the Editors

JOHN D. DUNNE holds the Distinguished Chair in Contemplative Humanities, a recently endowed position in the Center for Healthy Minds and the Department of Asian Languages and Cultures at the University of Wisconsin–Madison. He attended Amherst College and in 1999 received his PhD in Sanskrit and Tibetan studies from Harvard University. Before being appointed in his current position, John was a professor at Emory University, where he helped to establish the Collaborative for Contemplative Studies (now the Center for Contemplative Science and Compassion-Based Ethics). He also previously held research positions at the University of Lausanne, Switzerland, and the Central University of Higher Tibetan Studies in Sarnath, India. He is a fellow and former member of the Board of the Mind and Life Institute. His academic work includes teaching and advising for the Rangjung Yeshe Institute in Kathmandu, Nepal. He frequently serves as a translator for Tibetan scholars, and as a consultant, he is involved in various scientific studies of contemplative practices.

Daniel Goleman is a psychologist and science journalist, and a cofounder of the Collaborative for Academic, Social, and Emotional Learning. Dan attended Amherst College and received his doctorate in psychology from Harvard University, where he later was a visiting lecturer. A science journalist, he covered the brain and behavioral sciences for the *New York Times* for many years. Dan is the author of more than a dozen books, including the international bestsellers *Emotional Intelligence*, *Working with Emotional Intelligence*, and *Social Intelligence*, and he is the coauthor of *Primal Leadership*. He has moderated several Mind and Life meetings with the Dalai Lama and was editor of the proceedings of two: *Healing Emotions: Dialogues with the Dalai Lama* (Shambhala, 1996) and *Destructive Emotions: How Can We Overcome Them?* (Bantam Books, 2003). To honor the eightieth birthday of the Dalai Lama, Dan wrote *A Force for Good: The Dalai Lamas's Vision for Our World* (Bantam Books, 2015).

What to Read Next from Wisdom Publications

Zen on the Trail
Hiking as Pilgrimage
Christopher Ives

"Like John Muir, Chris Ives knows that going out into the natural world is really going inward. This book about pilgrimage is itself a pilgrimage: we accompany the author as he leaves civilization behind to enter the wilderness and encounter his true nature and original face."
—David R. Loy, author of *Money, Sex, War, Karma: Notes for a Buddhist Revolution*

Money, Sex, War, Karma
Notes for a Buddhist Revolution
David R. Loy

"A flashy title, but a serious and substantial book."—*Buddhadharma*

Landscapes of Wonder
Discovering Buddhist Dhamma in the World Around Us
Bhikkhu Nyanasobhano
Foreword by Bhikkhu Bodhi

"...one of the most melodious new voices in Western Buddhism to come along in some while."—Amazon.com

A Buddhist Response to the Climate Emergency
John Stanley, David R. Loy, Gyurme Dorje

"If you read only one Dharma book, make it this one."—*The Mirror*

Imagine All the People
A Conversation with the Dalai Lama
on Money, Politics, and Life as It Could Be
His Holiness the Dalai Lama with Fabien Ouaki

"In this inspiring book...the Dalai Lama expresses his thoughts on a wide range of topics of contemporary concerns and answers questions about his personal life and his method of handling problems."
—*The Beacon*

Sleeping, Dreaming, and Dying
An Exploration of Consciousness
His Holiness the Dalai Lama
Francisco Varela

"The book is a most stimulating and informative work...offers important insights for those genuinely interested in meaningful contacts between Buddhism, psychology, and neuroscience."
—*The Tibet Journal*

MindScience
An East-West Dialogue
His Holiness the Dalai Lama with Herbert Benson, Robert Thurman, Howard Gardner, and Daniel Goleman

"A lively and interesting description of the dynamic interaction between Buddhism and mainstream science...full of pearls..."
—*Shambhala Sun*

About Wisdom Publications

Wisdom Publications is the leading publisher of classic and contemporary Buddhist books and practical works on mindfulness. To learn more about us or to explore our other books, please visit our website at wisdompubs.org or contact us at the address below.

Wisdom Publications
199 Elm Street
Somerville, MA 02144 USA

We are a 501(c)(3) organization, and donations in support of our mission are tax deductible.

Wisdom Publications is affiliated with the Foundation for the Preservation of the Mahayana Tradition (FPMT).